The labour market in Africa

International Institute for Labour Studies   Geneva

The labour market
in Africa

Jean-Pierre Lachaud

Research Series   102

Research Series

The aim of the Research Series of the International Institute for Labour Studies is to publish monographs reflecting the results and findings of research projects carried out by the Institute and its networks. The Series will also occasionally include outside contributions. The monographs will be published in moderately priced limited offset editions. The Institute thus hopes to maintain a regular flow of high-quality documents related to its areas of continuing interest.

ISBN 92-9014-534-X

First published 1994

The responsibility for opinions expressed in signed articles, studies and other contributions rests solely with their authors, and publication does not constitute an endorsement by the International Institute for Labour Studies of the opinions expressed in them.

Copies of this publication can be ordered directly from: ILO Publications, International Labour Office, CH-1211 Geneva 22 (Switzerland).

Preface

In the mid 1980s, the International Institute for Labour Studies (IILS) launched a new programme on labour market issues. It was a time when the institutions of the labour market were under severe pressure. In the Third World, poverty had started to increase again in the face of deep recession and increasing indebtedness. In many cities, open unemployment was emerging alongside persistent underemployment and low productivity. In industrialized countries, unemployment was rising to levels unknown since the 1930s, and traditional systems of industrial relations were in retreat. The causes of these trends were contested, but labour market malfunctioning was widely viewed as an important factor: Some argued that wages were too high or too inflexible, that government policy created distortions, that trade unions prevented the market from functioning effectively... But these were presumptions and suppositions. Little hard evidence existed on the functioning of labour markets in low-income settings, on the role played by different institutions, on the significance of unemployment and its relationship with underemployment and poverty.

The IILS developed its work in Africa in this field on the basis of two observations. First, there was a serious lack of empirical research into labour market functioning in the continent; and second - and partly the source of the first — there was a dearth of scholars and research institutions with capabilities and interest in this field. It was clear that a research effort was required, but if it was to have more than a short term effect, it had to be built around support to individuals and institutions in Africa. So the idea of a network was born, in which research into labour markets could be carried on in a comparative framework, involving the participation of researchers from several African countries, alongside a series of activities aimed at the development of empirical and analytical skills. The lack of research on labour markets partly reflected the paucity of suitable data, so it was also essential for the network to generate fresh information, specifically designed to permit analysis of the most important labour market issues.

This network, under the direction of Jean-Pierre Lachaud of the University of Bordeaux I, an IILS consultant since 1986, has produced a series of papers and publications on labour market issues in Africa. But because its work has been concentrated in Francophone countries, little material has appeared in English. Yet much of the research which has been undertaken appears to be relevant to anglophone countries of Africa and indeed elsewhere. This volume makes available to an English speaking audience translations of three representative selections from this work, each due to Jean-Pierre Lachaud. The first, which draws on the work of the network as a whole, summarizes the findings from six countries on the structuring of the urban labour market and its relationship with poverty. This work highlights the critical state of labour markets in many African countries, and shows the linkage between poverty and unemployment, labour supply and labour market status. It draws on new data collected by network participants for the purposes of this project. The second chapter is a more general analysis of the relations between structural adjustment and the labour market - an issue which continues to be a major preoccupation in the Francophone countries of Africa with the recent devaluation of the Franc CFA. The third chapter is a detailed analysis of the labour market patterns in Tunisia, undertaken as background for the development of a network for labour market analysis in the Maghreb.

The crisis in African development continues. Success stories are few, and the declining capacity of the State to promote development has gone in hand with growing unemployment, underemployment and poverty. These problems will not be solved by labour market policy. There are fundamental development issues, both internal and international, which also need to be tackled. But labour market policy is surely a crucial ingredient of development strategy, if it can mobilize labour and make employment creation an effective instrument for both promoting growth and ensuring that the benefits from growth reach the population at large. A better understanding of labour market mechanisms is important if such goals are to be achieved, and it is to be hoped that research such as that reported here will stimulate others to pursue these matters further.

Gerry Rodgers
International Institute for Labour Studies
Geneva, April 1994

Table of contents

Peface, by Gerry Rodgers v

**1. Poverty and the urban labour market
in sub-Saharan Africa: A comparative analysis** 1

I.   Introduction 1
     A. The macro-economic context, the labour market
        and poverty 1
     B. The research method 3

II. The identification of poverty: Incidence and profile 7
     1. The determination of poverty 7
        A. The conceptual and methodological options 7
        B. The incidence of poverty 10
     2. Poverty and the profile of individuals and households 13
        A. The profile of persons 13
        B. The profile of households 14

III. The stratification of the labour market 18
     1. Basis and method of analysis 18
     2. The stratification of the labour market and poverty 21

IV. Urban unemployment 28
     1. The incidence of urban unemployment 28
     2. Profile of unemployment and poverty 32

V.   The labour supply 37
     1. Concepts and method 38
     2. Labour supply structure 40
     3. Labour supply strategy 43

VI. Access to employment, mobility and segmentation 48
     1. Access to employment 48
     2. Career profile and segmentation 54

Conclusion 59

Bibliographical references 62

Appendices 65

2. **Structural adjustment and the labour market
    in French-speaking Africa** 83

I.   Introduction 83

II. Structural adjustment, employment
     and unemployment 88
     1. Structural adjustment and employment 88
     2. Labour market mobility and informalization 93
     3. Unemployment and structural adjustment 99

III. Structural adjustment and labour market
     distortions 103
     1. Real wages and labour market flexibility 103
     2. Labour market segmentation in the modern sector 109

IV. Structural adjustment and labour market institutions 118
     1. Informal labour market institutions and social
        adjustment 119
     2. Structural adjustment and the efficiency
        of formal labour market institutions 122
        A. Changes in the institutional context
           of the labour market 123
        B. The uncertain efficiency of the new
           institutional content of the labour market 129

Conclusion 132

Bibliographical references 134

Appendices 137

3. **The labour market in Tunisia: structure imbalance
    and adjustment** 153

I.   Introduction 153

II. The stratification of the labour market 155
     1. Employment structure 155
     2. Income structure 159

III. Labour market imbalances 162
      1. Decline in the absorption capacity of employment 162
      2. The inadequacy of the educational system 166

IV. Labour market dysfunctionings 167
      1. Institutional environment   167
      2. Static imbalances in the labour market 169

 V. Labour market adjustments 171
      1. Growth of urban unemployment   171
      2. Employment stagnation in the modern sector 172
      3. The drop in real wages 172
      4. Employment and the informal sector 173
      5. Migration 174

Conclusion   175

Bibliographical references 176

List of tables

**Chapter 1. Poverty and the urban labour market
in sub-Saharan Africa: A comparative analysis**

Table 1   Dependency ratio and size of households
by standard of living   16

Table 2   Structure of household income   17

Table 3   Urban unemployment rate by education and age
– 15 years and above (percentage of active
population) 31

Table 4   Distribution of unemployed by reason
for job-seeking (percentage)   33

Table 5   Probability (Pi) of unemployment
by standard of living 37

Table 6   Methods of access to present employment
of employees by standard of living 49

Table 7   Present status of work of heads of households:
principal parameters of discriminant analyses 53

Table A   Some socio-economic indicators in French
speaking African countries from the present sample 65

Table B   Incidence, depth and inequality of poverty
in households by status of head of household 66

Table C   Incidence, depth and inequality of poverty
in households by stratification of the labour market
– status of breadwinner   67

Table D   Relative distribution of labour status
by earner type and country   68

Table E   Regression equations coefficients of the
multivariate analysis of poverty and status
of work of heads of households   69

Table F   Urban unemployment rate by situation in the
household and standard of living – 15 years
and above (percentage of active population) 71

Table G   Regression coefficients of the logistic estimate
of determinants of unemployment 72

Table H   Employment and labour supply rates of adults
– 15 years and above – by marital status
and level of income (percentage) 73

Table I   Labour supply rate by marital status
and age (percentage) 74

Table J   Distribution of the male population aged 15
and above by labour market status and age
(percentage) 75

Table K   Distribution of the female population aged 15
and above by labour market status and age
(percentage)...................................... 76

Table L   Regression coefficients of probit structural
equations of labour supply of household members 77

Table M   Regression coefficients of logistic equations
of labour supply of married women 79

Table N   Access to capital by self-employed workers
– present employment (percentage) 81

Table O   Occupational transition matrix – Burkina Faso,
Cameroon, Côte d'Ivoire and Mali 82

**Chapter 2. Structural adjustment and the labour market
in French-speaking Africa**

Table 1   Net variation in real wages in Côte d'Ivoire,
1979-1989 107

Table 2   Breakdown of wage differentials between
the public and private sectors in French-speaking
Africa 115

Table 3   Breakdown of wage differentials between
the para-public and private sectors in Côte d'Ivoire,
1979-1989 118

Table A   Gross variation in real wages in Côte d'Ivoire,
1979-89 137

Table B   Coefficients of regression equations for all employees
in the modern production – tradeables and
non-tradeables sectors – sector in Côte d'ivoire,
1979-89 138

Table C   Coefficients of regression equations for newly
recruited employees in the modern production
– tradeables and non-tradeables sectors
– sector in Côte d'ivoire, 1979-89 140

Table D   Coefficients of regression equations for all
employees in the modern production
– para-public and private sectors – sector
in Côte d'ivoire, 1979-89 142

Table E   Coefficients of regression equations for newly
recruited employees in the modern production sector
– para-public and private sectors – in Côte d'ivoire,
1979-89 144

Table F   Breakdown of wage differences in the modern
production sector Côte d'Ivoire in 1979 and 1989 146

Table G   Descriptives statistics on wages and employment
in the public and private sectors in French-speaking
Africa 146

Table H   Comparaison of salaries in the public service
and public enterprises in French-speaking Africa 147

Table I   Descriptive statistics on samples 148

Table J   Coefficients of regression equations of salaries
in the public and private sectors in French-speaking
Africa 150

Table K   Coefficients of regression equations of employees
in the para-public and private sectors in Côte d'Ivoire,
Abidjan, 1979-1989 152

**Chapter 3. The labour market in Tunisia: structure imbalance
and adjustment**

Table 1   Breakdown of production systems and employment
in Tunisia, 1984-89 156

Table 2   Distribution of active employed population
by status in occupation in Tunisia, 1975-1989 158

Table 3   Evolution of the total population, active population
and participation rate by urban/rural distribution
and sex in Tunisia, 1975-89 163

Table 4   Employed active population by sex and urban/rural
distribution in Tunisia, 1975-89 164

List of figures

**Chapter 1. Poverty and the urban labour market
in sub-Saharan Africa: A comparative analysis**

Figure 1   Incidence of poverty in households, by country
and status of head of household on the labour market 11
Figure 2   Relative contribution to poverty of households
by measure of poverty, country and labour market
status of head of household 12
Figure 3   Incidence of poverty in households by country
and labour market market of the breadwinner 23
Figure 4   Relative contribution to poverty of households
by measurement of poverty, country and labour
market status of the breadwinner 24
Figure 5   Poverty incidence curves and stratification
of the labour market – breadwinner – Conakry 1991   25
Figure 6   Urban unemployment rate by country, situation
in household and standard of living – percentage
of active population 29
Figure 7   Irregular employment during occupational career,
by country and standard of living – workers aged 15
and above taken together (percentage) 57

**Chapter 2. Structural adjustment and the labour market
in French-speaking Africa**

Figure 1   Evolution of wage employment in enterprises
in the modern sector in Côte d'Ivoire 90
Figure 2   Unemployment by age and sex, Abidjan, 1978-1987 98
Figure 3   Unemployment by education, Abidjan, 1978-1987 98
Figure 4   Means of subsistence of unemployed persons
in African capitals in the early 1990s 122

Chapter 3.   The labour market in Tunisia: structure imbalance and adjustment

Figure 1   Log of income by employed active persons
in Tunisia, 1971-88 161
Figure 2   Evolution of minimum and average nominal wage
in Tunisia, 1971-89 161
Figure 3   Real wage indices in Tunisia, 1971-89 173

1 Poverty and the urban labour market in sub-Saharan Africa: A comparative study

I. Introduction[*]

A. The macro-economic context, the labour market and poverty

Over the last two decades the economic, social and political climate of sub-Saharan Africa has deteriorated significantly. Several major events would seem to explain the precarious nature of this situation. In many countries, governments have been confronted with a domestic environment which has not helped the development process: unfavourable geographic and climatic conditions, a low level of human capital, the weakness of the administrative and institutional structures, political instability, limited potential markets and, in some cases, a weak banking system. The international situation has also played a major role in making the crisis worse, with the increase in the prices of cereals and oil, the recession and inflation in the industrialized countries, the increase in real interest rates, fluctuations in exchange rates and the drop in commodity prices. Lastly, some blame must also be attached to domestic policies in the evolution of the crisis. Poor choice of investments, the inadequate nature of overall policies, the lack of financial discipline and poor management have all reducing potential in the public production sector. Thus, in sub-Saharan Africa, the average annual GDP growth was only 2.1 per cent in the 1980s, whereas between 1965 and 1980 it was 4.2 per cent.[1] With account being taken of the strong population growth – an average of 3 per cent a year – the per capita income fell in real terms each year by 0.9 per cent in the period 1980-1990.[2]

This slowdown in the economic transition process explains the introduction in the 1980s of structural adjustment programmes with the support

---

[*] The author is grateful to G. Rodgers and J. B. Figueiredo of the International Institute for Labour Studies for their comments on this research.

[1] World Bank [1992].

[2] World Bank [1992]. Per capita real income fell by 1.0 per cent in 1991. Furthermore, per capita GNP rose by only 0.2 per cent between 1965 and 1990.

of the International Monetary Fund and the World Bank. However, these new economic reforms, which called into question state intervention in the social and economic spheres by the introduction of structural changes and allow the market to determine the social order, may undermine social systems and create open conflict or hidden pockets of resistance.[3]

The labour market is an important indicator of the social cost of adjustment and many elements appear to confirm the increasing imbalances on the labour market which were inherent in the destabilization of the African economies in the 1980s. At the macroeconomic level, the capacity to absorb labour fell during this period, with the appearance of a fundamental imbalance between the labour demand – poor growth of production and structural changes – and labour supply – marked growth in the total population and the economically active population. Other sources of imbalance have compounded the employment problem: the surplus of graduates from higher education and the shortage of skilled workers; the decline of the role of agriculture, accompanied in many countries by an excessive growth in services; the relative importance of precarious employment.

Several adjustments seem to have occurred in recent years on the urban labour markets of most of the sub-Saharan African countries.[4] First, the urban unemployment rate has substantially increased – doubling between 1975 and 1990, from 10 per cent to around 20 per cent – and employment has become increasingly precarious. Secondly, employment in the modern sector, especially in the public sector, has stagnated and even declined. In 14 countries in sub-Saharan Africa, the annual growth rate of salaried employment was estimated at 3 per cent between 1975 and 1980, but only 1 per cent during the first half of the 1980s. Thirdly, if employment growth in the modern sector has remained positive, this may well be due in part to the drop in real wages – on average, real wages in 27 African countries appear to have fallen by around 30 per cent between 1980 and 1986. Fourthly, the increase in employment in the rural and urban informal sector – estimated at 6.7 per cent between 1980 and 1985[5] – has been an essential factor in determining the absorption of surplus urban labour. Furthermore, in some countries[6],

---

[3] For example, the events which occurred in Mali in May 1991 were not unrelated to the social and economic situation of the country.

[4] For Africa in general see Ghai [1987]; Vandemoortele [1991]. For Mali see Lachaud [1990].

[5] Vandemoortele [1991].

[6] In particular the Sahel countries.

emigration has been another factor which has brought about adjustment on the labour market. Finally, labour market regulations have been amended to ensure that they are not an obstacle to the functioning of the market, particularly in the private and para-public modern sectors.

This situation has been compounded by the high level of poverty in sub-Saharan Africa. The World Bank estimated that in 1985, 47 per cent of the population in the region was living below the poverty threshold, whereas the figure in other developing countries was 33 per cent.[7] Human development data seem to bear out these figures. According to the UNDP, the average level of the human development index for sub-Saharan Africa is 0.35, compared to 0.62 for other developing countries.[8] Furthermore, poverty seems to have become more widespread over the last two decades; between 1975 and 1985, the number of destitute persons increased by two thirds, whereas poverty in the developing world as a whole rose by only one third. In addition, forecasts show that sub-Saharan Africa is the only region in the world where poverty is likely to worsen during the decade 1990-2000.[9]

The recent evolution of the macro-economic situation in sub-Saharan Africa has thus led to a significant increase in the extent and depth of poverty and the precarious nature of the labour market, particularly in urban areas. If political leaders really want to implement strategies to combat this poverty, it is essential to identify the roots of the problem. Although poverty is influenced by a number of factors, the adjustments which occurred during the 1980s indicate that labour market status is one of the main factors of poverty. This link is close enough to merit an in-depth study, in particular with a view to the implementation of policies to promote social progress.

B.   The research method

In most countries of sub-Saharan Africa any analysis of the labour market is made difficult by the lack of available statistical data. This handicap, which becomes particularly evident when attempts are made to determine the labour market mechanisms which underlie poverty, appears at

---

[7] The poverty threshold in 1985 PPA dollars is 370 US dollars per inhabitant per year. See World Bank (1990a). This estimate seems to be confirmed by those of the ILO and UNDP, according to which 50 per cent of the population in sub-Saharan Africa live in absolute poverty (JASPA [1991]).

[8] The index measures average hardship in each country as regards life expectancy, adult literacy and minimum purchasing power. UNDP [1990].

[9] UNDP [1990]. According to the World Bank, by the year 2000 the number of poor will reach 304 million, i.e. 49.7 per cent of the population. World Bank [1992].

three levels.[10] First, information on the labour market is fragmentary. In the case of the urban labour market, studies carried out by the statistical services of the ministries of planning or labour – censuses, household or establishment surveys – are very few in number and permit only a partial exploration of the labour market mechanisms.[11] Of course, other studies are sometimes available;[12] but given their nature or date, they are of relatively limited interest.[13] Secondly, conceptual deficiencies only emphasize the quantitative inadequacies of the statistical data on the labour market. Most studies try to adapt employment categories taken from standard international classifications.[14] Although this approach may be justified by the need to make comparisons over time, it is not appropriate for an analysis of the stratification of the labour market as related to poverty. The labour categories used fail to identify the precarious forms of work which overlap the formal-informal dichotomy and which, in the context of the adjustments resulting from the new economic policies, are closely linked with poverty. Furthermore, the concept of income is frequently absent from the available studies. Moreover, relatively little recent information on remuneration from self-employment and on the bonuses and benefits of wage earners in the modern production sector. Thirdly, the methodological weaknesses of available studies[15] compounds the precarious nature of labour market data.

In an attempt to fill these gaps – the lack of statistics and the weakness of labour market analyses – a series of pilot household studies was carried out between 1986 and 1992 in several African capitals – Abidjan (Côte d'Ivoire), 1986-87; Antananarivo (Madagascar), 1989; Yaoundé (Cameroon), 1990-91; Conakry (Guinea), 1991-92; Bamako (Mali), 1991; Dakar (Senegal), 1991; Ouagadougou (Burkina Faso), 1992.[16] These different studies were carried out within the framework of the Network for the Analysis of the Labour Market in Africa (NALMA), on the initiative of the

---

[10] For a more in-depth analysis, see Lachaud [1988] – Côte d'Ivoire; Lachaud, Sidibé [1993] – Mali.

[11] The long time lag – of several years – between the date of the survey and the publication of results is another obstacle to the labour market analysis.

[12] For example, some research carried out in academic circles.

[13] For example, the priority surveys of the DSA programme of the World Bank include little data on the labour market.

[14] See, for example, ILO [1990].

[15] Representativity; processing of data.

[16] Table A in the appendix gives some socio-economic indicators for these various countries.

International Institute for Labour Studies in Geneva.[17] The studies examined the links between the structure of the labour market and urban poverty, in other words, those factors likely to shed light on the functioning of the labour market: limited access to employment, high unemployment rate, vulnerability of certain groups to unemployment and poverty, growth of precarious employment. New information on the labour market was collected in order to examine the internal structure of the latter without recourse to the dualist approach of the informal and modern sectors. Some recent preliminary studies[18] of this kind have shown that not all poor persons are necessarily to be found in the informal sector and that not all the non-poor belong to the modern sector. Homogenous groups can be found outside this informal-modern division; thus subordinate employees in enterprises in the private and para-public sectors are not necessarily any different in this respect from some workers in the informal sector.

In each case, the random samples comprised approximately 300 households. The surveys used of a relatively extensive questionnaire containing six sections: identification of persons; family background; transfers and special household consumption; education and training; employment – principal and secondary – during the preceding seven days and preceding 12 months; occupational profile. Furthermore an unemployment module and an apprenticeship module were also included.

The basic idea underlying this research is to use the comparative data to highlight specific national characteristics, enhance the analytical conclusions and increase the veracity of the results obtained. The data collected under the NALMA programme may strengthen the comparative analysis. All the surveys were relatively homogenous as regards sampling, statistical support, concepts used[19] and the procedures for processing the data

---

[17] With financial support from USAID and ILO technical cooperation. Furthermore, several African local institutions collaborated in these surveys: ONFP (Côte d'Ivoire); OSIPD (Madagascar); Directorate of Statistics and ENSUT (Senegal); Ministry of Planning and Regional Development (Cameroon); ONMOE (Mali); ONEMO (Guinea); INSD (Burkina Faso).

[18] Harris, Kannan, Rodgers [1990]; Lachaud [1988].

[19] The household groups together two categories of members. First, members who are related to the head of the household, i.e. all the persons who live and eat on a permanent basis in the household: persons present who live and eat on a permanent basis in the household; persons temporarily absent (less than three months) during the last twelve months, but who usually live and eat in the household; persons regularly absent (less than nine months) but who usually live and eat in the household. Secondly, the group comprises other members of the household not related to the head of the household, but who regularly live and eat in the household. This second category is excluded from the present research. The concept

generated.[20] Thus despite the relatively heterogeneous nature of the countries included – four low income economies and two intermediate level economies[21] – the strength of this analytical approach is reinforced by the homogenous nature of the statistical sources used. The small size of the samples suggests, however, the need for some caution in the interpretation of the results.

The following pages will examine successively the identification of poverty, the stratification of the labour market, unemployment, the labour supply, access to employment, mobility and the segmentation of labour.

---

is based on cohabitation and the sharing of meals, and the incomes of the households come from outside; thus domestic staff who earn their income from the household itself and pensioners are excluded. Household income is made up of the amount of the incomes of all members of the household – except possible income from apprenticeship – including net transfers. Although the determination of income – generally, in the form of wages – is relatively easy in the case of employees, it is much more difficult to determine in the case of other occupational categories. For non-wage workers, a distinction must be made according to the regularity of the sale of goods and services during the year. The reference period is the last week. For persons whose sale of goods and service is regular throughout the year – the questionnaire reduces data to the level of the week - incomes are obtained by deducting costs from the amount of sales. On the other hand, if activity is irregular throughout the year – which is usually the case – it was necessary to weight the different volumes of sales by the number of "good", "average" and "bad" weeks. The sum total is divided by 52 to obtain the weekly income on an "annual basis". Furthermore, it should be noted that bonuses, allowances, gratifications and family benefits are added to wage incomes.

[20] The collection, control and analysis of data were backed up by training courses provided by the International Institute for Labour Studies. An initial course was organized in April-May 1989 in Abidjan (Côte d'Ivoire), in collaboration with the National Office of Vocational Training of Côte d'Ivoire, the DSA Unit of the World Bank, and the Programme for Employment and Technical Skills in Africa, and with financial assistance from the ILO Technical Cooperation Branch. A second, more ambitious course was held in Yaoundé (Cameroon) in September-October 1990 and July-August 1991, with financial support from USAID, the EEC and the ILO Technical Cooperation Branch; the DSA Unit of the World Bank also collaborated in its organization. Finally, a third training course in the comparative analysis of the labour market was organized in Ouagadougou (Burkina Faso) in November 1992, with support from the ILO Technical Cooperation Branch.

[21] Data on Senegal will not be used because of the poor quality of some of the information. This paper is based on three elements: (i) studies already published: Lachaud [1988]; Inack, Ndiffo, Nkwayeb, Lachaud (with the participation and under the direction of) [1992]; Rakotobé, Lachaud (with the participation and under the direction of) [1992]; Dioubaté, Lachaud (with the participation and under the direction of) [1992]; Lachaud, Sidibé [1993]; (ii) papers from the course in training in the comparative analysis of the urban labour market in Africa, Ouagadougou; (iii) additional processing of data by the present author.

II.   The identification of poverty: Incidence and profile

It is important at the outset to define on the one hand the conceptual and methodological options inherent in the determination of poverty and on the other, certain basic elements concerning the profile of poor persons and households.

1.   The determination of poverty

A.   The conceptual and methodological options[22]

A priori, it is relatively easy to define poverty. In a given society, the existence of poverty presupposes that one or more persons are unable to attain a level of material well-being considered an acceptable minimum by the standards of that society. In reality, however, the determination of poverty raises two major problems: one of identification and one of aggregation.[23]

The problem of identification concerns the evaluation of individual well-being and the determination of the threshold below which a person may be said to be poor. Irrespective of whether the comparisons of well-being are made on the basis of individual levels of usefulness, evaluated by the individuals themselves – the "welfarist" approach - or virtually independently of data on individual usefulness – the "non-welfarist" approach[24] – it is important to stress that the standard of living[25] of a person is generally determined in terms of his or her consumption of private – and, where applicable, public – goods available. Current consumption is in most cases considered as the preferred indicator of well-being, with income being used only as an approximation of consumption. In fact, these two indicators are the most frequently used, although consumption is often preferred when the question of variation over time arises.[26]

However, in as far as households differ in size and composition, a standardized process must be established which accounts for economies of scale in consumption terms. Indeed, some empirical studies have shown that the level of well-being of large families does not fall in exact proportion to the increase in the size of the family. Thus it is usual to use an "adult

---

[22] The following points have been taken from: Lachaud, Sidibé [1993].

[23] Ravallion [1992].

[24] Sen [1979]; Ravallion [1992].

[25] "Potential consumption" could be considered instead of current consumption.

[26] Consumption varies less than income over time. On the other hand, consumption may be a poor indicator of wellbeing in the long term.

equivalent scale" to determine the adult equivalent consumption or income. This procedure may include two aspects of distribution within households: the real differences in needs by age and sex and inequalities as regards outside opinions or "bargaining power". Unfortunately, it is very difficult for the latter not to be included in the analysis, which therefore increases the existing inequality.[27]

Despite the variety of methods for determining the standard of living of households – proportion of expenditure spent on food and nutritional indicators – this research project uses adjusted per capita income as an approximation of consumption.[28] Household income is composed of wage income (including bonuses, allowances, gratifications and social benefits), non-wage income from a main or secondary activity, exercised during the reference week by members of the household aged seven and above, and net transfers accruing to households. Weighting coefficients of 0.5 and 1 were used respectively for persons under the age of 15 and aged 15 and above.[29]

After specification of standard of living criteria, the poverty threshold or "poverty line" below which persons are considered to be poor must be determined. In developing countries, analysis has often been carried out in terms of absolute poverty, i.e. by reference to a poverty threshold fixed according to the standard of living indicator used. This approach implies an estimation of the cost of a volume of goods which satisfies the basic consumption needs of the domain of comparison of poverty. Despite the uncertainty of such an approach[30] and the existence of alternative analytical options[31], this is the method employed in this study. Thus the concept of poverty used is based on just the consumption of rice. In most countries of Africa, rice is the most common foodstuff. Furthermore, this item has the advantage that data are available on its equivalent in calories and on prices.

---

[27] Ravallion [1992].

[28] The relative amount of consumption expenditure cannot be determined from the employment surveys of households inherent in this research project. However, a standard of living was prepared on the basis of the specific consumption of households, the results of which are not presented here. See the in-depth comparative analysis in Lachaud (ed.) [1993].

[29] This procedure was suggested by Rodgers. See Rodgers [1984]. In some countries, different coefficients were used. See, for example, Glewwe [1987], for Côte d'Ivoire. However, no theoretical argument can actually justify the validity of the latter approach.

[30] Difficulty of determining energy needs; problems of non-food consumption. In this context, the x per cent of the poorest of the distribution are sometimes considered as "poor".

[31] For example, the determination of relative or subjective poverty lines. For a summary presentation, see Ravallion [1992].

If it is assumed that an adult – aged 15 or above – needs a minimum of 2 400 calories per day to live, that a kilogram of rice is equal to 3 500 calories, and that non-food consumption is equal to half a person's food consumption, it is possible, on the basis of the price of rice, to determine the weekly expenditure per adult equivalent (D_m) below which individuals can be said to be in "absolute poverty".[32] Moreover, $2D_m$ can be considered as constituting a "poverty" threshold[33]. For analytical purposes, the 30 per cent of households with the highest incomes are classed as "not poor", whereas the others are designated as "intermediate".

Once the poverty line is defined, the information obtained must be incorporated to express the measure of poverty. The incidence of poverty within a population or its sub-groups is usually indicated by stipulating the percentage of persons affected. In fact, recent analyses have revealed three main ways of measuring poverty: the incidence of poverty, the depth of poverty and inequality within poverty.[34] These three measures have been taken from those proposed by Foster, Greer and Thorbecke.[35] Given the intrinsic significance of these new conceptual approaches to the determination of poverty, they have been used in this study.

The simplest approach is to measure the incidence of poverty P0, which may be expressed as the rate between p, the number of poor households or persons, and n, the total number of households or persons.[36] However, a better measure of poverty is to determine the difference with respect to the poverty line – i. e. the depth of the poverty. Reference is thus not made exclusively to the number of poor persons but to the scope of the poverty. With P0, no account will be taken of whether a household or a person is very poor. Thus the depth of the poverty P1 encompasses the average proportional gap in income in relation to the poverty line, and the incomes of those who are not poor are not taken into account.[37] However, this index takes account of only the situation of the average poor person, without reference to the

---

[32] $D_m = 1.5* [(2400/3500)*p*7]$, if p = price of kilo of rice at the time of the survey.

[33] The poverty thresholds – per week and per adult equivalent – for the different countries are as follows: Burkina Faso (1992): 2,222 FCFA; Cameroon (1990-91): 2,880 FCFA; Côte d'Ivoire (1986-87): 2,286 FCFA; Guinea (1991-92) 2,757 FG; Madagascar (1989): 5,787 FMG; Mali (1991) 1,892 FCFA.

[34] Foster [1984]; Ravallion [1992].

[35] Foster, Greer, Thorbecke [1984].

[36] The poverty index is expressed by: $P0 = (p/n)$.

[37] If Z is the poverty line and R_i the adjusted per capita income of the household or the individual i, the depth of poverty P1 can be expressed by the following formula: $P1 = 1/n \Sigma [(Z-R_i/)/Z]$ with $Z \rangle R_i$.

inequality of the poverty. This is why it is sometimes proposed to widen the P1 measure by including a parameter x of "aversion to poverty". This measurement increases the preceding proportional gap to the power of x, the value of which reflects the degree of concern inherent in this gap.[38] The interest of these forms of measurement is that they are additive and may be broken down into sub-groups.[39]

B.   The incidence of poverty

Figure 1 shows the incidence of poverty in some capital cities in French-speaking Africa, by different measures of poverty and different sub-groups of households.[40] Poverty is measured at the household level in terms of the occupational situation of its head. The categories of workers used are conventional ones, taken directly from the survey. Despite the methodological and analytical interest of this approach, the present study will subsequently show a stratification of the labour market in terms of vulnerability which is substantially different.

If per capita income is used as a criterion of poverty, the incidence of urban poverty – PO – is correlated to the per capita GDP. Thus in the low income economies – Burkina Faso, Guinea, Madagascar and Mali – between one third and one half of the households are poor, whereas in the intermediate income economies – Cameroon and Côte d'Ivoire – the proportion is between one fifth and one quarter. In all the countries surveyed, the incidence of poverty appears highest in households where the head does not participate in the labour market. In two thirds of the countries – Burkina Faso, Cameroon, Côte d'Ivoire and Guinea – households where the head is unemployed are poor in 75 to 90 per cent of cases; in the other countries – Madagascar and Mali – the proportion is 50 per cent. An almost identical pattern can be verified if the head of households is inactive. The different surveys also showed that the incidence of poverty amongst persons who participate in the labour market is highest in households where the head is self-employed,

---

[38] Thus the measure Px can be written: $Px = 1/n \Sigma [(Z-R_j)/Z]^x$. It will be seen that the value of x is equal to 0 if no account is taken of the scope of poverty, to 1 if there is a uniform concern with the depth of poverty and is greater than 1 – for example 2 – if the aim is to propose a measure of poverty which is more sensitive to the situation of the poor.

[39] For example, if P_{xj} is the poverty indicator x of the sub-group j in the total population, Px the x poverty indicator for the total population, the relative contribution C_j is: $C_j = (P_{xj} *k_j)/P_x$ since $P_x = \Sigma k_j * P_{xj}$.

[40] See also table B in the appendix.

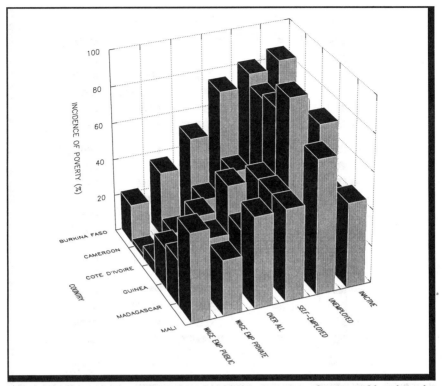

Figure 1: Incidence of poverty in households by country and status of head on the labour market

except in Mali[41]. The vulnerability of self-employed persons is moreover inversely related to the level of development; for example, in Burkina Faso, Guinea and Madagascar, between 50 and 75 per cent of households where the head is self-employed are poor, whereas this proportion is only between 20 and 38 per cent respectively in Côte d'Ivoire and Cameroon. Lastly, except in Mali, households whose heads are employees, particularly in the public sector, are the least vulnerable to poverty. But once again there are profound differences according to the level of development. The incidence of poverty in households where the head is an employee in the public sector is less than 10 per cent in intermediate income economies, whereas it is around 25 per cent in the least advanced countries. In this context, it is important to stress that the relative contribution to poverty – Cj – is highest in households where the head is self-employed – between 30 and 50 per cent in five out of the six

---

[41] The particularity of this situation will become clearer below.

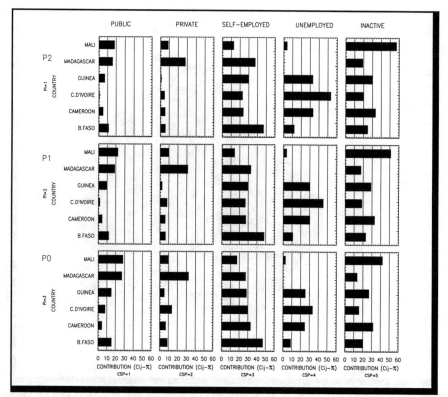

Figure 2: Relative contribution to poverty of households by measure of poverty, country and labour market status of head of the household

countries – unemployed – between 25 and 35 per cent in three countries out of five[42] – or inactive – higher than 20 per cent in four countries out of six (figure 2).

Table B in the appendix shows the variation in the depth and inequality of poverty according to the groups taken into account in the analysis. If the value of x – P1 and P2 – is increased, the relative contribution to poverty rises for households whose head is unemployed or inactive (figure 2). For these households, which are essentially made up of secondary workers or which subsist on transfers, the depth and inequality of poverty are an acute problem, irrespective of the level of development. For example, if the value of x is increased from 0 to 2, the relative contribution to poverty in households where the head is unemployed rises by around 50 per cent in three out of five countries – Cameroon, Côte d'Ivoire, Guinea. If the head of

---

[42] Madagascar was not taken into account.

the household is self-employed, the depth and inequality of the poverty remain relatively stable in the poorest countries and decrease in the intermediate income economies. On the other hand, in households headed by employees, there is a systematic decrease in the seriousness of the poverty as the value of x increases.[43]

2.   Poverty and the profile of persons and households

A.   The profile of persons

The microeconomic approach to the labour market generally gives special attention to the head of the household, who is presumed to play a fundamental role in contributing to the income for the group. However, the surveys show that the correspondence, in terms of contribution to the household income, between the status of head of the household and that of breadwinner – i. e. the person who has the highest income within the household – is sometimes fairly blurred. While in four countries out of six, around 80 per cent of the heads of households are at the same time bread-winners, the correspondence is somewhat tenuous in the other two countries: Mali (55 per cent) and Guinea (62 per cent). In both these cases, the household members who contributed the most to the group's income were above all single males. Thus, a dissociation may exist between the economic function and the social function of the head of the household, which is not the result of chance. In Mali and Guinea, households are relatively large[44] and many adult children live with their parents, one of whom – generally the father – is the head of the household or the family. Many such heads of households are inactive – the figure is 30 per cent in Mali. From an analytical point of view, this situation is especially relevant, in particular for identifying the link between poverty and participation on the labour market.

· Despite the diversity of the countries in the sample, several common factors help establish a relatively homogenous profile of the heads of households in the capitals of French speaking African countries. Most of the heads – 80 per cent – are married, whether monogamous or polygamous – a feature which shows the essentially patrilineal character of African society – and former migrants – between 75 and 80 per cent, except in Antananarivo-.[45]

---

[43] These results can be globally verified by using a consumption index as a criterion of poverty. See Lachaud (ed.) [1994].

[44] 12 and 11 persons respectively. See below.

[45] Migrants are persons not born in the capital. However, only in Côte d'Ivoire is there a large proportion of non-autochthonous migrants.

However, the proportion of poor households increases when the head of the household is a woman. Special attention needs to be given to this finding, which can in part be ascribed to the conceptual differentiation between the status of head of household and that of breadwinner.[46] Except in Mali and Guinea, for the reasons noted above, between 40 and 50 per cent of the heads of households are under the age of 40, and, if Cameroon and Madagascar are excluded, between 40 and 50 per cent are also without any education. However, irrespective of the country, the age of the heads of households tends to decrease as the standard of living increases, whereas the reverse is the case as regards education. Thus in poor households, lack of education and difficulty of access to higher education are respectively twice and three times higher than in non-poor households. A similar tendency can be seen concerning the diplomas obtained. Finally, in all the African capitals, on average more than 60 per cent of the heads of households are employed in the service sector, and the proportion tends to increase as the level of income rises.

An analysis of breadwinners in households shows that they are on average younger and better educated than the heads of households and that the proportion of women amongst them is higher. On the other hand, an analysis of profiles by standard of living reveals situations comparable to those noted previously.

The characteristics of the secondary members of the household – persons aged 15 or above – are, of course, considerably different from those of the head of the household. More than half the secondary members of the household are women, and in most cases, poor households have as many women as do non-poor households. In general, secondary members are relatively young – around two thirds are under 30 – and most of them have been born in the capital and are single – 60 per cent. Secondary members are better educated than the head of the household and their level of education increases along with that of the standard of living, particularly as regards secondary education. Finally, the employment exercised by the secondary members is closely linked to services.

B.   The profile of households

From the point of view of labour market analysis, an examination of the profile of households in terms of standard of living highlights a number of

---

[46] Many female heads of households are widows, single or divorced and do not contribute to the household income. For an analysis of this question in the case of Peru, see Rosenhouse [1989].

important factors.

First, although the economic crisis which is now raging in Africa may lead to a regrouping of households around those in which at least one person is working, traditional social structures, centred around an extended family, are the primary explanation for the large households typical of Mali and Guinea (table 1). However, irrespective of the country in question, the average size of households decreases as the level of income rises. The gap is particularly clear between the poor and the non-poor. An analysis of the composition of households shows that the proportion of adults is around two thirds, irrespective of the level of income. The dependency ratios also fall as the latter increases.[47] Thus in most French-speaking African countries, a worker from a poor household has twice as many dependents as a worker from a non-poor household.[48]

Secondly, income is very unevenly distributed between the different categories of households and the vulnerability of the poorest tends to be inversely correlated to the level of development. In Burkina Faso, Guinea and Mali, 50 per cent of the poorest households obtain between 10 and 20 per cent of income, whereas in Cameroon and Côte d'Ivoire, between 20 and 25 per cent of the poorest households have access to only 2 to 3 per cent of income (table 2). In most cases, the individual contribution to household income is higher for the head of the household. In fact, if the contribution of the various members to the household income is broken down by status, an average contribution by household and an average contribution by individual can be established.[49]

If account is taken of the demographic structure of households, the contribution of the head of the household is even higher in five countries out of six – between 50 and 80 per cent – but the role of secondary workers – in particular in countries characterized by traditional social structures – is essential. This means that the level of well-being of an average household

---

[47] The dependency ratio is the ratio between individuals without any monetary income in a household and those with such an income, including apprentices. The inclusion of the latter as providers of income probably results in an underestimate of dependency ratios. Children are taken into account in the calculation of the overall dependency ratio.

[48] Analysis also shows that the contribution of adults to the total dependency is twice as high as the contribution of children under the age of 15.

[49] Although for the head of the household, present in each of the latter, these two approaches are similar, this is not the case for secondary workers, distributed in a non-uniform way by household; and particularly as regards households comprising just one individual. Furthermore, there may be several secondary workers of a certain category in the same household.

Table 1. Dependency ratio and size of households by standard of living

Standard of living Country/parameter	Poor	Intermediate	Non-poor	Total
Burkina Faso (N)	154	101	48	300
Average size[1]	7.7 (5.2)	7.3 (4.3)	5.0 (3.0)	7.1 (4.7)
Adults (> 14 years)	4.4	4.5	3.1	4.2
Overall dependency ratio	3.2	2.6	2.0	2.8
Cameroon (N)	81	129	91	301
Average size[1]	8.3 (4.5)	8.2 (3.9)	6.8 (3.2)	7.8 (3.9)
Adults (> 14 years)	5.0	4.8	4.3	4.7
Overall dependency ratio	7.0	3.8	2.4	3.9
Côte d'Ivoire (N)	57	147	88	292
Average size[1]	7.1 (4.3)	6.2 (4.9)	4.3 (2.6)	5.8 (3.7)
Adults (> 14 years)	4.0	3.7	3.1	3.6
Overall dependency ratio	2.2	1.4	0.8	1.3
Guinea (N)	150	59	91	300
Average size[1]	12.3 (5.3)	11.8 (5.6)	8.5 (4.7)	11.1 (5.4)
Adults (> 14 years)	7.8	7.3	5.4	7.0
Overall dependency ratio	3.9	2.5	2.0	3.0
Madagascar (N)	61	64	54	179
Average size[1]	5.6 (1.9)	4.4 (1.7)	4.3 (1.5)	4.8 (1.8)
Adults (> 14 years)	4.0	3.2	3.3	3.5
Overall dependency ratio	2.4	1.3	1.0	1.5
Mali (N)	151	58	91	300
Average size[1]	12.1 (4.2)	12.7 (5.5)	11.2 (5.4)	11.9 (5.0)
Adults (> 14 years)	7.9	8.1	7.3	7.8
Overall dependency ratio	4.0	2.5	2.0	2.9

(1) The standard deviation is indicated in brackets.
Source: Pilot employment surveys in households in the capitals of: Burkina Faso, 1992; Cameroon, 1990-91; Côte d'Ivoire, 1986-87; Guinea, 1991-92; Madagascar, 1989; Mali, 1991.

is the result of a multiple labour supply. Table 2 shows that the contribution of the head of the household to group income increases along with the standard of living of the latter in two thirds of the countries, suggesting that the labour supply of these secondary members becomes greater as the household becomes poorer. Whereas in most countries the contribution of secondary activities to household income is on average low – less than 10 per cent – it is around three times higher in poor households than in well-off households. Finally, a more detailed analysis of these secondary workers shows that, except in Mali, most of supplementary household income comes from women – and, in particular, from married women.

Table 2. Structure of household income[1]

Level of income	Poor		Intermediate		Non-poor		Total	
Status	Avg /h	A v g /ind	Avg /h	Avg /ind	Avg /h	Avg /ind	Avg /h	Avg /ind
Head of household								
Burkina Faso	3.1	3.1	21.2	21.2	65.1	65.1	18.4	18.4
Cameroon	2.9	2.9	30.8	30.8	185.9	185.9	70.2	70.2
Côte d'Ivoire	3.2	3.2	18.1	18.1	49.5	49.5	24.7	24.7
Guinea	6.0	6.0	17.1	17.1	34.5	34.5	16.8	16.8
Madagascar	11.4	11.4	18.6	18.6	42.4	42.4	23.3	23.3
Mali	4.1	4.1	12.0	12.0	69.5	69.5	25.5	25.5
Second. workers								
Burkina Faso	2.5	0.7	7.8	2.1	53.9	22.7	11.7	3.4
Cameroon	3.9	0.9	14.3	3.5	44.4	12.2	20.4	5.1
Côte d'Ivoire	2.1	0.5	8.5	2.1	31.4	9.9	13.8	3.5
Guinea	9.5	1.4	18.8	3.0	23.5	5.2	15.5	2.6
Madagascar	4.0	1.3	12.1	1.9	35.2	14.7	16.2	6.2
Mali	4.6	0.7	12.8	1.8	111.4	17.7	38.7	5.7
Contribution of head of household (%)[2]								
Burkina Faso	55.1		74.1		57.6		62.7	
Cameroon	45.8		69.6		82.1		78.7	
Côte d'Ivoire	61.7		69.5		64.3		66.1	
Guinea	38.9		47.6		60.0		52.2	
Madagascar	74.6		62.0		56.1		60.1	
Mali	47.5		48.5		38.4		39.9	
Share of categories in total income (with transfers) (% households)[3]								
Burkina Faso	9.8 (51.3)		33.0 (33.7)		57.2 (15.0)		100.0	
Cameroon	1.8 (26.9)		20.6 (42.9)		77.6 (30.2)		100.0	
Côte d'Ivoire	2.7 (19.5)		34.1 (50.3)		63.2 (30.1)		100.0	
Guinea	20.8 (50.0)		30.7 (19.7)		48.5 (30.3)		100.0	
Madagascar	13.7 (34.0)		22.3 (35.8)		64.0 (30.2)		100.0	
Mali	7.5 (50.3)		7.7 (19.3)		84.8 (30.3)		100.0	

(1) Thousands of FG/week for Guinea; thousands of FM for Madagascar; thousands of F.FCA/week for the other countries. (2) For each income category, ratio between income from work generated by one (head of household) or more persons (secondary members) and the sum of household income derived from this category. (3) Ratio between the total household incomes from one category, including transfers, and the total income of households of the sample as a whole.
Source: Pilot employment surveys in households in the capitals of Burkina Faso, 1992; Cameroon, 1990-91; Côte d'Ivoire,1986-87; Guinea, 1991-92; Madagascar,1989; Mali,1991.

However, the relative weight of the contribution to income by women seems to be greater in non- poor households. This is because women from the former are more frequently employees and married women from well-off households are frequently protected women.

Thirdly, as a correlative, the analysis shows that in all the countries, the proportion of employed adults and, above all, differences between individual incomes have a greater influence than the demographic structure of households in explaining their standard of living.[50]

These preliminary results suggest the need for a deeper examination of the kind of participation in the labour market by persons from the poorest households.

III. The stratification of the labour market

1. Basis and method of analysis

The transition from traditional society to modern society in most African countries, by accelerating the concentration of society around urban centres, is giving rise to an entirely new long term process which, to a large extent, explains the complex and manifold evolution of the urban labour market. This new course of development, accentuated by the intensification of rural-urban migration, is accompanied by major changes in types of jobs and access to employment. New forms of work organization are emerging, the conventional protection of jobs in terms of status and/or remuneration – particularly in the public sector – is changing, the size of groups with low incomes and precarious jobs is increasing and open or hidden unemployment is spreading.

For two decades analysis of these fundamental changes has mainly been referred to the dualist model.[51] The formal/informal sector dichotomy

---

[50] R = total household income from the employment - principal and secondary – of its members ; Q = number of adult equivalents in the household; A = number of adults in the household; E = number of persons with principal or secondary employment in the household. The adjusted per capita income of the household R/Q may be broken down as follows: R/Q = $(A/Q)*(E/A)*(R/E)$. The A/Q ratio measures the numerical size of adults in the household and depends to a large extent on the age structure of the latter. The E/A ratio measures the proportion of employed adults and is in part determined by socio-cultural and economic factors. The R/E ratio measures in absolute terms the average contribution of each employed person to the household income. It is therefore influenced by the personal characteristics of individuals – education – and certain institutional factors – socio-occupational category and employment status. The relative importance of each of these three factors may be quantified by multiple classification analysis. In each case there is an absence of interaction effects, a beta coefficient which is much higher for the R/E factor and, as regards the latter, substantial deviations from the main average when checked against the other factors. See Lachaud (ed.) [1994].

[51] The analysis by Hart [1993], Todaro's model (Todaro [1969]) and the ILO report on

– parallel to the primary/secondary distinction of labour markets in the industrialized countries – is supposed to reflect the complexity and evolution of labour within the African urban economy. This distinction, incorporating the concepts of free entry and the productive system, is based on the idea that the differences in earnings between the two segments are only partially due to the human capital differential of persons. Other factors may help keep the inherent earnings of the informal sector below those of the modern sector. This approach to the urban labour market in Africa has been reinforced by the relatively large scope of the informal sector and the possibility of implementing economic policies for its promotion. Despite criticisms of the supposed homogeneity of the informal sector – in terms of activities and earnings[52] – and the dichomotization of forms of work, the dualist method would appear to reflect the diversity of forms of employment within the urban economy. A recent study affirmed that, alongside public and private employment in the large enterprises in the formal sector, co-exist four types of employment specific to the informal sector: casual work; wage employment in small enterprises in the informal sector; the employers of these small enterprises; and self-employed persons.[53]

The dualist approach refers back to the allocation of resources while the distribution of income and well-being depend essentially on the realloca-tion of work through the mechanism of relative prices – with unemployment implying a statistical imbalance on the labour market. However, the type of labour market segmentation which is assumed in the dualist analysis is pro-bably only one of the factors which help explain the persistence of low in-comes in certain segments of the urban economy. The recent drop in real wages and the accompanying increase in unemployment and poverty show that particularly precarious forms of employment transcend the formal/informal dichotomy and are closely linked with poverty. Thus the deter-mination of the labour market mechanisms which underlie urban poverty requires an understanding of how the labour market is stratified and, where applicable, segmented.

The idea of a segmentation of the urban labour market, independent of the formal/informal dichotomy is not a new one. During the second half of the 1970s, some writers, following Marx's analyses of relative overpopula-tion, tried to emphasize the functional character of some segments of the

---

Kenya (ILO [1972]) have greatly contributed to the development of the dualist model.

[52] Kannappan [1985].

[53] Mazumdar [1989].

labour market vis-a-vis peripheral capitalism.[54] In fact, the approach to labour market segmentation within the framework of a labour value theory showed some weaknesses as an economic policy to reduce poverty. Although based on case studies, the proposed approach remained relatively theoretical. Another more practical research line was proposed, in which the labour market segments were centred around the concepts of protection, regularity and autonomy.[55] The first attempt in this direction seems to have been made by Rodgers,[56] who made the following classification of forms of work – taken up by Lachaud[57] in the case of Côte d'Ivoire:[58] (i) wage employment protected by contracts of employment, legal constraints and barriers to entry inherent to the labour market; (ii) competitive, regular, wage employment which is exposed to labour market forces, but carried out on a continuous basis and probably on the basis of contracts of employment; (iii) non-protected, relatively heterogenous wage employment (casual work, wage employment in the small trade sector, etc.) characterized by job insecurity and/or irregularity; (iv) self-employment and family work within small production units; (v) "marginal" activities, above all low production activities carried out on the street or semi-legal or illegal activities.

This methodological orientation is based on the data recently collected in French-speaking Africa and on the cluster analysis method to define the strata in the labour market. This approach uses the Quick cluster procedure SPSS/PC+, based on an algorithm inherent to the centroid criterion. A case is assigned to the group for which the distance between the case and the centre of the group – the centroid – is the lowest. The cluster analysis was carried out with the use of 34 dichotomic variables drawn from 16 parameters: occupational category; sector – public, para-public, private; non-migratory nature of the work; irregularity of the work; type of contract of employment; proportion of employees in the enterprise; size of enterprise; liability to taxation; hours of work per week and day; type of remuneration; existence of bonuses; existence of benefits in kind; amount of capital used; ownership of premises; subcontracting; regularity of sales.

---

[54] See, for example, Gerry [1979].

[55] The idea of emphasizing vulnerable segments of the labour market also appears in other analyses. See Weeks [1986]; Aryee, Mhone [1986].

[56] Rodgers [1986].

[57] Lachaud [1988], p. 67.

[58] This classification has been used in all the studies carried out in Africa with support from the International Institute for Labour Studies.

2.   The stratification of the labour market and poverty

At the statistical level, for all the countries, the hierarchical cluster analysis shows that the different household members employed – with the exception of apprentices and family help – are divided into five homogenous groups corresponding to a logical structure of the labour market.[59] This result justifies the establishment of groups of workers on the following hypotheses: (i) irregular workers: all irregular workers; (ii) protected workers: regular wage employment; contracts of indefinite duration; monthly remuneration; at least skilled labourer; (ii) marginal self-employed persons: regular self-employment; capital below a certain amount K; (iv) self-employed persons with capital: self-employment; regular worker; capital equal to or more than K; (v) non-protected workers: regular wage employment; at most fixed term contract; monthly or variable remuneration; at most semi-skilled worker. It will be noted that this stratification of the labour market is independent of the dualist dichotomy. Thus self-employed persons with capital may perfectly well belong to the "informal" sector or the modern sector. The same is true for the group of irregular workers and non-protected employees. Table C shows the relative distribution of labour status by earner type and country.

An examination of labour market stratification according to adjusted per capita level of income leads to a number of observations. First, a comparative analysis shows a very close association between the incidence of poverty and certain forms of employment. In the case of heads of households, in all the countries, with the exception of Côte d'Ivoire, irregular workers and marginalized self-employed persons belong predominantly to poor households and, to a lesser extent, so-called intermediate households. In four countries out of five, around 50 per cent of the heads of households with this status come from poor households.[60] Furthermore, in the four low income countries, 40 to 50 per cent of non-protected employees are the heads of poor households – with only between a quarter and a third belonging to non-poor households. In the middle income economies – Cameroon and Côte d'Ivoire – heads of households who are non-protected employees account for a significant proportion. This situation can be

---

[59] In the case of Madagascar, only four groups were identified. The classification into 5 groups is the best in statistical terms (F test). For details of the statistical procedures, see Lachaud (ed.) [1994].

[60] The proportion is 38.9 per cent in Mali, with account being taken of the specificity of commercial activities. An extreme case is Burkina Faso, where 80 per cent of irregular or marginal self-employed heads of households belong to poor households.

explained by the specific character of the economic structures of the two countries, and in particular, the high proportion of workers in the private sector. In Côte d'Ivoire and Cameroon marginal self-employed persons have a level of capital approximately twice as high as in the other countries of the sample. This undoubtedly explains the loosening of the link between poverty and marginal self-employment in these two countries. Conversely, it is mainly the heads of households who are self-employed workers with capital and protected employees who appear in non-poor households. In five out of the six countries, the proportion is around 50 per cent.[61] If account is taken of secondary household members, a similar situation appears in the case of the non-poor. On the other hand, poverty declines slightly in households where secondary workers are irregular workers and marginal self-employed persons – they are in the majority in three countries out of five – and more markedly if they have the status of non-protected employees – a category found more frequently in households with an average, even high standard of living. Some forms of employment are present to a significant extent in poor households: in the four low-income economies, marginal self-employment, irregular employment and non-protected wage employment are between 35 to 75 per cent, 35 to 55 per cent and 35 to 50 per cent respectively. These same categories predominate above all in households with an intermediate standard of living in Cameroon and Côte d'Ivoire. But for all the countries, self-employed persons with capital and protected employees are the least present in the poor households. Given the relative weight of the contribution to income made by the heads of households, the influence of labour market vulnerability on the poverty of households can be measured. Figure 3, which shows the incidence of poverty in households according to the status of the principal breadwinner, confirms these tendencies.

Secondly, although the depth and inequality of poverty of households tend to reinforce the preceding analysis, they do suggest that the vulnerability associated with work status is heterogeneous. In this connection, table D in the appendix shows the stratification of the labour market for the breadwinner,[62] by standard of living of the household to which the latter belongs. In all the countries concerned, the depth of poverty (P1) and the inequality of poverty (P2) are highest in households in which the bread-

---

[61] Except in Burkina Faso, where this category predominates in intermediate groups, for both heads of households and secondary members.

[62] Given the proportion of inactive or unemployed heads of households in some country, it appears more appropriate to focus analysis on the breadwinner of the household.

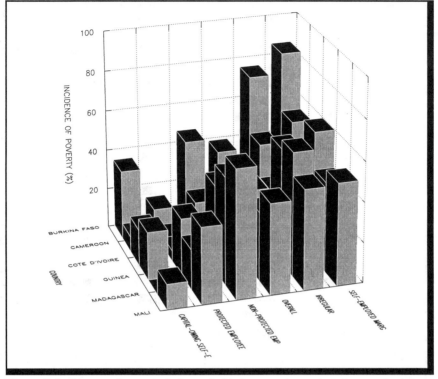

Figure 3: Incidence of poverty in households by country and status on the labour market of breadwinner

winner is an irregularly or marginally self-employed person. Except in Côte d'Ivoire, vulnerability in terms of the poverty of non-protected employees is also very marked. Marginally self-employed workers and, to a lesser extent, non-protected employees most contribute to the poverty of house-holds. In all countries of the sample, the relative contribution to poverty increases significantly with the degree of aversion to the latter for marginal independent workers (figure 4). This segment of the labour market is the most vulnerable in the urban regions of Africa. The relative contribution to poverty of irregular workers, increases slightly with the value of x in half the countries and remains stable in the others. The relative contribution to poverty of non-protected employees falls substantially with the degree of aversion to the latter in two thirds of the countries and increases slightly in the remaining third. In two countries – Madagascar and Mali – households in which the breadwinner is a subordinate employee in the private and public sectors contributes to more than 40 per cent of the poverty. This fact highlights the social impact of institutional changes concerning the labour

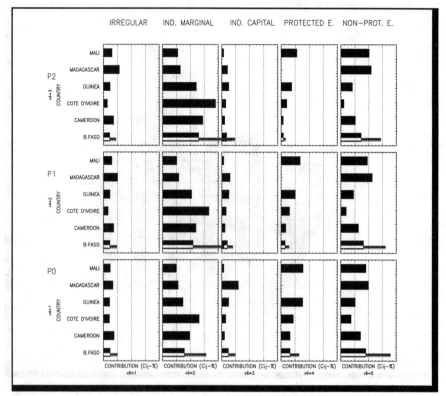

Figure 4: Relative contribution to poverty of households by measure of poverty, country and status on the labour market of breadwinner

market for which provision is made in structural adjustment programmes. These results can be illustrated by the development of the poverty incidence curves in a fairly representative country, Guinea[63] (figure 5). Only in households where the breadwinner is a marginal self-employed person is the incidence of poverty not very sensitive to the determination of the poverty line. Indeed, if the poverty line is reduced by 25 per cent, the incidence of poverty for this segment of the labour market falls slightly.

Thirdly, this stratification of the labour market explains the specificity of the labour market integration and income-generating processes. A

---

[63] Each point on a curve indicates the proportion of the population of households whose adjusted income is below the amount appearing on the horizontal axis. The projection on the vertical axis of each intersection of each curve with a poverty line indicates the incidence of poverty - equal to P0 with a poverty line 1 of 12,209 FG per month. Poverty line 2 corresponds to 75 per cent per cent of the line adopted in the present study.

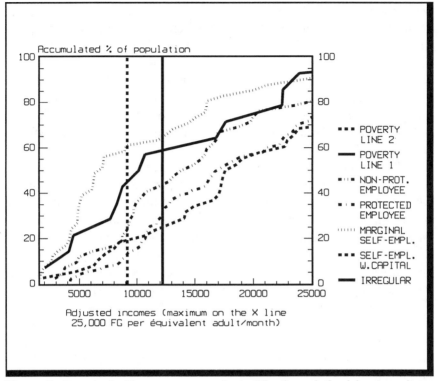

Figure 5: Poverty incidence curves and stratification of the labour market - breadwinner - Conakry 1991-92

predominant proportion of heads of households are employees,[64] except in poor households where self-employment is the main form of activity – with the exception of Mali. Furthermore, public employment – in public administration and public enterprises – predominates in intermediate and non-poor households in four out of the six countries – Cameroon, Guinea, Madagascar and Burkina Faso. In all the countries around 90 per cent of heads of households have a regular job, although irregularity of employment is relatively more marked in poor households.[65] Other data show that the heads of households in the categories of higher and middle management

---

[64] Self-employment accounts for 40.9, 26.5, 25.0, 41.4 and 37.9 per cent respectively of total employment in Mali, Cameroon, Côte d'Ivoire, Madagascar, Guinea and Burkina Faso.

[65] However, this result is relative in so far as regularity does not automatically mean stability of income - for self-employed persons - but rather the exercise of the same activity in a continuous manner over a given period.

work in the administration on contracts of indefinite duration. Verbal contracts and fixed-term contracts are generally obtained by manual and semi-skilled workers. Finally, more than two thirds of senior and middle management and skilled manual workers have more than ten years' seniority of employment. On the other hand, it is in the category of manual and self-employed workers that the most recent integrations into the labour market have occurred. This result must be related to the weak labour demand which prevailed during this period of structural adjustment of African economies.

The structure of the employment of secondary members by standard of living of households shows that a high proportion of married and single women are employees. However, there is a notable difference between the two groups. Married women from poor households are essentially self-employed, whereas single women are mainly self-employed, apprentices or family help workers. Most male secondary members of households are employees. Irregularity of employment affects occupational categories which are fairly close to those affected in the case of heads of households. Furthermore, an analysis of the types of contracts tends to show the relative protection of women employees as compared with secondary male members for whom verbal contracts are more usual. In addition, the existence of contracts of unlimited duration increases as the standard of living of the household rises.

In this context, the close link between forms of employment within the household is interesting. In general, between 60 and 70 per cent of the secondary members – except self-employed persons with capital – have status identical to that of the principal breadwinner.[66] This situation probably has important repercussions on methods of access to employment. In Africa, access to protected and non-protected wage employment of secondary

---

[66] The analysis does not distinguish between persons who work in the same family enterprise as the breadwinner from those who work in a different enterprise. However, this is of little importance. By definition, there is a self-employed worker - the employer - in each enterprise and the employer owns the capital; since the case of associates is relatively rare, the other workers of the family enterprise will have a different status. In Burkina Faso, 89.6 per cent and 63.0 per cent of the secondary members of households are, respectively, protected employees and non-protected employees, when the breadwinner has the same employment status. This is also the case - with percentages above 50.0 per cent - with Mali, Guinea and, to a lesser extent, with Cameroon and Côte d'Ivoire. In the same way, in Mali, 73.0 per cent and 55.6 per cent of secondary workers are, respectively, irregular and marginal self-employed workers when the breadwinner is from the same labour market segments. This is also the case in Côte d'Ivoire, Cameroon, Guinea - with the exception of irregular workers - and Madagascar.

members of households suggests that privileged personal relations are involved. It should be remembered in this connection that the public sector employs most of the employees in the six countries studied. Except in Burkina Faso, when the breadwinner is a self-employed worker with capital, the methods of acquiring technical capital – the family, savings – and its relative scarcity probably restrict its access for other secondary members. In these circumstances, wage employment within or outside the family is the most likely method of employment. Of course, in households where the breadwinner has a precarious job – as an irregularly or marginally self-employed worker – secondary members have little chance of gaining access to other segments of the labour market.

Not surprising, the lowest earned incomes are those of marginal self-employed persons, irregular workers and, to a lesser extent, non-protected employees[67] and the income – independently of status of work – of women which are lower than that of their male counterparts. In this connection, multiple classification analysis shows that in five countries of the six, persons who have irregular employment are penalized in terms of income.[68]

Empirical data confirm the marked dependency of the household's standard of living on the labour status of the head of the household. An analysis of the relationship between the adjusted level of income of the household and a set of independent variables inherent to the head of the household – labour status, education, training, age, nationality – and to the group to which the head belongs – size of household, percentage of employed persons in the household – shows that the labour status accounts for most of the variation in the standard of living in five countries out of six (table E in the appendix). All other things being equal, if the head of the household moves from irregular employment into protected wage employment, the earnings of the group increase by 225, 131, 76, 128 and 70 per cent respectively in Burkina Faso, Cameroon, Côte d'Ivoire, Guinea and Madagascar. The special situation of Mali should once again be noted.

---

[67] It is self-employed workers with capital who have the highest incomes in urban areas: however, income distribution is very wide in the case of self-employed persons.

[68] Approximately 70.0 per cent as compared with the principal average, all other things being equal. The only exception is Mali. See Lachaud (ed.) [1994].

IV. Urban unemployment

1. The incidence of urban unemployment

In the urban areas of Africa, unemployment, as defined by the International Labour Organization,[69] does not fully encompass the scope of inactivity. Some persons exercise a secondary and/or main activity while they are looking for a different job. They are for the most part persons who have either lost their job and have taken up self-employment or who have never worked before and believe that the job they have is not commensurate with their skills. These persons may be considered as under-employed, because their present employment implies an opportunity cost, since the remuneration which they receive is below what they could obtain in other employment. Although sub-optimal employment is difficult to define, empirical research has shown that many persons take up activities which they consider marginal compared to their qualifications. Some persons exercise no activity and are not looking for a job. Logically, they are not members of the active population. However, some of them would like to work but take no steps to do so for particular reasons: "there are no jobs"; "it is difficult to find a job if you have no skills"; "I plan to set up business when I get the capital"; "I am waiting for a reply to my application", etc. These are potential job-seekers who would become members of the active population if labour market conditions changed. They are marginal, unemployed persons who are usually classified amongst the inactive population. However, a marginal unemployment rate can be calculated by incorporating this category of persons into the active population.

The analysis of unemployment rates calls for several comments. First, unemployment is a major form of adjustment on the urban labour market in Africa[70] (figure 6 and table F in the appendix). In general, between one fifth and one quarter of the active population aged 15 and above are unemployed in five countries out of the six and between 20 and 40 per cent of secondary members of households are unemployed. Furthermore, despite the conceptual uncertainties inherent in comparisons over time, this process seems to have become more marked over the last 15 years. For example, in Mali, in 1976 and 1988, the unemployment rates for the active population aged 10

---

[69] Lack of principal or secondary employment, fit for work and looking for work. See ILO [1990].

[70] The effect of this kind of adjustment would tend to increase as the level of development rises.

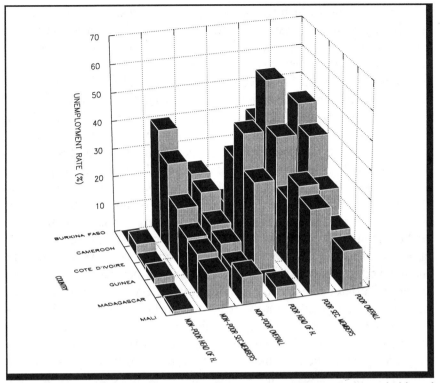

Figure 6: Urban unemployment rate, by country, situation in household and standard of living - % of the active population

and above were, respectively, 8.1 per cent and 16.0 per cent.[71] In the same way, in Abidjan, the unemployment rate increased threefold between 1978 and 1986-87.[72] The recent destabilization of the macroeconomic situation, the acceleration in population growth and dysfunctionings in the educational system to a large extent explain the significant effects which this kind of adjustment has on the urban labour market. A different picture of the adjustment process in terms of unemployment appears in table F in the appendix. Thus, marginal unemployment affects a high proportion of women. In two thirds of the countries concerned, between one fifth and almost half of all secondary women members are potentially active. Although in some countries – Mali, Guinea – this is partially due to

---

[71] See Lachaud [1990].

[72] According to Vandemoortele, unemployment rates in sub-Saharan Africa have doubled over the last 15 years - from 10 to 20 per cent. See Vandemoortele [1991].

traditional structures which restrict the participation of women on the labour market, the economic crisis may well have significantly accentuated the phenomenon of discouraged workers. The level of under-employment is not insignificant amongst secondary male members.

Secondly, empirical research shows single secondary male and female members are the most vulnerable to unemployment. Thus the unemployment rates for secondary male and female members are between 20 and 50 per cent; in two thirds of the countries, more than 40 per cent of single men are without jobs and in five countries out of six at least one third of unmarried women are looking for a job. If these rates are added to those of marginal unemployment, the loss of the level of well-being can be measured in terms of the non-participation in the labour market of an essentially young population. This result is not surprising given the relative number of graduates with this matrimonial status. On the other hand, except in a few cases, the proportion of heads of households and married women who are unemployed is relatively low: between 5 and 10 per cent. However, an important difference exists between the two categories: the incidence of marginal unemployment is much greater for married women than for heads of households. Several factors may easily explain the scope and differentiation of these unemployment rates. In most African countries, social structures give the head of the household a role which is both social and economic. Thus, heads of households tend to be the oldest persons in a household and are either inactive, or have been employed for a very long time. As regards married women, their effective labour market participation rate is lower and many of them would like to be able to exercise any kind of activity. Those who join the labour market do so as a result of real opportunities, in particular the exercise of an independent commercial activity; on the other hand, when no such opportunities arise – because of their low level of education – they become part of the potentially active population.

Thirdly, in all the countries concerned, the unemployment rate is inversely related to the standard of living (figure 6). Whereas in poor households between one fifth and almost one half of individuals are without employment, the proportion is between 10 and 20 per cent in more affluent households. In general, the incidence of unemployment is between two and three times higher in poor households than in non-poor households. Thus one of the causes of poverty in the urban areas of Africa seems to be the lack of participation in the labour market. Irrespective of the country, marginal unemployment falls markedly as the standard of living rises. The fact that the incidence of marginal unemployment is on average twice as

Table 3: Unemployment rate by education and age – 15 years and above (percentage of active population)

Country Parameter		Burkina Faso	Came-roon	Côte d'Ivoire	Guinea	Mada-gascar	Mali
No	15-29 years	30.1	0.0	11.9	12.6	-	19.4
schooling	30-39 years	10.9	16.7	6.7	1.8	-	8.3
	> = 40 years	4.7	0.0	12.2	10.0	-	2.1
	Overall	15.0	8.0	10.8	9.3	-	9.9
Primary	15-29 years	42.1	54.1	35.3	12.9	8.3[2]	20.1[1]
	30-39 years	17.2	21.7	9.1	19.3	0.0	8.5
	> = 40 years	19.2	7.1	3.4	23.3	2.2	9.1
	Overall	34.7	28.8	25.4	16.3	2.7	16.2
Secondary	15-29 years	60.5	50.5	45.0	23.9	-	-
1st cycle	30-39 years	40.0	11.7	13.0	18.9	-	-
	> = 40 years	13.3	18.6	22.2	20.0	-	-
	Overall	43.4	30.9	35.2	21.9	-	-
Secondary	15-29 years	56.0	45.2	43.5	38.2	40.4	45.2
2nd cycle	30-39 years	0.0	14.3	8.3	21.4	10.4	12.5
	> = 40 years	0.0	13.0	0.0	12.8	1.3	9.4
	Overall	24.6	27.7	30.1	26.0	14.5	24.4
Higher	15-29 years	21.0	60.9	42.9	68.0	42.9	64.3
	30-39 years	7.7	20.8	12.5	29.2	10.5	34.2
	> = 40 years	0.0	0.0	0.0	7.4	0.0	0.0
	Overall	8.1	31.7	25.0	32.5	20.9	29.7
Overall	15-29 years	43.3	51.8	33.3	23.2	37.0	25.6
	30-39 years	10.1	16.7	9.3	19.1	8.5	13.9
	> = 40 years	6.7	9.6	11.3	13.3	1.4	4.2
	Overall	25.0	29.3	22.8	19.0	13.1	16.9

Note: The unemployment rate has been calculated as follows: unemployment rate = [(unemployed)/(employed + under-employed + unemployed)].
Source: Pilot employment surveys in households in the capitals of Burkina Faso, 1992; Cameroon, 1990-91; Côte d'Ivoire, 1986-87; Guinea, 1991-92; Madagascar, 1989; Mali, 1991.

high in poor households as in non-poor households is another special adjustment process on the labour market. For some categories of persons, who are often underprivileged in terms of human capital, the difficulties of access to the labour market force them to become marginalized from the active population. Thus the lower effective participation in the labour market leads to lower incomes at the household level.

Fourthly, the different surveys confirm the high rate of unemployment amongst young persons and graduates in the African capitals (table 3). In four out of the six countries, between one third and half of persons aged between 15 and 29 are unemployed; in the two other countries – Guinea and Mali – the proportion is one quarter. Probably the high rate of marginal unemployment in these two latter countries explains the lower rate of unemployment amongst young persons. On the other hand, for persons above the age of 30, the unemployment rate fall substantially. Irrespective of sex, unemployment rates increase as the level of education rises, especially from the secondary level. Thus, if the unemployment rate of persons without schooling is only 10 per cent on average, it is between 25 and 40 per cent for persons who have attained the secondary level. To one of the basic questions – whether youth unemployment is transitory or permanent – the analysis answers that it is more structural than transitory. Of course, that the unemployment rate falls as age increases could mean that lack of experience makes young persons more vulnerable on the labour market. However, several factors tend to confirm the structural nature of youth unemployment. First, the duration of the unemployment is at least as long for those who become integrated into the labour market for the first time as for those who have already some occupational experience. Secondly, young unemployed persons are willing to review their wage expectations in three quarters of cases. Thirdly, the unemployment rate amongst women is as high as that of men – even higher in the case of young women. Finally, as noted above, the unemployment rate is virtually correlated with the level of education, and the inverted U curve appears clearly in some countries. In this connection, it must be emphasized that the vulnerability of young persons is not unrelated to their level of education, which means that young persons are unemployed not because they are young but because they are educated. Thus, for the 15-29 age group, the unemployment rate increases substantially as the level of education rises. In the case of the countries of sub-Saharan Africa, these unemployment rates amongst graduates are not surprising. Indeed, the educational system is poorly adapted to market needs at three levels: a surplus of graduates of higher education, a lack of adaptation and shortage of technical skills and an absence of any technical component in the basic educational system.

2. Profile of unemployment and poverty

In the urban areas of sub-Saharan Africa, as noted above, the precarious nature of employment status is not the only cause for the low standard of living of households, as unemployment and poverty are also closely linked. Several other elements tend to reinforce this idea and should be taken into account in this context.

Table 4: Distribution of unemployed persons by reasons for seeking job (%)

Country Parameter	Burkina Faso	Came- roon	Côte d'Ivoire	Guinea	Mada- gascar	Mali
Unemployment (N)	197	224	217	226	64	176
Loss of employment	14.7	27.2	28.6	41.6	7.8	18.2
New entry	85.3	72.8	71.4	58.4	92.2	81.8
Total	100.0	100.0	100.0	100.0	100.0	100.0
Other reasons (N)	67	31	65	44	45	25
Change of employ- ment[1]	22.0	11.4	17.4	7.0	40.4	4.5
Extra work[1]	3.4	0.8	8.9	9.3	0.9	7.9

(1) Percentage of all the reasons for seeking employment.
Source: Pilot employment surveys in household in the capitals of: Burkina Faso, 1992; Cameroon, 1990-91; Côte d'Ivoire, 1986-87; Guinea, 1991-92; Madagascar, 1989; Mali, 1991.

First, various surveys clearly show that the difficulty of obtaining a first job is the main reason for urban unemployment (table 4). In five countries out of six, at least 70 per cent of unemployed persons were looking for their first job.[73] Even in Guinea where the public sector restructuring has had a greater impact than everywhere else, the proportion of unemployed persons entering the labour market for the first time is around 60 per cent. The large proportion of young people in the total population and the imbalance between aspirations and job opportunities are the main reasons for this situation. The phenomenon has probably become more marked since the beginning of the 1980s when recruitment into the public service was restricted, and especially since the second half of the 1980s when public service recruitment was frozen in many African countries. However, the role of restructuring in the public productive sector must not be underestimated in the rise of urban unemployment in Africa. In Guinea, almost 40 per cent of job losses can be ascribed to the winding up, restructuring and privatization of public enterprises, compared with 34.4 , 6.3, 18 and 13.7 per cent respectively in Mali, Côte d'Ivoire, Cameroon and Burkina Faso.

The heterogenous nature of urban employment encompasses both disparities and similarities. In the first case, a number of unemployed persons with occupational experience are male. The proportion of heads of households and secondary workers is relatively balanced on average, but the

---

[73] Unemployed persons without any occupational experience are aged between 23 and 26, whereas those who have lost their jobs are, on average, between 30 and 40 years old.

share of the former is much higher in the case of poor households. In these circumstances, and given the economic weight of the latter within the household, it is not surprising to see that there is a close link between unemployment and poverty.

On the other hand, women make up a much greater proportion of young unemployed persons – mainly secondary workers: between 35 and 40 per cent depending on the country, except in Mali for well-known reasons. Furthermore, unemployed persons with occupational experience are less well educated than those who enter the labour market for the first time,[74] although in both cases the less well educated are proportionally more represented in poor households. Finally, young unemployed persons seem to be more inclined to work in the public sector than their counterparts with occupational experience. Indeed, almost 50 per cent of new job seekers apply to the administration and public enterprises, whereas the figure is around 25 per cent in the case of unemployed persons with occupational experience. It is true that many of the latter have been laid off as a result of the winding up, restructuring or privatization of enterprises in the public productive sector and they perhaps are no longer able to meet the requirements set for entry into the public administration. Despite the introduction of new economic policies, the public sector in Africa always attracts young persons in search of a first job. However, their aspirations are now at least equally directed towards the private sector, something which would have been unimaginable ten years ago. This result appears to confirm those analyses which have tended to show that there is no segmentation of the labour market between the public and private sectors. Employees in the public sector receive a substantial bonus only in two countries: Cameroon – 38.4 per cent – and Mali – 34.8 per cent.[75]

Irrespective of the reason for unemployment – the loss of a job or new entry on to the labour market - persons in search of employment have two points in common. First, most of them – between 50 and 75 per cent – are looking for permanent wage employment and the proportion of those who are indifferent is higher than the proportion of those who would like to be self -employed. Secondly, irrespective of the country, at least two thirds are prepared to revise downwards their wage aspirations if they continue to be

---

[74] Although it varies considerably between countries, the proportion of persons with at least a secondary level of schooling can be estimated as being 50 per cent higher amongst unemployed persons without any occupational experience than amongst those who already have occupational experience.

[75] Lachaud (ed.) [1994].

unemployed. The length of unemployment does not vary significantly between the types of unemployed persons[76] – it is on average between 24 and 36 months – although there appear to have been more job offers made to unemployed persons with occupational experience.

These results might indicate that the lack of experience of young persons on the labour market is not a convincing explanation of unemployment. The rigidity of the labour market for graduates seems to be based on hypotheses which are becoming increasingly invalid in the African context.[77] Age-earnings profiles in the public service have become increasingly uncertain and recruitment criteria have been diversified. The coexistence of unemployment amongst graduates and the strong demand for education may be partly explained by changes in the recruitment procedures in the productive system.[78] The reduction in expenditure and the growing privatisation on education and the many strikes which have been held in universities have lowered the quality of the educational system. As a result, despite the increasing supply of graduates, a gulf has emerged between the nominal and real value of the diplomas received. Thus, employers give greater attention to recruitment procedures which means that the wage offered to those who are recruited is unchanged, whereas those who fail to meet the standards remain unemployed. The slowness in the transmission of this information could well explain the persisting high demand for education.

Secondly, whether or not unemployment is explained in terms of supply or demand, in terms of well-being it is closely linked to poverty. The results outlined earlier – the inverse relationship between the unemployment rate and the standard of living of households, and the growth of the relative contribution to poverty of households in which the head is unemployed when the x value increases – can be made more explicit. First, poor households proportionally have the most unemployed persons and the ratio between the number of unemployed persons and the number of persons providing income is approximately twice as high as in non-poor households. The surveys show that in households with unemployed persons, the

---

[76] It is two to six months longer for unemployed persons with occupational experience in three countries out of five; it is two to eight months shorter in the other two countries. Madagascar was not included because of the small number of unemployed persons with occupational experience.

[77] In other words, the labour supply cost is rigid if there is a manpower surplus, and unemployment does not give the expected signal to young persons who want to invest education.

[78] A similar hypothesis is proposed by Mazumdar [1989].

employment status of the other active members is more precarious in poor households than in non-poor households. The former, for example, include relatively more marginal self-employed workers. In addition, persons belonging to poor households, have undoubtedly more difficulty reaping benefit from their diploma or qualifications on the labour market than do persons from a higher social background. The processes governing access to employment which will be examined below confirm this view.

Thirdly, the incidence of unemployment on a worker's career tends to be greater for those from poor households and/or those with a precarious status on the labour market. Although data are available for only four countries in the sample, several results can be cited. In all the countries, the frequency of short term unemployment – the last twelve months – is the highest for persons from poor households and for currently irregular workers, marginalized self-employed persons and non-protected employees. On the other hand, the frequency of long term unemployment – prior to the last 12 months – is less related to the standard of living, type of worker and country. However, in the three countries for which data were relatively satisfactory – Burkina Faso, Cameroon and Côte d'Ivoire – the length of short term and long term unemployment is the highest for workers from poor households and from those who have a precarious form of employment.

Finally, to evaluate the relation between unemployment and poverty, a logistic model expressed by the following equation has been estimated:

[I] $NV_i = f(I_i, F_i, S_i, E_i, E^2_i, C_i, T_i, TC_i, DM_i)$

where NV_i, TC_i, DM_i, I_i, F_i, S_i, E_i, C_i, and T_i, represent, respectively, standard of living, unemployment rate and size of households, education, training, sex, general experience – current and previous job experience – unemployment and vulnerable labour status of head of household. Thus the model takes account of factors concerning both individual persons and households.[79] The dependent variable NV_i of the previous equation is coded 1 for poor households, and 0 if they are intermediate or non-poor. The logistic form of the model implies an estimate by maximum likelihood and the generation of related tests.

The results are contained in table G in the appendix and show, in particular, that the probability of becoming poor is greater in the case of households from which the head is unemployed; all other things being equal, the log of the chances of becoming poor increases by country from

---

[79] The selection bias has not been taken into account.

Table 5: Probability (Pi) of poverty by unemployment and labour market status [1]

Country Parameter	Burkina Faso	Came- roon	Côte d'Ivoire	Guinea	Mali
Status of head of household					
Unemployed	0.766	0.592	0.500	0.733	n.a.
Employed	0.489	0.173	0.122	0.433	n.a.
Vulnerable labour status	0.613	0.333	0.157	0.531	n.a.
Non-vulnerable labour status	0.441	0.167	0.149	0.496	n.a.

(1) Means of variables.
Source: based on table G in the appendix.

1.2 to 1.9, which means that if Pi = 0.5, the variation in Pi is between 0.3 and 0.5.[80] On the other hand, the log of chances of becoming poor increases by country from 1.4 to 1.7 when the unemployment rate within households increases of 1 per cent.

Table 5 gives the probability of becoming poor by unemployment and labour status of the head of household. In the four countries concerned, the proposed model shows that, all other things being equal, the probability of becoming poor is between two and three times higher in the case of households from which the head is unemployed than for households from which the head is employed. We also note, as it has been said before, that the vulnerable labour status is a factor which influences poverty.[81]

V. The labour supply

The analysis of the labour supply is essential to an understanding of the functioning of the urban labour market, and in particular of the mechanisms which contribute to the emergence or spread of poverty. The present research offers an opportunity to explore this analytical approach. After a review of some conceptual and methodological aspects, the following paragraphs examine labour supply structure and strategies.[82]

---

[80] On the basis of the relation: $dP_i = \beta(P_i-(1-P_i))$.

[81] Lachaud (ed.) [1994].

[82] In the context of sub-Saharan Africa, relatively little use has been made of this kind of approach for two main reasons. First, the analysis of the labour supply has been concentrated above all on an examination of the factors leading to the modification of participation rates in the context of strong population growth; secondly, the fragmentary

1. Concepts and methods[83]

For classical economists, discussions on the determinants of growth in the active population, in particular the influence of variations in real wages, used to be the main features of any analysis of the labour supply. Today, without abandoning the examination of population growth, labour economists believe that the analytical approach should be inverted. Thus, specific attention is given to the labour supply process of a population of a given size. In this connection, one of the components of the labour supply is the participation rate of the active population, i.e. the percentage of the population which has or which is seeking paid employment. Thus, persons making up the "labour supply" are those who have an economic activity or who are engaged in the process of looking for a job. Although empirical research shows that the volume of the labour supply is very varied,[84] in the present study the "supply" refers to persons aged 15 and above who have an economic activity or who are in the process of looking for a job during the reference week. To the extent that urban unemployment is relatively high in sub-Saharan Africa, an examination of the labour market mechanisms linked to poverty means that account is taken of active persons as a whole. The determination of the labour supply implies choices as regards age, activity and reference period. Several elements justify the choices made in this study: the gap between the labour supply of persons aged 7 and above, and those aged 15 and above, is marginal;[85] the account taken of secondary activities is justified in as far as married women reported that they exercised a

---

nature of the micro-economic data on the labour market - particularly at the household level - has been a serious obstacle to research in this sphere. See in particular: Anker, Knowles [1977]; Standing [1978]; Fallon [1985].

[83] This part follows the analysis made by Lachaud [1991].

[84] Thus some analyses examine the determinants of the "employment rates" by specifying the position of persons in terms of their status on the labour market and by referring to "participation rates" (Mazumbdar [1981]). To the extent that persons are classified as "employed" or "non-employed", the participation rate excludes the unemployed. Other studies determine labour supply in a more restrictive manner, by emphasizing the explanatory factors of the "participation rates" of persons aged 16 or above, who have been in wage employment, whether principal or secondary, during the previous year (Appleton, Collier, Horsnell [1990]). See also the approaches in the Western countries based on Killingworth, Heckmann [1986]. Some studies carried out in Western countries define the labour supply as "per capita work input", i.e. the product of the employment-population ratio by the weekly hours performed by employed workers.

[85] But, when this is not the case, it might be appropriate to taken into account the active population aged at least 7 years.

secondary activity without being engaged in a principal activity; the reference period of the preceding week has no special significance.[86] Thus at the practical level, the labour supply rate for a given stratum is obtained by comparing the number of active persons – employed, under-employed and unemployed – with that of the total population of the group.[87]

At the econometric level, an examination of the labour supply functions implies choices concerning the underlying model and the estimation procedure used. Since these methodological elements are relatively well-known, only a few brief remarks will be made here. The use of the linear probability model is possible, but it implies an estimation which eventually leads to predicted values outside the 0-1 interval, i.e. unacceptable values. Thus the limits imposed on the binary variable – for example, 0 and 1 – are ignored if the standard multiple regression model of the least squares is used. Although there are several possible ways of overcoming this difficulty in the linear probability model, it seems preferable to use models for which predictions are consonant with the appropriate interval. Thus the problem can be reformulated in such a way that the predictions no longer refer to a binary variable, but rather to a continuous variable which of course remains within the O/1 interval. The two models most commonly used are the logit and probit models. The choice of estimation procedures also determines the analysis of the labour supply and two difficulties must be mentioned here. First, there is the problem of the selection bias. The sample of active persons may be "self-determined" and thus non-random, with the first choice concerning the decision of participating or not in the labour market. In other words, the coefficients of the earnings function may be biased, since they reflect not only the effects of cause variables on incomes, but the probability of being employed. In accordance with Heckman,[88] the correction of this bias implies an estimation of the Mills (Lambda) inverse ratio on the basis of the probit estimation of the participation equation and its inclusion in the earnings equation. Although this problem arises above all in identifying the determinants of participation in wage employment,[89] Heckman's correction

---

[86] In general, more than 90 per cent of persons employed have exercised the same activity over the last 12 months.

[87] In the same way, a potential labour supply rate could be obtained by including marginal unemployed persons, as well as an employment rate, i.e. for each stratum, the ratio between the number of employed persons - those who are in wage employment or self-employment - and the total number of the stratum in question.

[88] Heckman [1976].

[89] In this case, persons have the choice between wage employment and self-employment. The argument in favour of excluding self-employment persons is based on the

can be maintained in the analysis of the labour supply as a whole. In this case, the Lambda coefficient expresses the probability of being included in the sample as an active person. Secondly, the income from the earnings in structural labour supply equations is not really exogenous, since it is determined by the labour supply and demand. If it is used directly in the structural participation equation, a bias may result. It is therefore important to use the predicted value of income inherent in the earnings equation in the structural participation equation. With account being taken of these two difficulties, an analysis of labour market participation implies an estimation of the model expressed by the equations [2] to [4]:

[2] $V_i = f(I_i, DIP_i, F_i, DE_i, CF_i)$ $(i = I...n)$

[3] $R_i = g(I_i, DIP_i, F_i, DE_i, \Lambda_i)$ $(i = I...n)$

[4] $Os_i = h(I_i, DIP_i, F_i, DE_i, CF_i, EXPREV_i)$ $(i = I...n)$

The equations [2], [3] and [4] represent, respectively, the reduced labour supply equation, the earnings equation and the structural labour supply equation. The variables I_i, DIP_i, F_i, DE_i, CF_i, Lambda (Λi) and $EXPREV_i$ represent respectively education, training, demographic factors, family background, Mills inverse ratio and the expected income. The list of variables is explained in tables L and M in the appendix. Thus the estimation of [2] on the basis of the probit model allows a determination to be made of the inverse Mills-Lambda ratio. This latter is used in equation [3] – estimated by the least squares – which leads to the determination of expected income – EXPREV. Finally, an estimation of [4] on the basis of maximum likelihood allows the parameters of the structural labour supply equation to be determined. In the present research, this latter is also estimated by standard of living of households. Furthermore, an analysis of the labour supply of secondary members of households will also be made on the basis of simplified, logistic probability models.

2.   The labour supply structure

Tables H, I, J and K in the appendix make it possible to determine the basic elements of the labour supply structure in the urban areas of French speaking Africa.

---

idea that earnings represent income from both capital and labour.

First, the research indicates that the overall labour supply varies significantly from country to country; the rates range approximately from 40 per cent – in Mali – to 70 per cent – in Côte d'Ivoire (table H). These disparities can be easily explained by the very heterogenous nature of the labour market participation of the different members of the household which, in turn, reflects the unequal incidence of traditional structures. Thus it is no accident that the overall about supply is lowest in countries such as Mali and Guinea. The participation of women – especially single women – in the labour market in these countries is very low for the reasons already noted. But in general, it is clear that the labour supply of women in Africa is much lower than that of men. In this respect, the gap is very marked between secondary members, since in two thirds of the countries, the labour supply rates of secondary male members are twice as high as those of secondary female members. This undoubtedly explains the marked incidence of marginal unemployment in the case of the latter (tables F and K). Unequal access to the educational system plays a major role in this process.

Secondly, the taking account of age produces an expected result. Irrespective of the country and type of worker, the labour supply rates show an inverted U curve which depends on age. However, marginal unemployment affects at least 50 per cent of young persons – men and women – under the age of 25 and between 70 and 80 per cent of those under 30. This means that the gap between the potential and actual labour supply is greatest for the youngest age groups. Thus many young persons – especially women – would like to participate in the labour market, but are dissuaded from looking for any kind of job because of the conditions in the labour market – in particular, the high rate of unemployment.

Thirdly, irrespective of the country, the labour supply increases as the standard of living of households rises. In three countries of the sample – Cameroon, Madagascar and Mali – the labour supply rate of non-poor households is between 40 and 60 per cent higher than that of poor households; in the three other countries – Burkina Faso, Côte d'Ivoire and Guinea – the proportion is between 20 and 35 per cent. This result is partly due to the demographic structure of households, and in particular the evolution of the dependency ratios which are inversely related to the standard of living of households. In actual fact the evolution is not homogenous by type of worker. In the case of heads of household and married women, labour market participation rates systematically increase with the rise in adjusted income. Furthermore, the participation rate ratio between heads of households and married women decreases as standard of living increases.[90] On the other hand, the evolution is less marked in the case of secondary workers, since in one third of the countries the labour supply rate falls as the standard of living of the household rises. This result is particularly interesting since it has already been shown that, irrespective of the country, marginal unemployment is twice as low in well off households as in poor households.

The data indicate a relative differentiation in the effective participation in the labour market by sex and age (tables J and K). In Africa, women participate to a much less extent than men in wage employment. In most of the countries, around one third of the total male population of households works in wage employment – protected and non-protected – whereas the proportion for women is only between 10 and 15 per cent. On the other hand, the relative incidence of self-employment amongst men and women is very similar; but, when this form of employment requires a substantial amount of capital, it is more often undertaken by men. These observations explain the extent of inactivity and marginal unemployment amongst women.

Neither sex nor age seems to be the major determinants of the incidence of vulnerability on the labour market. Irrespective of sex, in five countries out of six – the exception being Côte d'Ivoire – around 80 per cent of protected employees and self-employed persons with capital are at least 30 years old. This is logical in so far as these employment statuses require the acquisition of some degree of human capital and, in the second case, the availability of a large amount of technical capital. Furthermore, it is above all married women and heads of households who are protected employees. In the same way, around two thirds of marginal self-employed and irregular workers are at least 30 years old. Young persons are more often non-protected employees in posts which required much lower skills.[91] However, non-protection of employees is exclusive to the youngest workers; between one quarter and one third of non-protected male employees are over 39 years old.

Labour supply structure, then, requires an analysis of the different strategies implemented, followed by an examination of the processes governing access to employment and career profiles.

---

[90] Except in Mali, the figure falls from around 2 for poor households to 1.2/1.5 for non-poor households.

[91] Non-protected wage employment may sometimes offer a point of entry to the labour market leading to protected wage employment.

3.   Labour supply strategies

Econometric analyses clarify some of the basic characteristics of the labour supply of households.

First, let us consider the labour supply of household members as a whole. Table L in the appendix shows the parameters of the probit structural equations of labour supply and suggests a number of comments.[92] First, the labour supply increases with age; all other things being equal, if the age increases by one year there is an increase in the probability of participation in the labour market of between 0.21 and 0.36 in three countries, and by 0.09 in one country. The sign and significant value of the variable (Age)^2 imply that the probability of participation in the labour market rises up to around the age of 35-40 years. Secondly, in five countries out of six, the availability of training, in particular apprenticeship in micro-enterprises and large enterprises, is positively related to labour market participation. This means that access to employment is linked to the informal and formal transmission of technical skills. In this connection, the relatively high value of the apprenticeship coefficients in the different countries – between 0.8 and 2.4 – is worth noting. This result, coupled with those from the logistic estimation of unemployment – table G – should be taken into account in the formulation of economic policies. In four countries, the probability of participation in the labour market is positively related to education or diplomas, especially as regards secondary and higher education. These results are consonant with economic theory: the higher the age and level of education and/or training, the higher the potential earnings which persons may acquire on the labour market, leading to a substitution of work for leisure. However, it should be noted that in the case of Cameroon, the education coefficients are all significant and negative. This is largely due to the high proportion of educated persons in the population. Table A in the appendix shows that in this country the percentage of the relevant age group receiving primary education is 101 per cent, whereas in three countries out of four where the

---

[92] The reduced equations and earnings equations are not reproduced. It will be noted that the Lambda coefficient of the earnings equations is significant and negative in all the countries, which suggests the existence of a self-selection bias for the type of data used. It will be recalled that this coefficient represents the covariance between the errors of the reduced equation and the errors of the earnings equation. A negative coefficient indicates that the non-observable characteristics which increase propensity to participate in the labour market also contribute to the probability that a person will obtain lower earnings. Normally, since persons seek to maximise their anticipated earnings, the coefficient should be positive. A negative coefficient might imply the existence of obstacles to entry or that the labour market selection process is biased. See: Lachaud (ed.) [1994].

education coefficients are positive, this percentage varies between 20 and 30 per cent.[93]

Finally, family situation also affects the labour supply. In all the countries, all other things being equal, the secondary members of households – in particular, married women who are not heads of households – are less inclined to participate in the labour market than the heads of households, who are generally men. Thus, in the urban areas of Africa, the role of the head of the household – and thus of men – is essential in terms of labour supply. This result was in no way surprising, given the structure of household incomes – table 2. The lower propensity of women to participate in the labour market in Africa is to be explained, a priori, both on the supply side – the low level of human capital, social and cultural obstacles to entry which lead to a high labour supply cost – and on the demand side – discrimination on the labour market. Although the low human capital of married women reduce their opportunities of access to the labour market in most of the countries, in some cases – Mali, Guinea – social and cultural are probably the main factors in reducing the propensity of women to participate in the labour market. The other factors of the family situation lead to mixed results. The variable relating to the number of adult women in the household is significant in three countries, but has a negative sign in two of them; in the same way the variables concerning family background are significant in only two countries and produce contrasting results. Table L also shows that the coefficient of the attributed wage is significant in three countries and positive in two of these. In this latter case, the result seems logical since it means that the labour supply increases with income and that the substitution effect is greater than the income effect. Furthermore, it is consonant with the above-mentioned remarks on the evolution of the labour supply by standard of living. It is in Cameroon and Mali that the gap between the labour supply of poor households and the labour supply of non-poor households – in particular as regards heads of households – is the highest (table H). There remains the reason for these differences between the countries. In fact, one of the elements to be taken into consideration could be the inequality of incomes. Table 2 shows that in countries where income distribution is very uneven – Cameroon, Mali – the labour supply increases as attributed income rises.[94]

---

[93] In Côte d'Ivoire, the percentage of the pertinent age group receiving primary schooling is 70 per cent. It will also be noted that in the case of Madagascar this percentage is 92 per cent and that the coefficients concerning education are negative, although not significant.

[94] It should also be noted that these two countries have different levels of development.

Secondly, despite the great uncertainty of the econometric results, an analysis of the labour supply according to the standard of living of households does produce some additional results for four countries in the sample.[95] On the one hand, it seems that age has a different effect on the labour supply according to standard of living. For non-poor households, the labour supply is, as noted above, positively related to age; on the other hand, for poor groups, the relationship is either inverted or not significant, or suggests an earlier entry into the labour market.[96] One of the reasons for this difference probably lies in the acquisition of skills. In three of the four countries concerned, the variables concerning secondary education diplomas or training are positively related to the labour supply for non-poor groups. This result must be set alongside what was noted above concerning the stratification of the labour market. In three countries out of four, in the non-poor households the propensity to participate in the labour market is inversely and significantly related to the status of a married woman who is not head of a household. The logical result is that, all other things being equal, the relative labour supply of the latter increases as the household becomes poorer. In other words, even if, as noted earlier, the relative level of the labour supply of married women – in particular, as compared with the head of the household – is lower in poor households than in affluent households, the relative variation is much less in the former than in the latter. It is perfectly logical that, in two countries, the attributed income coefficient is positive and significant only for poor groups.

Thirdly, the above results suggest that the labour supply of secondary members of the household should be further explored. Despite the use of simpler models than those previously employed,[97] several elements must be

---

[95] The results of the probit models for the poor and non-poor are not presented; the stratum of intermediate households has been omitted. Furthermore, it should be noted that two types of tests were carried out to examine the structural stability of the coefficients - the coefficients are the same for the different samples - of the various sub-samples. Chow's test was calculated for the different equations and the likelihood ratio test was systematically applied to the probit equations. The results of these texts refute the structural non-stability of the coefficients of the appropriate equations for four countries: Cameroon, Côte d'Ivoire, Guinea and Mali.

[96] But this does not mean that the real entry into the labour market - i.e. other than as family help - is before the age of 15 years.

[97] An examination of the determinants of the labour supply was carried out on the basis of logistic functions, and the models were corrected in several directions. First, the models were estimated for each secondary member of the household. Thus, by estimating separately regression equations for each class of secondary adults, the present analysis makes a major conceptual simplification. Indeed, it is accepted that within each household, the decisions to

emphasized in this connection. First, as regards married women,[98] the lack of education or training systematically reduces the propensity to participate in the labour market in all the countries (table M). This result should be set alongside the low participation of women in the labour market, in particular at the level of wage employment. This seems to concur with the fact that age has a positive influence on the labour supply of married women in two thirds of the countries; many older married women are protected employees. Other elements concerning the demographic situation of the household must be taken into account. In half of the countries of the sample, the probability of participation in the labour market decreases with the reduction of the relative number of women in the household. On the other hand, the hypotheses of traditional theory concerning the influence of the number of children appear to be confirmed in practice only in one country – precisely in one of the countries where the influence of the number of adult women can be observed. Labour market participation by married women is influenced by the status of the head of the household. Participation increases if the latter has a paid activity – as is the case in four countries – and, in particular, if the head is an employee – as in three countries. This is not really surprising since more unemployed heads of households are from poor households and protected or non-protected wage employment is least common in the latter. Thus the labour supply of married women is probably influenced by external factors which can be ascribed directly or indirectly to the form of employment of the head of the household. Initial capital for self-employment, the existence of skills and a network of personal relations permitting access to jobs increase if the head of the household exercises a paid activity, in particular wage employment. The coefficient of the income of the other members is significant in 50 per cent of cases, but the expected negative sign appears in one case only.

---

participate in economic activity are made individually. However, the account taken in the regression equations of variables which might reflect collective decision processes allows this bias to be limited. Thus, in each equation, the employment status of the head of the household, the incomes of the other household members (including transfers) and the level of unemployment of the latter are independent variables. Moreover, the present analysis does not take into account selection biases.

[98] It will be recalled that according to traditional theory, in the case of married women, the decision to participate in the labour market, preferably in leisure or domestic activities, is positively related to age and education, and negatively linked to the income of the other members if the leisure is a normal good with a positive income elasticity. In the same way, it might be concluded that the number of adult women and the number of children in the household affect the propensity to participate in the labour market.

The inclusion of other secondary members reveals similarities and divergencies compared with married women. In the large majority of the countries, single secondary members' participation in the labour market is positively related to age. However, for secondary female members, the age coefficients are much lower and their labour supply increases up to around the age of 41, compared to the maximum secondary male members reach towards the age of 37, suggesting a later entry. For single women, the effect of the number of children in the household is also different than the married women. As for married women, single men's lack of training has a negative effect on participation in the labour market. In most of the countries, the participation in the labour market of secondary male and female members is negatively related to the level of education. Such a result is to be expected as a higher level of education means a later entry into the labour market. On the other hand, many marginal unemployed persons have completed at least secondary education.[99] The analysis also shows that, unlike married and unmarried women, the labour supply of secondary male members is influenced by the unemployment rate of the other members of the household – except the head – in half of the cases. Although the work status of the head of the household seems to influence the labour supply of secondary members, a difference by sex is evident. The labour supply of secondary male members seems to be more influenced by the self-employment status of the head of the household than by that of an employee status. The reverse is the case for women, although it should be noted that in two countries out of three, the presence of married self-employed women in the household increases the propensity of young girls to join the labour supply. In both cases, there is a positive influence on the labour supply especially if the head of the household has a precarious job. This result concurs with the relationship between age and vulnerability on the labour market noted earlier. Even if the existence of technical skills is taken into account, the form of employment of the head of the household is a major determinant of the nature of the social relations which structure the work environment, and in particular the processes governing access to employment. The breadwinner's vulnerability on the labour market may well create external negative factors in terms of employment and income for the other members of the household. Thus, the individual mechanisms of the labour market in Africa have an indirect social effect far beyond individual well-being. The taking into account of the income of other household members shows the existence of a negative link

---

[99] For example, 75 per cent in the case of Cameroon and almost 50 per cent in Côte d'Ivoire and Guinea.

between the labour supply and the income of the other members of the household in the case of single men. Thus, even with a simple model, the analysis reveals not only the influence of personal characteristics on the labour supply of the secondary members of the household, but the existence of an interaction between the individual supply within households.

VI. Access to employment, mobility and segmentation

The hypothesis of a segmented labour market leads to an analysis of the processes of access to employment and career profiles.

1. Access to employment

In the urban areas of French speaking Africa, the processes governing access to employment seem to be characterized by several factors.[100]

First, access to the present wage employment is related to two basic elements (table 6). The ability of individuals – tests, occupational trial periods – accounts for between one-quarter and one-half of the procedures for access to wage employment in five countries out of six. The possession of a diploma is not necessarily a passport to employment as has often been claimed; in two thirds of the countries, a diploma accounts for only 10 to 15 per cent of the methods of access to employment. This might confirm the previously proposed hypothesis that employers are conscious of the increasing gap between the apparent skills attested by the diploma and the real skills which the diploma is supposed to confirm. The other element, which may be ascribed in 25 to 40 per cent cases is family or ethnic relations. In fact the procedures for access to employment vary according to standard of living and thus by status of work. Table 6 shows that the incidence of traditional institutions is much greater in the case of persons from poor households, twice as many of whom use the channels offered by traditional society to obtain a job as compared with persons from affluent households. The contrary is the case as regards the role of the diploma and the verification of technical skills. Of course, these differences of access to employment can also be seen as regards the status of persons on the labour market. Access to employment through the intermediary of social institutions

---

[100] As regards access to principal employment. In general, around 10 per cent of individuals with a principal activity have a secondary activity. Methods of access to secondary employment are essentially through non-official channels. See Lachaud (ed.) [1994].

Table 6: Methods of access to present employment of employees
by standard of living (%)

Country Parameter		Burkina Faso	Came- roon	C ô t e d'Ivoire	Guinea	M a d a - gascar	Mali
Poor	Fam/ethnic gr.	46.7	40.0	53.3	28.9	36.7	47.3
	Diploma	6.7	15.0	0.0	27.5	2.0	23.0
	Test/trial period	28.0	30.0	13.4	23.1	42.9	12.2
	Employer cond.	16.0	15.0	6.7	13.1	14.3	11.5
	Other cases	2.6	0.0	26.7	7.2	4.1	5.7
	N	75	20	15	69	49	139
Non-poor	Fam/ethnic gr.	15.3	18.0	36.1	21.1	32.0	27.2
	Diploma	18.6	23.0	18.9	47.8	18.7	39.6
	Test/trial period	57.5	36.7	39.3	23.0	44.0	12.3
	Employer cond.	1.7	16.5	3.3	3.5	4.0	13.6
	Other cases	6.8	5.7	2.4	3.6	2.7	7.1
	N	59	139	122	113	75	154
Over-all	Fam/ethnic gr.	28.1	24.7	42.3	25.6	31.9	36.9
	Diploma	11.5	14.1	13.0	40.2	12.7	32.1
	Test/trial period	48.5	43.5	35.0	22.6	43.2	12.2
	Employer cond.	8.5	11.2	6.9	7.5	8.8	12.0
	Other cases	3.5	6.6	2.9	4.3	3.5	6.9
	N	260	304	277	254	204	393

(l) Including employer's apprentice
*Source: Pilot employment surveys in households in the capitals of: Burkina Faso, 1992;
Cameroon, 1990-91; Côte d'Ivoire, 1986-87; Guinea, 1991-92; Madagascar, 1989; Mali,
1991.*

is positively related to vulnerability on the labour market. On the other hand,
an inverse correlation appears as regards diplomas and tests of technical
skills. This result must be set alongside earlier remarks on the valorization of
education or diplomas in the case of persons from poor households. Given the
importance of subordinate jobs performed by secondary workers of
households, it is not surprising that access to employment through non-
official channels should be particularly high in the case of the latter – in
particular, for single men and women. Traditional social institutions play a
major role in the dissemination of information on employment and the role
of the Manpower Offices is becoming increasingly small – accounting for
around 10 per cent. These results are consonant with the fact that for the large
majority of protected workers – more than 80 per cent – according to the
persons surveyed, technical skills are appropriate for the job which they
perform. However, this is the case for around only 40 per cent of non-
protected employees and irregular workers. For these workers, social
institutions thus play a key role in their access to employment, with specific
training either being acquired subsequently on the job – the most frequent

case – or not being required for the exercise of precarious jobs. Protected workers have the necessary technical skills – which are verified on recruitment or confirmed by a diploma – which may be complemented by subsequent training.[101]

Secondly, access to a person's present self-employment depends on the availability of capital and training. In all the countries of the sample, these two factors account for more than 80 per cent of the methods of access to self-employment, with training being the main factor for men and capital playing the main role in the case of women. This result has now become classic in the African capitals. The channels provided by traditional society – the household, the family – more frequently facilitate the acquisition of capital for marginal self-employed persons and irregular workers than for self-employed persons with capital (table N in the appendix). Informal loans are more common amongst the most vulnerable self-employed persons. This phenomenon is important in as the cost of access to capital is often higher when it comes from non-institutional sources. If the role of savings is undeniably important in the method of access to capital, irrespective of the type of worker, it is substantially more important in the case of small enterprises with a certain volume of capital. This role tends to show the involution – low income and small accumulation of capital – of marginal self-employed workers. Job vulnerability may be substantially reduced if there is access to capital.[102]

Access to training is heavily dependent on relations within traditional society, family background and the macro-economic context. Indeed, 70 to 80 per cent of self-employed workers who acquired their trade through apprenticeship were self-employed persons.[103] Furthermore, between one half and two thirds underwent their apprenticeship with an employer who was a member or friend of the family or from the same ethnic group; many – between 15 and 35 per cent – learn their trade in family micro-enterprises, which does not exclude the payment of apprenticeship in some countries –

---

[101] This differentiation in the processes of access to wage employment might explain the special incidence, amongst the poor, of a gap between job aspirations and opportunities. In poor households - and amongst vulnerable, irregular or non-protected employees - it is above all "the need to obtain resources" - amongst long-term job-seekers, persons with low incomes - which leads to the acceptance of their present job.

[102] However, this question must be examined in the context of other assets of the persons concerned.

[103] Approximately three quarters in micro-enterprises and one quarter in large enterprises.

Cameroon, Côte d'Ivoire, Madagascar.[104] In the latter countries, the payment of apprenticeship is most common – 70 to 75 per cent – in enterprises with between 1 and 9 persons. Finally, access to apprenticeship also depends on family relations as regards financing. The surveys show that between 50 and 75 per cent of apprenticeships were financed by parents or members of the family. It is likely that access to apprenticeship will become increasingly difficult in the years to come. The demand for apprenticeship will increase under the impetus of demographic factors (the growth of the population) social factors (rising unemployment) and economic factors (reduction in the purchasing power of households). This, together with the relative reduction in the supply of formal training, the implicit subsidizing of apprenticeship costs by traditional society and the reduction in real incomes of enterprises and the gradual transformation of social structures will lead to a growing shortage of apprenticeship places. Even if apprentices receive a small payment in more than half of the cases, it is likely that a mechanism of rationing by cost or number of places will weaken the role of traditional African structures and that the cost of this kind of training will become a growing burden which poor households will find it increasingly difficult to bear.

Thirdly, as far as the factors governing access to a first job – different from current employment – are consonant with the above-mentioned observations, it may be useful to examine the factors which influence the choice between different methods of employment. A statistical procedure called discriminatory analysis can be used to examine to what extent certain personal and family characteristics of persons accurately predict the different employment status of individuals. Given the importance of the contribution of heads of households to family income, the analysis must first of all be carried out at the level of the head. The groups of the discriminant analysis are those which have been identified by the use of hierarchical classification analysis. The explanatory variables refer to the characteristics of the persons – education ($EDUC_i$); training ($FORM_i$); age (AGE); sex (SEXE); place of birth (LNAI) – and family background – father's education (PED_i); father's training (PFO_i); occupational category of father (CSP_i).[105] The principal parameters of the discriminatory analyses are set forth in table 7 and call for a number of observations.

---

[104] Apprenticeship is paid for in 47.8 per cent, 30.0 per cent and 44.0 per cent of micro-enterprises respectively in Cameroon, Côte d'Ivoire and Madagascar; in non-family micro-enterprises, the proportions increase by around 50 per cent.

[105] All the variables are dichotomic, except age.

The variance analysis – test F – shows that for at least 45 per cent of the variables, the hypothesis that the averages of all the groups are identical may be rejected in four countries of the sample.[106] The analysis of total variability between the employment status groups shows that the first discriminant function accounts for at least two thirds of the variance – at a level of signification of 0.0000 – in all the countries – and for at least three quarters in three countries – whereas the other functions contribute only to an insignificant degree to differences between the groups. Indeed, the Wilks lambda coefficient associated with function 2, if the former has been omitted, is significant in only two countries – Côte d'Ivoire and Madagascar. On the basis of the average discriminant canonical functions, it can be seen that, in all the countries, the first function discriminates the most between marginal self-employed workers and protected employees and discriminates the least amongst self-employed persons with capital and non-protected employees and between marginal self-employed people and irregular workers. The coefficients of correlation between the values of the functions values of the variables allow the relative contribution of the different variables to be identified. As regards the first function, it can be seen that in all the countries, the variables related to the education and training of the head of the household have the highest correlation coefficients. However, the level of education of the father of the head and/or his status on the labour market have an effect in five countries out of six. Sex is a poor indicator of future employment status, and migration is not a determinant. The level of education and type of training of the head of the household, as well as the educational and occupational background of the family, seems to determine to a large extent access to a given employment status. This is not surprising in the light of the earlier observations on the profile of individuals. Finally, table 7 gives the classification results of the discriminant analyses – comparison between present groups and a posteriori probabilities – and shows that the variables used provide a correct classification of a fairly high percentage of cases, of between 51.6 and 63.4 per cent. The percentage of correctly classified cases is highest for workers with a precarious status or a protected status. In five countries out of six, between 50 and 65 per cent and 50 and 75 per cent respectively of irregular workers and marginal self-employed workers were correctly classified, whereas the figures are between 65 and 80 per cent for protected workets in all countries; this was expected given the canonical

---

[106] The Wilks Lamba coefficient leads to the same observations, since it hardly varies from 1 for most of the prediction variables with few differences by groups.

Table 7. Present status of work of heads of households: principal parameters of discriminant analyses

Country Parameter		Burkina Faso	Cameroon	Côte d'Ivoire	Guinea	Mada-gascar	Mali
F: $H_i \neq H_j$, $< =0.05$; % variables[1]		85.0	25.0	47.4	29.2	44.4	55.0
% of variance explained-by function 1		85.4	64.1	62.7	72.3	66.2	80.5
(Sig F)		(0.000)	(0.000)	(0.000)	(0.000)	(0.000)	(0.000)
Wilks Lambda associated-with function 2		0.770	0.732	0.722	0.656	0.729	0.771
(Sig F)		(0.156)	(0.232)	(0.001)	(0.154)	(0.067)	(0.550)
% of corrected classed cases[2]		55.9	55.4	51.6	58.6	63.4	56.4
Average discriminant functions (func. 1)[3]							
Gr 1: irregular		0.67680	-0.80428	0.67894	1.32388	-0.65258	0.83820
Gr 2: marg self-emp.		1.52175	-1.24533	0.96948	1.33094	-1.22572	1.13553
Gr 3: self-emp. capital		0.70174	-0.48067	0.14494	0.53813	-	0.57697
Gr 4: prot. employee		-1.43304	0.75631	-0.83319	-1.20924	0.81454	-1.37893
Gr 5: non-prot. emp.		0.56741	-0.48310	0.20498	0.31727	-0.46279	0.60857
Relative contribution of variables - by coef-ficients of correlation between the values of the functions and the va-lues of the variables (in decreasing order)	Function 1	EDUC1 EDUC5 FORM3 PED1 EDUC4 PED2 PFO3 PCSP1	EDUC5 EDUC2 EDUC1 FORM3 PCSP4 PED2	FORM3 EDUC1 EDUC3 EDUC4	EDUC1 FORM2 EDUC5 EDUC4 FORM1 PED3	EDUC2 EDUC3 FORM1 PED2 EDUC4 FORM2 SEXE FORM3 PED1	EDUC1 EDUC4 EDUC3 PED1 FORM2 PCSP1 PED2
	Function 2	-	-	SEXE PCSP2	-	PCSP3 PFO1 PFO2 PCSP2	-
Number of cases		247	242	244	191	153	202

(1) Percentage of variables in the hypothesis that the averages of all the groups are identical; (2) comparison of present groups and a posteriori probabilities; (3) canonical functions (centroid groups).

Note: the variables are as follows: EDUC1=without education; EDUC2=primary education; EDUC3=secondary, first cycle (Côte d'Ivoire), secondary (Madagascar, Mali); EDUC4= secondary, second cycle (Burkina Faso, Côte d'Ivoire, Guinea), higher (Madagascar, Mali); EDUC5=higher (Burkina Faso, Cameroon, Guinea); FORM1=without training; FORM2= apprenticeship in enterprises; FORM3=modern training; PED1= father of head, without education; PED2=father of head, > = primary (Burkina Faso, Cameroon, Mali), primary (Madagascar); PED3= > =secondary (Madagascar); PFO1=father of head, without training; PFO2=father of head, apprenticeship in enterprises; PFO3=father of head, modern training; PSCP1=executive; PCSP2=father of chief, employee (Côte d'Ivoire), executive and supervisory staff (Madagascar); PCSP3=manual worker; PCSP4=self-employed, subsistence agriculture; SEXE male.

Source: Pilot employment surveys in households in the capitals of: Burkina Faso, 1992; Cameroon, 1990-91; Côte d'Ivoire, 1986-87; Guinea, 1991-92; Madagascar, 1989; Mali, 1991.

average values of the various functions l.[107]

2. Career profile and segmentation

An analysis of the occupational profile of persons provides a deeper understanding of the link between status on the labour market and poverty.[108]

First, a number of observations can be made about the occupational career of the different members of the household on the basis of the number and type of jobs held, both short term and long term.[109] Empirical research shows that most employed persons have had only one job – the one they hold – in the last twelve months. Indeed, during this period, approximately 90 per cent of the persons have had only one job. On the other hand, if account is taken of long term employment, then there is some degree of labour mobility, which is apparently positively correlated to the level of development. In Cameroon and Côte d'Ivoire respectively, 17.9 and 85.7 per cent of employed persons have had at least three jobs during the course of their occupational careers, whereas this proportion is between 5 and 7 per cent in the other two countries.[110] Statistical uncertainties probably account to some extent for the wide differences in these figures. Whereas in Burkina Faso, Cameroon and Mali, the proportion of secondary employment and irregular employment is around only 10 per cent, in Côte d'Ivoire it appears that only 37.7 and 45.9 per cent of persons have not had any secondary and irregular employment, respectively, during their careers.

---

[107] It should be noted that the analysis was carried out with respect to the current employment of heads of household, without any distinction being made between individuals who have had only a first job and those who have already acquired career experience. Thus current employment encompasses persons with very different kinds of occupational experience. When the analysis is differentiated by career, the results are more or less the same, both at the econometric and explanatory levels. Thus, the family educational and occupational background - in particular, the father of the head of the household - and the education and training of the head of the household may be considered as essential factors which influence the choice of points of entry into the labour market.

[108] Because of the quality of data on this subject, the analysis refers only to four countries: Burkina Faso, Cameroon, Côte d'Ivoire and Mali.

[109] Short-term jobs are those held during the last twelve months and long-term jobs are the short-term jobs and others also held before the last twelve months - entire occupational career.

[110] In Burkina Faso, 30.2 per cent of individuals have two jobs; in Mali, the proportion is 8.8 per cent.

Of course, the number of jobs held varies according to the characteristics of workers. As regards long term employment, it is above all self-employed persons with capital and irregular workers who have held the most number of jobs during their careers, with the mobility of the former being due to capital and that of the latter being inherent in the method of employment. On the other hand, the relative mobility in terms of jobs of protected workers, non-protected employees and marginal self-employed persons is approximately twice as high irrespective of the country. These results probably explain why the number of long term jobs bears little relationship with the standard of living of households and why no clear trend is discernible by level of education.

As regards the kinds of job held, currently irregular workers have held irregular jobs during their occupational careers. In the four countries surveyed, more than 50 per cent of irregular workers have held jobs of which between one half and three quarters were in themselves irregular. On the other hand, the survey shows no significant differences with respect to the other kinds of work status. Irregularity of employment tends to be a characteristic of poor rather than affluent households, although in some countries – Mali, in particular[111] – the differences are not really significant (figure 7). To some extent the link between vulnerability on the labour market and poverty is once again evident, and the existence of segmentation in the labour market, identified in terms of the special incidence of irregular employment in poor households, is probable in most French-speaking countries of Africa. A multiple classification analysis to highlight the factors which explain the number of long term jobs, shows that when the existence of irregular employment during the course of a worker's occupational career is set alongside certain personal characteristics – age, education, training – individual mobility increases significantly. Thus all other things being equal, the existence of irregular employment increases the number of long term jobs from 33 to 59 per cent, depending on the country, as compared with the principal average. But as was to be expected, the number of jobs held during a worker's occupational career is positively correlated with age.

Secondly, the occupational transition matrices provide another means of assessing occupational careers. For the purposes of the present study, these matrices refer to persons with job different from their first job (table N in the appendix). Furthermore, the career is examined over a relatively long period, since the average age on the labour market is around twenty

---

[111] For reasons related to the structure of activities, in particular the importance of commerce. In Mali, it is not irregular workers who contribute the most to the poverty of households. See Lachaud, Sidibé [1993].

years.[112] Despite the sometimes fragmentary nature of the data available, a number of observations can be made on table O. Depending on the country, 60 to 80 per cent of persons who entered the labour market as protected workers continue to hold such employment.[113] In this connection, it must be emphasized that non-protected employees, the majority of whom are skilled and unskilled manual workers, account for almost all the mobility towards protected wage employment; for these workers protected wage employment may, according to the sector or enterprise, constitute a normal form of promotion towards seniority. This explains why between one-quarter and one- half of currently protected employees have entered competitive wage employment in three countries. The occupational stability of non-protected employees is thus less marked, since between 40 and 50 per cent of those who have acquired this status still retain it today. Although between 25 and 30 per cent of these have become protected employees, a substantial proportion – between 25 and 30 per cent – still hold jobs which are essentially precarious – irregular work and marginal self-employment; furthermore, many of these irregular employees are former apprentices. Non-protected employment seems to provide a bridge towards either precarious employment or protected employment, a sign of its relative homogeneity. The former apprentices of small enterprises often become employees – or quasi-employees – in these same enterprises before embarking on an occupational career as regular or non-regular self-employed workers. On the other hand, those who have acquired training in larger enterprises or who have been directed recruited into subordinate posts in the public service may expect promotion to more protected jobs.

Thirdly, the stability of self-employment is more or less comparable to that of non-protected employees; between 50 and 60 per cent of persons who began their occupational careers as self-employed persons still have the same status today – as marginal self-employed persons and self-employed persons with capital. A few have become protected workers, the rest have swollen the ranks of irregular employment and competitive wage employment. It should also be noted that, except in Burkina Faso, two-thirds of self-employed persons with capital have entered wage employment,

---

[112] The average between the present age of individuals and the age at which they obtained their first job. These averages are 22.1, 17.1, 21.7 and 24.1 years respectively for Burkina Faso, Cameroon, Côte d'Ivoire and Mali; furthermore there are no real differences by status of employment.

[113] This result confirms observations already made in India and Malaysia. See: Mazumdar [1989].

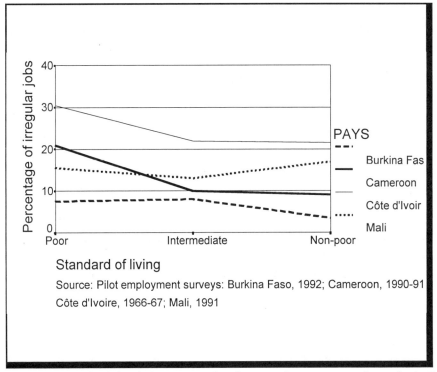

Figure 7: Irregular jobs during occupational career, by country and standard of living – workers aged 15 above taken together (percentage)

above all in non-protected employment. Thus, when the first job is on an independent basis, the activities exercised are often of an involuted kind and not likely to lead to the accumulation of capital. Above all, table O shows that the proportion of precarious jobs – irregular workers and marginal self-employed persons – seems to have increased in the urban areas of Africa. Discounting both apprentices – first employment – and self-employed persons with capital – current employment – from this cohort of persons employed, it can be seen that over the last twenty years, the net gains as a percentage of the total of irregular workers and marginal self-employed persons – as compared with protected and non-protected employees – were 13.9 per cent, 10.8 per cent, 5.2 per cent and 25.4 per cent respectively for Burkina Faso, Cameroon, Côte d'Ivoire and Mali. This evolution is independent of the level of development of the country. Thus, in Cameroon, 19.0 and 51.1 per cent of current marginal self-employed persons entered the labour market as protected and non-protected workers respectively. In the same way, between one fifth and one third of current irregular workers in Abidjan, Bamako and Yaoundé had their first job in protected wage employment. This result has some importance in the current macro-economic context: the reduction in the employment absorption capacity of the modern sector, the restructuring in the public productive system and the drop in real incomes, all imply deep-seated changes on the labour market and in particular, the existence of a low level of protection.

The type of mobility which has just been described may be the result of a free choice. Self-employment is far from having the residual nature which is often ascribed to it and it may reflect some degree of upward mobility.[114] But this type of mobility can probably be explained by the withdrawal of the State. It will be recalled that, according to the different surveys, between 10 and 30 per cent of job losses are probably due to the winding up, restructuring and privatization of public enterprises. If the labour market ensures the occupational promotion of some persons, the above observations clearly show the existence, on the one hand, of a segmentation related to a very strong marked mobility within precarious forms of employment and, on the other, of adjustments in terms of increasing vulnerability. Although the intensity of these adjustments varies from country to country, they are one of the factors to be taken into account in analysing current transformations on the labour market.

Finally, an analysis of occupational transition according to the standard of living of households tends to reinforce the link between the precarious nature of employment and poverty. Two major differences can be seen between households which are at present poor and those which are well off. In the former, the points of entry onto the labour market are much more frequent in terms of precarious jobs – in particular as regards irregular employment and marginal self-employment – than in the latter. Furthermore, in poor households, mobility essentially occurs in the vulnerable categories, in particular as regards apprentices and non-protected female workers who frequently become irregular workers or marginal self-employed persons. In poor households, in addition to the marked stability of protected workers, mobility frequently takes the form of non-protected employees moving to more stable jobs. In these circumstances, persons are poor not only because their points of entry onto the labour market are vulnerable in terms of status of employment and income, but because these points of entry virtually exclude them from any future career development. When seen from this perspective, the segmentation of the labour market

---

[114] Very appropriately, Mazumdar recalls that self-employment may enable a worker who is at the bottom of the wage scale to exploit his capacities to the full, make social and occupational gains and provide protection against monetary erosion. Mazumdar [1989].

highlights an essential aspect of the link between poverty and in the labour market.

Conclusion

This research has identified a number of points of analysis concerning the urban labour markets in French-speaking Africa.

First, independently of any reference to the dualist schema, there is a close association between, on the one hand, the incidence of poverty and, on the other, certain forms of employment and unemployment. In all the countries studied, the incidence, depth and inequality of poverty are highest in households where the breadwinner is an irregular worker, a marginal self-employed person or even a non-protected employee, and in households where the head is unemployed or inactive. The relative contribution to poverty increases substantially for these same categories of households if the degree of aversion to poverty increases. Thus to the extent that heads of households – who in most cases are breadwinners – provide between 50 and 80 per cent of the group's income, their exclusion from segments of the labour market characterized by protection, regularity and autonomy, or their non-participation in the labour market, are the main factors determining the marginalization of many households as regards social progress.

Secondly, although self-employment and irregular employment are predominant in poor households, particular groups of households, which are often excluded from the scope of conventional policies, appear to be relatively vulnerable. On the one hand, in the least advanced countries, the incidence of poverty in households where the head is an employee in the public sector is around 25 per cent; furthermore, in these same countries, between 40 and 50 per cent of non-protected employees also head poor households. On the other hand, the level of well-being is even lower in households where the head is a woman, with account being taken of the demographic structure of these households – where there is often only one income earner – and the lower participation of women in wage employment as compared with men – married women in poor household are mainly self-employed. The vulnerability of these groups is further increased by the fact that, in general, between 60 and 70 per cent of the secondary members of urban households have an identical status to that of the breadwinner.

Thirdly, the precarious nature of the urban social system is highlighted by the massive incidence of unemployment. In five countries out of six, between one-fifth and one-quarter of the active population aged 15 and above are without work and between 20 and 40 per cent of the secondary members of households are unemployed. Furthermore, in four countries out of six, between one-third and one-half of persons aged between 15 and 29 are unemployed – in the two other countries the proportion is one-quarter – and for those who have received secondary education, the inactivity rate is between 25 and 40 per cent. In addition, whereas unemployment brings about an increasing adjustment on the labour market in all the countries studied, the incidence of unemployment is between two and three times higher in poor households than in well off ones. This situation is further compounded by the fact that, in two-thirds of the countries, between one-fifth and almost half the secondary female members are potentially active and that marginal unemployment, which affects above all young men and women under the age of 25 – around 50 per cent – falls significantly as income rises. While in some countries – Mali, Guinea – this may be partially due to the marked incidence of traditional structures which restrict the participation of women on the labour market, it may well be that the economic crisis discourages workers even more.

Fourthly, an examination of the dependency of poverty on participation in the labour market reveals a number of important aspects. First, the level of education and training, as well as the educational, occupational and family background of the head of the household, to a large extent determine access to a given employment status. In poor households, the incidence of the lack of schooling and non-access to higher education is, respectively, twice and three times as high as compared with non-poor households and, in five countries out of the six, an econometric analysis shows that the existence of training, and in particular apprenticeship in micro-enterprises and large enterprises, is positively linked to participation on the labour market. The difference in the process of access to employment is quite logical, with the role of traditional institutions increasing as employment becomes more precarious. In addition, these mechanisms are probably reinforced by the existence of external factors within the household which spring, directly or indirectly, from the form of employment of the head of the household. The participation of secondary workers in the labour market – married women, single men and women – is influenced by the status of the head of the household and becomes increasingly marked if the latter has a paid activity. This means that the individual mechanisms of the labour market in Africa have a social effect which indirectly goes well beyond individual well-being. The interaction of the individual labour supply within a household is undoubtedly an expression of this social effect. But in addition, the relative labour supply of married women becomes increasingly greater in poorer households. Finally, an examination of the occupational careers of persons reinforces the idea of a segmentation of the labour market. The very marked stability of protected wage employment, the high mobility within vulnerable groups and the differentiated mobility of non-protected employment – as a point of transition towards either precarious employment or protected employment – appear to confirm the idea that the segmentation of the labour market is in part due to factors related to demand. For this reason, undoubtedly, the number of jobs held is positively correlated to the precarious nature of employment, in particular irregular employment. As a result, people are poor not only because their points of entry onto the labour market are vulnerable in terms of employment status or revenue, but also because these points of entry virtually exclude them from any future career development. The incidence of unemployment during the occupational career tends to be greater for workers in poor households and/or with a precarious status.

Fifthly, the lack of experience by young persons on the labour market is not a convincing explanation of unemployment. Even if the growing insta-bility of the macro-economic situation and the increase in population growth have accentuated the incidence of unemployment, the fact that between 25 and 40 per cent of persons with secondary level education are unemployed, and that at least 70 per cent of unemployed persons are looking for their first job, shows that the educational system is unadapted to the needs of the labour market. This gap is apparent at several levels: in the surplus of graduates of higher education, the inappropriateness and shortage of tech-nical skills and the lack of a technical component in the basic educational system. The rigidity of the labour market for diploma holders seems to be based on hypotheses which are becoming less and less valid in the African context. Age-earnings profiles in the public sector have become increasingly uncertain and recruitment criteria have been diversified. It is conceivable that the coexistence of unemployment amongst graduates and the high demand for education can be explained by changes in recruitment procedures in the productive system. Budgetary restrictions in education and the withdrawal of the State from this sphere – where there is growing privatization – have probably eroded the quality of the educational system. As a result, despite the growth in the supply of graduates, the gap between the technical skills attested by their diplomas and the skills which graduates actually possess has become increasingly wide. Thus employers now give increasing attention to recruitment procedures. This means that the wage offered to those recruited is unchanged, whereas those whose skills are below standard remain unemployed. The slowness in the transmission of this information may explain the continuing strong demand for education, despite the high level of unemployment amongst graduates.

At the beginning of the 1990s, in most French speaking countries of Africa, the balance of the social system was extremely precarious. The slowdown in the process of economic transition, the increasing exclusion of many persons from any kind of social progress and the uncertain evolution of political systems were the main characteristics of the new approach to development. As balance in the social system is largely dependent on methods of participation in the labour market, particularly in urban areas, the present research could lead to preliminary work on the search for a better balance between economic and social adjustment. Flexibility, improved preliminary analysis and greater pragmatism in the implementation of structural adjustment programmes,[115] the re-examination of the promotion of self-employment, the reorganization of certain institutions linked to apprenticeship and the search for new policies based on the distribution of collective assets - in particular, education and health - appear to be the essential elements in the design of more effective policies to fight urban poverty.

Bibliographical references

Anker, R., Knowles, J.C. 1977. "Female labour participation in Kenya", in the work published under the direction of Standing, G., Sheehan, G.: *Labour force participation in low income countries: methodological issues and data requirements*, Geneva, ILO.

Appleton, S., Collier, P., Horsnell, P. 1990. *Gender, education and employment in Cote d'Ivoire*, Washington, working paper policy analysis No. 8, World Bank.

Aryee, G.A., Mhone, G.C.Z. 1986. *Vulnerable segments of the labour market in southern Africa*, Geneva, ILO/SATEP.

Dioubate, Z., Lachaud., J-P. (with the participation and under the direction of) 1992. *Pauvreté et marché du travail à Conakry (République de Guinée)*, Geneva, DP/49, International Institute for Labour Studies (French only).

Fallon, P.R. 1985. *The labor market in Kenya: recent evidence*, Washington, Labor market division, World Bank.

Foster, J. 1984. "On economic poverty: a survey of aggregate measures", *Advances in econometrics*, Vol. 3.

Fosteer, J., Greer, J., Thorbecke, E. 1984. "A class of decomposable poverty measures", *Econometrica*, Vol. 52.

Gerry, Ch. 1979. "Small-scale manufacturing and repairs in Dakar: a survey of market relations within the urban economy", in Bromley, R., Gerry, Ch. (eds.): *Casual work and poverty in the third world cities*, London, Chichester

---

[115] Distortions on the modern labour market of many African countries are perhaps less marked that is usually thought. On the gaps between wages in the public and private sectors, see: Lachaud [1993].

Ghai, D. 1987. *Economic growth, structural change and labour absorption in Africa: 1960-85*, Geneva, discussion papers, UNRISH.

Glewwe, P. 1987. *Distribution of welfare in Cote d'Ivoire in 1985*, Washington, Living standards measurement study, working document No. 29, World Bank.

Harris, J., Kannan, K.P., Rodgers, G. 1990. *Urban labour market structure and jobs access in India: a study of Coimbatore*, Geneva, Research series 92, International Institute for Labour Studies.

Hart, K. 1973. "Informal income opportunities and urban employment in Ghana", *Journal of Modern African Studies*, Vol. 11, No. 1, March.

Hechman, J. 1976. "The common structure of statistical models of truncation, sample selection and limited dependant variable and a simpler estimator for such models", *Annals of economic and social measurement*, Vol. 5, No. 4.

ILO 1972. *Employment, incomes and equality: A strategy for increasing productive employment in Kenya*, Geneva.

ILO 1990. *Employment, unemployment and underemployment. An ILO manual on concepts and methods*, Geneva.

Inack Inack, S., Ndiffo, J., Nkwayeb, R., Lachaud, J-P. (with the participation and under the direction of) 1992. *Pauvreté et marché du travail au Cameroun: le cas de Yaoundé*, Geneva, DP/47, International Institute for Labour Studies.

JASPA 1991. *African Employment Report 1990*, Addis Ababa, JASPA.

Kannnappan, S. 1985. "Urban employment and the labor market in developing nations", Economic development and cultural change, Vol. 33, No. 4, April.

Killingsworth, M.R., Heckman, J. 1966. "Female labor supply: a survey", in the work published under the direction of Ashenfelter, O., Layard, R.: *Handbooks of labor economics*, New York, Elsevier science publishers, Vol. 1.

Lachaud, J.P. 1988. *Pauvreté et marché du travail urbain: le cas d'Abidjan (Cote d'Ivoire)*, Geneva, DP/8, International Institute for Labour Studies (French only)

Lachaud, J.P. 1990. *Etude sur le marché de l'emploi au Mali*, Washington, International Management & Development Group, February.

Lachaud., J.P. 1991. *Pauvreté et offre de travail à Abidjan (Cote d'Ivoire): concepts, méthode et analyse*, Geneva, DP/39, International Institute for Labour Studies.

Lachaud, J.P. 1993. *Les écarts de salaires entre les secteurs public et privé en Afrique francophone: analyse comparative*, Geneva, discussion paper No 53, International Institute for Labour Studies.

Lachaud, J.P., Sidibe, E.B. 1993. *Pauvreté et marché du travail au Mali: le cas de Bamako*, Geneva, discussion paper No. 50, International Institute for Labour Studies.

Lachaud, J.P. (ed.) 1994. *Pauvreté et marché du travail en Afrique au sud du Sahara: analyse comparative*, Geneva, International Institute for Labour Studies (forthcoming).

Mazumdar, D. 1981. *The urban labor market and income distribution. A study of Malaysia*, Washington, World Bank.

Ministry of co-operation and development, 1992. *Les Etats d'Afrique, de l'Océan indien et des Caraïbes. Situation économique et financière en 1991*, Paris, Ministry of co-operation and development.

Rakotobe, F., Lachaud, J.P. (with the participation and under the direction of) 1992. *Pauvreté et marché du travail à Antananarivo (Madagascar)*, Geneva, DP/50, International Institute for Labour Studies (French only).

Ravallion, M. 1992. *Poverty comparisons. A guide to concepts and methods*, LSMS working papers, No. 88.

Rodgers, G. 1984. *Poverty and population. Approaches and evidence*, Geneva, ILO.

Rodgers, G. 1986. "Labour markets, labour processes and economic development", *Labour and Society*, Vol. 11, No. 2, May.

Rosenhouse, S., 1989. *Identifying the poor. Is "headship" a useful concept?*, Washington, LSMS working papers, No. 58.

Sen, A. 1979. "Personal utilities and public judgements: or what's wrong with welfare economics?", *The economic journal*, Vol. 89.

Standing, G. 1978. *Labour force participation and development*, Geneva, ILO.

Todaro, M.P. 1969. "A model of labor migration and urban unemployment in less developed countries", *American Economic Review*, Vol. 59, March.

UNDP 1990. *Human Development Report 1990*, New York, UNDP.

Vandemoortele, J. 1991. "Labour market informalisation in sub-Saharan Africa", in Standing, G., Tockman, V. (eds.): *Towards social adjustment*, Geneva, ILO.

Weeks, J. 1986. *Vulnerable segments of labour market: urban areas of the African studies*, Geneva, January, ILO.

WORLD BANK 1988. *World Development Report 1988*, Washington, World Bank.

WORLD BANK 1989. *Social development in Africa report. Statistical tables*, Washington, World Bank.

WORLD BANK 1990a. *World Development Report 1990. Poverty*, Washington, World Bank.

WORLD BANK 1990b. *Analysis plans for understanding the social dimensions of adjustment*, Washington, SDA unit, July.

WORLD BANK 1992. *World Development Report 1992*, Washington, World Bank.

Appendices

Table A: Some socio-economic indicators in French-speaking African countries from the present sample

Country Parameter	Burkina Faso	Cameroon	Côte d'Ivoire	Guinea	Mada-gascar	Mali
GNP per capita						
Level (dollars, 1991)	350	940	690	450	210	280
Growth 1965-90	1.3	3.0	0.5	1.1[1]	-1.9	1.7
Growth 1980-91	1.3	-0.9	-3.4	-0.1[2]	-2.4	-0.1
Poverty/income distribution in h.						
Incidence of poverty (% h.)[11]	51.7	26.9	19.5	50.0	34.1	50.3
Lowest quartile (% income)[12]	0.5	1.4	1.7	5.3	5.3	1.8
Highest quartile (% income)[12]	76.7	76.5	67.3	56.9	59.3	84.3
GDP in % (1965/90)						
Agriculture	37/32	33/27	47/47	56[4]/28	31/33	65/46
Industry	24/24	20/28	19/27	36[4]/33	16/13	9/13
Manufacturing	11/14	10/13	11/17[3]	-/4	11[5]/12	5/8
Services	39/44	47/46	33/26	8[4]/39	53/54	25/41
Population						
Total pop. (TP) 1991 (millions)	9.3	12.1	12.3	5.9	12.0	8.7
Growth rate TP 1980-90 (%)	2.6	3.0	3.8	2.5	3.0	2.5
Active pop. (AP) 1990 (millions)	4.2	4.4	4.6	3.1	5.0	2.9
Growth rate AP 80-85/85-90 (%)	1.9/2.0	1.8/2.0	2.7/2.6	1.6/1.7	1.9/2.1	2.5/2.6
Education (1989)						
% of respective age group in:						
Primary (total/girls)	35.0/27.0	101.0/93.0	70.0[6]/58.0	34.0/21.0	92.0/90.0	23.0/17.0
Secondary (total/girls)	7.0/5.0	26.0/21.0	20.0/12.0	9.0/5.0	19.0/18.0	4.0/.0
Hiher	1.0	3.0	3.0[7]	1.0	4.0	1.0[7]
Primary enrollment ratio - net (%)	28.0	75.0	48.9[7]	26.0	64.0	19.0
Urbanization						
Urban pop., 1990 (% total pop.)	9.0	41.0	40.0	26.0	25.0	19.0
Population capital, 1990 (millions)[8]	0.4	0.7	2.1[9]	1.3	0.7	0.7
Urban pop. growth rate (1980-90)	5.3	5.9	4.5	5.7	6.4	3.7
Employment						
% active pop., 1965-1985/87						
* Agriculture	89.0/86.6	86.0/74.0	81.0/65.2	87.0/80.7	85.0/80.9	90.0/85.5
* Industry	3.0/4.3	4.0/4.5	5.0/8.3	6.0/9.0	4.0/6.0	1.0/2.0
* Services	7.0/9.1	9.0/21.5	15.0/26.342	7.0/10.3	11.0/13.2	8.0/12.5
% women agric./non-agric. (1990)	46.1/47.0	39.8/23.0	.8/23.5	43.6/29.0	46.0/17.0	15.1/21.0
Wage employment in the capital (% active urban population)[10]						
Public sector	30.0	22.3	13.1	23.3	35.7	22.7
Private sector	15.2	21.7	35.0	9.0	31.7	15.0
Central government (% active population in 1990)	0.8	4.2	2.6	2.3	2.1	1.5

(1) 1965-84; (2) 1980-87; 1987-89: the growth rate was -0.3%; (3) 1989; (4) 1960; (5) 4% in 1960; (6) 1987; (7) 1986; (8) Estimated according to: World Bank (1992), except for Abidjan; (9) Abidjan; (10) Burkina Faso, 1992; Cameroon, 1990-91; Côte d'ivoire, 1986-87; Guinea, 1991-92; Madagascar, 1989; Mali, 1991; (11) see note 33 for the poverty thresholds; (12) including nul or negative incomes.
Source: World Bank (1980), (1986), (1989a), (1989b), (1992); PECTA (1991); Pilot employment surveys in households: Burkina Faso (Ouagadougou, 1992), Cameroon (Yaoundé, 1990-91), Côte d'Ivoire (Abidjan, 1986-87), Guinea (Conakry, 1991-92), Madagascar (Antananarivo, 1989), Mali (Bamako, 1991); Ministry of co-opération and developement (1992).

Table B: Incidence, depth and inequality of poverty in households by the status
            of household

Parameter	PO		P1		P2		N
Status head of h./country	Value	C_j (%)	Value	C_j (%)	Value	C_j (%)	
Burkina Faso	**0.517**	**100.0**	**0.341**	**100.0**	**0.281**	**100.0**	**288**
Employee public sector	0.215	15.4	0.108	11.8	0.084	11.1	107
Employee private sector	0.361	8.7	0.173	6.3	0.126	5.6	36
Self-employed	0.745	47.0	0.503	48.1	0.404	46.9	94
Unemployed	0.813	8.7	0.661	10.8	0.600	11.9	16
Inactive	0.857	20.1	0.645	23.0	0.569	24.6	35
Cameroon	**0.258**	**100.0**	**0.150**	**100.0**	**0.119**	**100.0**	**283**
Employee public sector	0.026	4.1	0.015	4.1	0.014	4.8	116
Employee private sector	0.106	6.8	0.053	5.9	0.038	5.3	47
Self-employed	0.381	32.9	0.183	27.1	0.126	23.6	63
Unemployed	0.750	24.7	0.533	30.1	0.464	33.1	24
Inactive	0.697	31.5	0.424	32.9	0.340	33.3	33
Côte d'Ivoire	**0.181**	**100.0**	**0.110**	**100.0**	**0.084**	**100.0**	**281**
Employee public sector	0.071	7.8	0.009	1.6	0.002	0.5	56
Employee private sector	0.065	13.7	0.023	8.0	0.010	4.5	107
Self-employed	0.195	29.5	0.107	26.7	0.070	22.8	77
Unemployed	0.773	33.4	0.633	45.1	0.570	53.1	22
Inactive	0.421	15.7	0.301	18.5	0.241	19.4	19
Guinea	**0.495**	**100.0**	**0.216**	**100.0**	**0.129**	**100.0**	**281**
Employee public sector	0.226	15.1	0.060	9.2	0.026	6.7	93
Employee private sector	0.368	5.0	0.074	2.3	0.018	0.9	19
Self-employed	0.494	28.1	0.226	29.4	0.135	29.4	79
Unemployed	0.897	25.2	0.468	30.1	0.307	33.0	39
Inactive	0.725	26.6	0.343	28.8	0.211	29.7	51
Madagascar[1]	**0.343**	**100.0**	**0.148**	**100.0**	**0.092**	**100.0**	**172**
Employee public sector	0.254	27.1	0.075	18.7	0.039	15.7	63
Employee private sector	0.333	32.2	0.139	31.0	0.077	27.8	57
Self-employed	0.500	27.1	0.261	32.8	0.184	37.3	32
Inactive	0.400	13.6	0.223	17.4	0.180	19.0	20
Mali	**0.495**	**100.0**	**0.244**	**100.0**	**0.159**	**100.0**	**293**
Employee public sector	0.483	28.3	0.178	22.2	0.092	18.0	89
Employee private sector	0.301	9.7	0.229	9.3	0.135	8.7	29
Self-employed	0.500	17.2	0.121	14.0	0.068	12.6	83
Unemployed	0.726	2.7	0.313	3.5	0.215	3.7	8
Inactive	0.461	42.1	0.434	51.0	0.308	57.0	84

(1) No head of household was registred as unemplyed.
*Source: Pilot employment surveys in households: Burkina Faso (Ouagadougou, 1992),
Cameroon (Yaoundé, 1990-91), Côte d'Ivoire (Abidjan, 1986-87), Guinea (Conakry, 1991-92),
Madagascar (Antananarivo, 1989), Mali (Bamako, 1991).*

Table C: Labour status by earner type – 15 years and above – and country in French-speaking Africa (%)

Country Parameter		Burkina Faso	Cameroon	Côte d'Ivoire	Guinea	Mada- gascar	Mali
Household head	Irregular	4.0	6.2	4.9	9.9	7.2	8.9
	Marginal self-emp.	17.4	12.0	26.6	17.8	16.3	17.8
	Self-emp.w. capital	11.3	10.3	3.7	15.2	-	17.9
	Protected employee	37.7	47.9	41.4	41.4	47.1	36.1
	Non-prot.employee	29.6	23.6	23.4	15.7	29.4	22.3
	Total	100.0	100.0	100.0	100.0	100.0	100.0
	N	247	242	244	191	153	202
Secondary males	Irregular	11.4	17.2	4.6	6.9	9.5	10.6
	Marginal self-emp.	29.1	6.1	17.2	27.6	19.0	10.6
	Self-emp.w. capital	1.3	1.0	4.6	7.6	-	3.5
	Protected employee	13.9	17.2	40.2	25.5	19.0	28.2
	Non-prot.employee	44.3	58.6	33.3	32.4	52.4	47.1
	Total	100.0	100.0	100.0	100.0	100.0	100.0
	N	79	99	87	145	21	255
Secondary married women	Irregular	9.8	11.4	1.2	1.4	14.3	15.7
	Marginal self-emp.	28.3	22.9	69.9	32.9	26.0	19.3
	Self-emp. . capital	10.9	6.7	0.0	11.0	-	0.0
	Protected employee	39.1	34.3	21.7	43.8	37.7	39.8
	Non-prot.employee	12.0	24.8	7.2	11.0	22.1	25.3
	Total	100.0	100.0	100.0	100.0	100.0	100.0
	N	92	105	83	73	77	83
Secondary unmarried women	Irregular	22.6	14.7	6.5	7.4	0.0	15.4
	Marginal self-emp.	29.0	20.6	41.3	25.9	16.7	10.8
	Self-emp.w. capital	3.2	2.9	2.2	3.7	-	1.5
	Protected employee	19.4	14.7	15.2	40.7	29.2	29.2
	Non-prot.employee	25.8	47.1	34.8	22.2	54.2	43.1
	Total	100.0	100.0	100.0	100.0	100.0	100.0
	N	31	34	46	27	24	65
Total	Irregular	7.8	10.2	4.3	7.3	8.7	11.2
	Marginal self-emp.	22.5	13.8	34.1	24.1	19.3	14.2
	Self-emp. . capital	8.9	7.1	3.0	11.2	-	6.6
	Protected employee	32.5	36.3	35.0	36.5	40.7	32.6
	Non-prot.employee	28.3	32.7	23.5	20.9	31.3	35.4
	Total	100.0	100.0	100.0	100.0	100.0	100.0
	N	449	480	460	436	275	605

Source: Pilot employment surveys in households: Burkina Faso (Ouagadougou, 1992), Cameroon (Yaoundé, 1990-91), Côte d'Ivoire (Abidjan, 1986-87), Guinea (Conakry, 1991-92), Madagascar (Antananarivo, 1989), Mali (Bamako, 1991).

Table D: Incidence, depth and inequality of poverty in households by labour market status – status of breadwinner

Parameter	PO		P1		P2		N
Status of breadwinner/country	Value	C_i (%)	Value	C_i (%)	Value	C_i (%)	
Burkina Faso	**0.387**	**100.0**	**0.172**	**100.0**	**0.103**	**100.0**	**238**
Irregular	0.750	9.8	0.331	9.6	0.186	9.0	12
Marginal self-employed	0.853	31.5	0.529	44.1	0.374	52.0	34
Self-employed with capital	0.346	9.8	0.128	8.1	0.066	7.0	26
Protected employee	0.128	13.0	0.026	5.9	0.008	3.1	94
Non-protected employee	0.458	35.9	0.182	32.4	0.098	29.0	72
Cameroon	**0.174**	**100.0**	**0.073**	**100.0**	**0.043**	**100.0**	**265**
Irregular	0.467	15.2	0.190	14.8	0.109	14.5	15
Marginal self-employed	0.563	39.1	0.291	48.3	0.205	57.9	32
Self-employed with capital	0.077	4.3	0.036	4.9	0.018	4.2	26
Protected employee	0.046	13.0	0.010	6.8	0.002	2.9	130
Non-protected employee	0.210	28.3	0.078	25.2	0.037	20.5	62
Côte d'Ivoire	**0.127**	**100.0**	**0.056**	**100.0**	**0.033**	**100.0**	**267**
Irregular	0.300	8.8	0.102	6.8	0.050	5.7	10
Marginal self-employed	0.243	52.9	0.134	66.8	0.090	75.9	74
Self-employed with capital	0.182	5.9	0.087	6.4	0.045	5.7	11
Protected employee	0.052	17.6	0.016	12.1	0.006	8.1	115
Non-protected employee	0.088	14.7	0.020	7.8	0.007	4.5	57
Guinea	**0.383**	**100.0**	**0.154**	**100.0**	**0.084**	**100.0**	**230**
Irregular	0.571	9.1	0.242	9.6	0.137	9.8	14
Marginal self-employed	0.634	29.5	0.362	41.8	0.230	48.7	41
Self-employed with capital	0.237	10.2	0.096	10.3	0.051	10.1	38
Protected employee	0.284	30.7	0.076	20.3	0.031	15.1	95
Non-protected employee	0.429	20.5	0.152	18.0	0.074	16.3	42
Madagascar	**0.343**	**100.0**	**0.148**	**100.0**	**0.086**	**100.0**	**155**
Irregular	0.615	13.8	0.352	20.0	0.232	22.7	13
Self-employed	0.448	22.4	0.183	23.1	0.116	25.4	29
Protected employee	0.200	24.1	0.039	11.9	0.016	8.3	70
Non-protected employee	0.535	39.7	0.240	44.9	0.135	43.5	43
Mali	**0.452**	**100.0**	**0.196**	**100.0**	**0.112**	**100.0**	**290**
Irregular	0.500	9.9	0.263	12.1	0.156	12.6	26
Marginal self-employed	0.510	19.8	0.226	20.2	0.138	21.8	51
Self-employed with capital	0.125	3.1	0.052	2.9	0.028	2.8	32
Protected employee	0.380	31.3	0.142	27.0	0.067	22.3	108
Non-protected employee	0.640	35.9	0.295	37.9	0.179	40.4	73

Note: The number of households covered in Table D is lower than those in Table B. Table 4 includes only households in which there is an income from activity (breadwinner).

Source: Pilot employment surveys in households in the capitals of: Burkina Faso, 1992; Cameroon, 1990-91; Côte d'Ivoire, 1986-87; Guinea, 1991-92; Madagascar, 1989; Mali, 1991.

Table E: Regression equation coefficients of the multivariate analysis of poverty and status of employment of heads of households[1]

Country	Burkina Faso		Cameroon		Côte d'Ivoire	
Independant variable	β	Sig T[2]	β	Sig T[2]	β	Sig T[2]
Status of work[3]						
Marginal self-employed	-0.37087	0.30	-0.22953	0.28	-0.06438	0.81
Self-employed with capital	1.54957	0.00	1.22848	0.00	0.71365	0.07
Protected employee	1.18053	0.00	0.83752	0.00	0.56719	0.04
Non-protected employee	0.72911	0.03	0.36575	0.03	0.22407	0.42
Instruction[4]						
Primary	-0.31703	0.08	0.03312	0.89	-0.23934	0.09
Secondary first cycle	0.16867	0.46	0.07313	0.77	-0.12235	0.46
Secondary second cycle	0.20737	0.37	0.21139	0.41	0.26664	0.16
Higher	0.06254	0.93	0.80809	0.00	0.89660	0.00
Training[5]						
Micro-enterprise	-0.05046	0.77	-0.2869	0.85	-0.15601	0.21
Large entreprise	-	-	0.10810	0.61	-	-
Modern training[6]	0.28814	0.11	-0.07573	1.56	0.15200	0.38
Demography 1						
Age	0.09592	0.03	0.06248	0.09	0.04648	0.32
(Age)²	-0.00120	0.01	-0.00057	0.18	-0.00053	0.35
Nationality	-	-	-	-	0.25309	0.07
Demography 2						
Size of household	-0.04425	0.00	-0.03074	0.06	-0.08069	0.00
% persons employed/household	0.00560	0.04	0.01112	0.00	0.00983	0.00
Constant	-1.41672	0.16	-0.59034	0.43	8.83778	0.00
Variations: R² (Sig F)						
Satus of labour	0.34933	0.00	0.29131	0.00	0.07836	0.00
Instruction/training	0.02983	0.13	0.06268	0.00	0.07417	0.00
Demography 1	0.03071	0.00	0.00562	0.32	0.03344	0.02
Demography 2	0.04005	0.00	0.08406	0.00	0.15101	0.00
R²/R² ajusted	0.44993	0.41218	0.44367	0.41182	0.33698	0.29336
F/Sig F	11.91877	0.0000	13.92938	0.0000	7.72540	0.0000
N	219		278		244	

Table E (contd.):   Regression equation coefficients of the multivariate analysis of poverty and status of employment of heads of households[1]

Country	Guinea		Madagascar		Mali	
Independant variable	β	Sig T^2	β	Sig T^2	β	Sig T^2
Status of work[3]						
Marginal self-employed	0.09871	0.46	0.86423[7]	0.00	-0.09769	0.71
Self-employed with capital	1.01135	0.00	-		1.32152	0.00
Protected employee	0.82763	0.00	0.53138	0.02	-0.16213	0.55
Non-protected employee	0.63997	0.00	0.26252	0.24	-0.25383	0.32
Instruction[4]						
Primary	-0.18531	0.17	0.43874	0.08	0.20282[10]	0.31
Secondary first cycle	0.00546	0.97	0.31381[8]	0.11	-	-
Secondary second cycle	0.18130	0.24	0.84755[9]	0.00	0.40232[11]	0.09
Higher	0.32395	0.05	1.00215	0.00	0.89570	0.00
Training[5]						
Micro-enterprise	0.06799	0.56	-0.18297	0.46	0.27094	0.10
Large entreprise	-0.17345	0.33	0.26618	0.35	-	-
Modern training[6]	0.12443	0.26	-0.06191	0.68	0.23845	0.16
Demography 1						
Age	0.00524	0.86	0.08459	0.03	-0.06665	0.12
(Age)^2	0.00005	0.85	-0.00083	0.05	0.00078	0.06
Nationality	-	-	-	-	-	-
Demography 2						
Size of household	-0.03003	0.00	-0.09518	0.01	-0.00639	0.63
% persons employed/household	0.01048	0.00	0.00725	0.00	0.01398	0.00
Constant	8.27469	0.00	6.05218	0.00	1.34477	0.24
Variations: R^2 (Sig F)						
Satus of labour	0.26551	0.00	0.10704	0.00	0.19971	0.00
Instruction/training	0.03705	0.04	0.09063	0.01	0.05421	0.02
Demography 1	0.00268	0.58	0.01639	0.19	0.02065	0.07
Demography 2	0.11359	0.00	0.11720	0.00	0.08027	0.00
R^2/R^2 ajusted	0.41882	0.38813	0.33126	0.27200	0.35485	0.31023
F/Sig F	13.64434	0.0000	5.59038	0.0000	7.95410	0.0000
N	300		173		202	

(1) The dependent variable is the log of adjusted income; breadwinner in the case of Madagascar; (2) Two-tailed probability that the coefficient is equal to zero; (3) Base = irregular work; (3) Without education = base; (4) Base = without education; (5) Base = without training; (6) Except apprenticeship; (7) All self-employed workers taken together; (8) Secondary incomplete; (9) Secondary complete; (10) Basic; (11) Secondary as a whole

Source: Pilot employment surveys in households in the capitals of: Burkina Faso, 1992; Cameroon, 1990-91; Côte d'Ivoire, 1986-87; Guinea, 1991-92; Madagascar, 1989; Mali, 1991.

Table F: Urban unemployment rate by situation in the household and standard of living – 15 years and above – (percentage of active population)

Country Parameter		Burkina Faso	Cameroon	Côte d'Ivoire	Guinea	Mada-gascar	Mali
Head of	Unemployment	6.0	9.0	8.1	15.7	0.0	3.7
household	Under-employment	0.8	4.5	5.9	8.0	3.1	0.5
	Marginal unempl.	1.9	1.8	0.0	3.5	0.0	2.3
Secondary	Unemployment	42.3	52.2	43.4	21.7	43.4	22.8
male	Under-employment	3.2	5.3	6.7	2.9	13.2	2.3
	Marginal unempl.	8.3	5.0	0.9	16.5	10.2	13.8
Women	Unemployment	19.2	22.6	9.0	10.2	5.8	5.8
married	Under-employment	1.3	0.0	1.9	0.9	2.3	1.0
	Marginal unempl.	15.2	13.8	5.2	16.9	9.5	18.9
Secondary	Unemployment	47.9	51.1	36.6	34.5	40.0	26.7
female	Under-employment	0.0	1.4	4.1	0.0	6.5	0.0
	Marginal unempl.	19.0	26.8	10.6	46.3	8.0	40.9
Secondary members - unemployment		35.8	42.4	30.8	24.3	24.3	20.7
Overall - unemployment		25.0	29.3	22.8	19.0	13.1	16.9
Head of	Poor	10.5	31.0	43.6	31.0	0.0	4.4
household[1]	Intermediate	3.1	7.5	2.8	3.7	0.0	6.3
	Non-poor	0.0	4.4	1.2	2.4	0.0	1.3
Secondary	Poor	38.9	56.9	41.1	23.8	32.7	29.4
members[1]	Intermediate	29.4	42.5	34.8	18.3	27.5	17.7
	Non-poor	39.2	31.6	20.3	14.8	14.1	12.3
Overall[1]	Poor	31.9	47.5	40.0	25.4	16.0	23.7
	Intermediate	19.4	26.8	22.8	14.8	15.3	15.1
	Non-poor	22.1	19.9	13.0	11.2	7.9	9.6

Note: The various unemployment rates were calculated as follows: Unemployment rate = [(unemployed persons)/(employed + under-employed + unemployed)];   under-employment rate = [(under-employed)/(employed + under-employed + unemployed)];   rate of marginal unemployment = [(marginal unemployed)/(employed + under-employed + unempoyed + marginal unemployed)].

(1) Unemployment.

Source: Pilot employment surveys in households in the capitals of: Burkina Faso, 1992; Cameroon, 1990-91; Côte d'Ivoire, 1986-87; Guinea, 1991-92; Madagascar, 1989; Mali, 1991.

Table G: Regression coefficients of logistic estimate of determinants of poverty[1]

Country	Burkina Faso		Cameroun		Côte d'Ivoire		Guinée		Mali	
Independant variable	β	Sig T²	β	Sig T²	β	Sig T²	β	Sig T²	β	Sig T²
Sex (1=men)	-1.1744	**0.02**	-1.4479	**0.00**	0.2027	0.73	1.0184	0.20	-0.2610	0.54
G.exp./100 (years)	-0.0272	0.55	-0.0274	0.55	-0.0186	0.72	0.0930	**0.05**	0.0243	0.52
(G.exp)²/100 (years)	0.0541	0.37	0.0847	0.23	0.0506	0.49	-0.1073	**0.06**	-0.0186	0.67
Education (years)	-0.1424	**0.00**	-0.0742	0.10	-0.0642	0.28	-0.0571	**0.03**	-0.0140	0.61
Training (years)	-0.0533	0.40	0.0256	0.78	0.0420	0.60	-0.0306	0.57	-0.0710	**0.08**
Unemploy-ment (1=yes)[3]	1.2305	**0.05**	1.9376	**0.00**	1.9696	**0.00**	1.2813	**0.00**	0.1583	0.80
Vul. labour stat. (1=yes)[4]	0.6968	**0.03**	0.9080	**0.00**	0.0594	0.88	0.1386	0.67	0.1478	0.59
Household unempl. rate	1.3805	**0.01**	1.4233	**0.00**	1.6003	**0.00**	1.7148	**0.00**	1.7206	**0.00**
Household size	0.0036	0.91	0.0309	0.47	0.1098	**0.02**	0.0565	**0.04**	0.0035	0.89
Constant	1.5096	0.14	-0.4601	0.63	-2.7503	**0.03**	-3.3309	**0.01**	-0.4779	0.62
-2 log likelihood	314.123		269.203		234.324		337.218		391.06124	
CHI²	100.123		81.380		53.988		78.670		.814	
Sig CHI²	0.0000		0.0000		0.0000		0.0000		0.000	
Cor.clas. cases	72.2%		80.4%		84.6%		42.0%		58.0%	
N	299		301		292		300		300	

(1) Except Madagascar. The dependant variable is the standard of living (1=poor; 0=intermediate and non-poor); (2) Two-tailed probability that the coefficient is equal to zero; Wald statistic with logit;; (3) included under-occupation and marginal unemploymentl; (4) Vulnerable status= irregular work, marginal self-employed and non-protected employee.
Source: Pilot employment surveys in households in the capitals of: Burkina Faso, 1992; Cameroon, 1990-91; Côte d'Ivoire, 1986-87; Guinea, 1991-92; Madagascar, 1989; Mali, 1991.

Table H: **Employment and labour supply rates of adults – 15 years and above – by matrimonial status and level of income[1]**

Parameter	Poor		Intermediate		Non-poor		Overall	
Status/country	Empl.	Supply	Empl.	Supply	Empl.	Supply	Empl.	Supply
Burkina Faso (N)	676	676	449	449	140	140	1265	1265
Head of household	72.1	80.5	93.1	96.1	97.8	97.8	83.0	88.3
Secondary men	35.7	63.9	31.9	50.4	23.3	46.7	33.3	57.8
Married women	30.6	37.8	42.4	49.2	53.9	76.9	37.4	46.3
Single women	26.2	50.8	15.8	28.4	11.5	26.9	20.7	39.7
Overall	40.8	58.3	45.0	55.7	53.6	67.9	43.7	58.4
Cameroon (N)	407	407	624	624	394	394	1425	1425
Head of household	49.9	71.6	89.9	93.0	96.7	98.9	81.1	89.0
Secondary men	13.3	34.7	19.8	43.9	26.6	44.8	19.8	41.4
Married women	25.4	36.5	31.9	43.7	57.3	67.1	37.9	48.9
Single women	7.1	23.9	12.2	18.2	10.3	21.8	10.0	20.5
Overall	20.6	39.3	35.1	47.9	45.9	57.4	34.0	48.1
Côte d'Ivoire (N)	227	227	537	537	273	273	1037	1037
Head of household	56.1	86.0	93.2	95.9	93.2	94.3	86.0	93.5
Secondary men	33.8	77.0	33.1	64.9	56.2	75.3	39.8	70.7
Married women	37.9	41.4	49.7	56.6	67.8	71.2	51.2	56.5
Single women	28.9	52.6	33.4	59.4	40.5	62.2	34.5	59.5
Overall	39.6	66.1	54.2	70.2	68.5	78.8	54.8	71.6
Guinea (N)	1179	1179	428	428	492	492	2093	2093
Head of household	52.0	75.3	45.6	91.5	51.4	90.1	39.1	83.0
Secondary men	34.2	46.1	49.0	59.5	47.3	56.5	39.8	50.9
Married women	31.2	35.3	40.9	44.9	52.3	58.3	39.8	42.8
Single women	14.7	23.5	20.6	33.0	21.1	27.8	38.4	26.5
Overall	31.5	42.3	45.6	53.5	51.4	57.9	17.4	48.3
Madagascar (N)	242	242	205	205	176	176	623	623
Head of household	88.5	88.5	85.9	85.9	92.6	92.6	88.8	88.8
Secondary men	14.3	34.9	25.0	47.7	24.4	39.0	20.3	39.9
Married women	36.5	53.8	58.5	67.9	70.5	70.5	54.4	63.8
Single women	10.8	27.7	17.8	33.3	35.9	43.6	19.4	33.6
Overall	36.9	50.6	51.0	61.7	59.0	80.9	47.8	55.2
Mali (N)	1191	1191	470	470	663	663	2324	2324
Head of household	57.0	59.6	77.6	82.8	84.6	85.7	69.3	72.0
Secondary men	31.0	45.9	42.3	52.0	50.6	57.3	38.9	50.4
Married women	10.4	10.8	22.5	24.5	30.4	32.3	19.0	20.2
Single women	12.8	18.2	21.1	27.2	16.3	21.8	15.3	20.9
Overall	25.2	33.5	37.2	43.8	42.8	47.4	32.7	39.3

(1) The employment rate for a given stratum is obtained by comparing the number of persons employed - employed and under-employed - with that of the total population of the group; the labour supply rate for a given stratum is obtained by comparing the number of active persons - employed, under-employed and unemployed, with that of the total population of the group.

Source: Pilot employment surveys in households in the capitals of: Burkina Faso, 1992; Cameroon, 1990-91; Côte d'Ivoire, 1986-87; Guinea, 1991-92; Madagascar, 1989; Mali, 1991.

Table I: Labour supply rate by matrimonial status and age (%)[1]

Country Parameter		Burkina Faso	Cameroon	Côte d'Ivoire	Guinea	Mada- gascar	Mali
Head of	15-29 years	97.2	95.3	95.2	100.0	92.3	100.0
household	30-39 years	97.0	94.8	97.3	100.0	94.3	96.2
	> = 40 years	82.8	82.4	88.9	78.8	85.8	66.2
	Overall	88.3	89.0	93.5	83.0	88.8	72.0
	N	300	301	292	300	179	300
Secondary	15-29 years	54.6	33.6	69.1	43.7	30.6	43.3
men	30-39 years	87.1	93.7	91.3	78.9	66.7	80.0
	> = 40 years	72.3	46.2	70.0	70.0	33.3	61.4
	Overall	57.7	41.4	70.7	50.9	35.8	50.4
	N	381	505	314	806	148	940
Married	15-29 years	44.4	41.4	59.5	35.3	44.4	18.7
women	30-39 years	57.7	61.5	58.1	52.1	49.1	28.0
	> = 40 years	36.7	44.9	44.4	40.7	69.6	15.9
	Overall	46.3	48.9	56.5	42.8	57.7	20.2
	N	337	280	260	549	149	510
Single	15-29 years	36.9	17.0	58.6	24.3	24.8	18.0
women	30-39 years	80.0	56.0	90.0	59.5	77.8	50.0
	> = 40 years	50.0	32.0	22.2	11.1	25.0	19.2
	Overall	39.7	20.9	58.5	26.5	31.3	20.9
	N	247	339	171	438	147	574
Overall	15-29 years	49.7	32.1	67.0	36.4	32.2	32.4
	30-39 years	78.4	81.0	83.1	69.2	71.6	59.5
	> = 40 years	63.0	64.3	73.5	57.7	77.3	40.6
	Overall	58.4	48.1	71.6	48.3	55.2	39.3
	N	1265	1425	1037	2093	623	2324

(1) The labour supply for a given stratum is obtained by comparing the number of active persons - employed, under-employed and unemployed - with that of the total population of the group. *Source: Pilot employment surveys in households in the capitals of: Burkina Faso, 1992; Cameroon, 1990-91; Côte d'Ivoire, 1986-86; Guinea, 1991-92; Madagascar, 1989; Mali, 1991.*

Table J: Distribution of male population aged 15 and above by labour market status and age (%)

Country / Parameter		Burkina Faso	Cameroon	Côte d'Ivoire	Guinea	Mada- gascar	Mali
Irrégular	15-24 years	23.5	3.3	31.3	13.8	8.3	18.2
	24-29 years	23.5	30.0	6.3	6.9	0.0	15.9
	30-39 years	41.2	46.7	50.0	13.8	50.0	29.5
	40-49 years	5.9	6.7	0.0	6.9	8.3	0.0
	> = 50 years	5.9	13.3	12.5	58.6	33.3	36.4
	Overall	2.8	4.0	3.0	3.2	4.2	4.0
Marginal self-employed	15-24 years	29.3	11.1	15.2	9.7	4.3	18.0
	24-29 years	8.6	14.8	16.7	22.2	17.4	6.6
	30-39 years	15.5	44.4	34.8	29.2	39.1	27.9
	40-49 years	22.4	18.5	19.7	12.5	4.3	13.1
	> = 50 years	24.1	11.1	13.6	26.4	34.8	34.4
	Overall	9.7	3.6	12.3	8.0	8.0	5.6
Self-employed with capital	15-24 years	0.0	0.0	0.0	7.9	_¹	0.0
	24-29 years	10.3	16.0	33.3	10.5	-	13.2
	30-39 years	27.6	36.0	8.3	28.9	-	18.4
	40-49 years	27.6	28.0	33.3	18.4	-	21.1
	> = 50 years	34.5	20.0	25.0	34.2	-	47.4
	Overall	4.8	3.3	2.2	4.2	-	3.5
Protected employee	15-24 years	2.0	0.0	9.8	0.9	1.4	3.5
	24-29 years	13.1	12.0	25.8	9.6	4.2	18.2
	30-39 years	54.5	48.7	37.9	40.4	29.2	40.6
	40-49 years	25.3	24.8	18.9	34.2	33.3	26.6
	> = 50 years	5.1	14.5	7.6	14.9	31.9	11.2
	Overall	16.5	15.4	24.7	12.6	25.1	13.0
Non-protected employee	15-24 years	18.4	18.7	17.1	7.8	12.2	22.2
	24-29 years	12.6	32.7	30.5	18.2	14.3	26.5
	30-39 years	32.0	27.1	34.1	39.0	30.6	25.3
	40-49 years	22.3	11.2	17.1	22.1	18.4	9.9
	> = 50 years	14.6	10.3	1.2	13.0	24.5	16.0
	Overall	17.1	14.1	15.3	8.5	17.1	14.8
Unemployed	15-24 years	57.9	30.5	49.6	16.4	43.5	33.6
	24-29 years	27.1	35.1	28.6	29.7	30.4	33.6
	30-39 years	5.6	23.7	10.9	23.4	26.1	25.0
	40-49 years	6.5	6.1	10.1	14.1	0.0	5.2
	> = 50 years	2.8	4.6	0.8	16.4	0.0	2.6
	Overall	17.8	17.3	22.2	14.2	8.0	10.6
Marginal unemployed	15-24 years	73.9	35.7	100.0	55.1	50.0	49.4
	24-29 years	8.7	28.6	0.0	18.0	16.7	29.6
	30-39 years	0.0	28.6	0.0	15.7	16.7	13.6
	40-49 years	0.0	7.1	0.0	2.2	0.0	2.5
	> = 50 years	17.4	0.0	0.0	9.0	16.7	4.9
	Overall	3.8	0.0	0.2	9.9	2.1	7.4
Inactive	15-24 years	72.7	78.5	77.6	69.3	59.8	66.6
	24-29 years	9.1	11.7	5.6	13.0	19.6	11.5
	30-39 years	3.0	1.3	3.7	4.5	7.8	4.9
	40-49 years	0.6	0.7	1.9	0.3	0.0	2.2
	> = 50 years	14.5	7.8	11.2	13.0	12.7	14.8
	Overall	27.5	40.5	20.0	39.4	35.5	41.2
Overall	15-24 years	40.1	40.9	34.6	37.4	28.9	40.1
	24-29 years	14.0	20.1	21.5	16.3	14.6	18.2
	30-39 years	20.3	21.1	23.7	19.1	23.0	18.0
	40-49 years	13.0	8.7	13.1	10.5	12.2	8.0
	> = 50 years	12.6	9.2	7.1	16.7	21.3	15.6
	Overall	100.0	100.0	100.0	100.0	100.0	100.0
		601	758	535	902	287	1097

(1) For Madagascar, the analysis does not distinguish between marginal self-employed persons and self-employed persons with capital.

Source: Pilot employment studies in households in the capitals of: Burkina Faso, 1992; Cameroon, 1990-91; Côte d'Ivoire, 1986-87; Guinea, 1991-92; Madagascar, 1989; Mali, 1991.

Table K: Distribution of female population aged 15 and above by labour market status and age (%)

Country Parameter		Burkina Faso	Cameroon	Côte d'Ivoire	Guinea	Mada- gascar	Mali
Irrégular	15-24 years	27.8	5.3	50.0	33.3	0.0	33.3
	24-29 years	38.9	10.5	0.0	33.3	16.7	12.5
	30-39 years	5.6	57.9	50.0	33.3	16.7	20.8
	40-49 years	27.8	15.8	0.0	0.0	16.7	16.7
	> = 50 years	0.0	10.5	0.0	0.0	50.0	16.7
	Overall	3.2	2.9	0.5	0.4	3.8	2.2
Marginal self-	15-24 years	14.0	12.8	27.8	18.2	3.3	8.0
employed	24-29 years	16.3	10.3	22.2	21.2	13.3	12.0
	30-39 years	11.6	35.9	24.4	21.2	20.0	24.0
	40-49 years	23.3	17.9	23.3	24.2	20.0	32.0
	> = 50 years	34.9	23.1	2.2	15.2	43.3	24.0
	Overall	7.7	5.9	23.0	4.1	9.6	2.3
Self-employed	15-24 years	36.4	0.0	0.0	9.1	-¹	50.0
with capital	24-29 years	9.1	11.1	0.0	0.0	-	0.0
	30-39 years	27.3	11.1	50.0	45.5	-	50.0
	40-49 years	9.1	44.4	50.0	27.3	-	0.0
	> = 50 years	18.2	33.3	0.0	18.2	-	0.0
	Overall	2.0	1.4	0.5	1.4	-	0.2
Protected	15-24 years	8.5	1.8	24.1	2.2	2.5	7.4
employee	24-29 years	14.9	14.0	41.4	8.9	5.0	11.1
	30-39 years	53.2	52.6	27.6	55.6	40.0	59.3
	40-49 years	21.3	24.6	6.9	33.3	37.5	18.5
	> = 50 years	2.1	7.0	0.0	0.0	15.0	3.7
	Overall	8.4	8.6	7.4	5.6	12.8	5.0
Non-protected	15-24 years	0.0	8.0	42.3	21.4	5.4	25.0
employee	24-29 years	41.7	34.0	26.9	14.3	21.6	32.7
	30-39 years	33.3	42.0	30.8	57.1	43.2	30.8
	40-49 years	12.5	14.0	0.0	7.1	16.2	7.7
	> = 50 years	12.5	2.0	0.0	0.0	13.5	3.8
	Overall	4.3	7.5	6.6	1.7	11.9	4.8
Unemployed	15-24 years	58.2	45.7	69.1	23.4	50.0	36.8
	24-29 years	21.5	38.6	20.0	35.9	27.3	47.4
	30-39 years	16.5	12.9	7.3	35.9	13.6	13.2
	40-49 years	3.8	2.9	1.8	3.1	9.1	2.6
	> = 50 years	0.0	0.0	1.8	1.6	0.0	0.0
	Overall	14.1	10.6	14.1	7.9	7.1	3.5
Marginal	15-24 years	52.8	48.0	55.6	51.7	30.8	58.9
unemployed	24-29 years	17.0	26.0	33.3	20.1	15.4	16.8
	30-39 years	18.9	20.0	11.1	12.8	38.5	11.2
	40-49 years	11.3	6.0	0.0	10.1	7.7	5.6
	> = 50 years	0.0	0.0	0.0	5.4	7.7	7.5
	Overall	9.5	7.5	4.6	18.4	4.2	10.0
Inactive	15-24 years	46.3	65.9	46.7	44.9	55.1	40.9
	24-29 years	13.0	7.0	14.8	9.0	10.1	10.8
	30-39 years	13.0	10.3	18.3	15.3	17.7	15.8
	40-49 years	12.6	6.2	11.2	11.6	5.7	13.6
	> = 50 years	15.1	10.6	8.9	19.2	11.4	18.9
	Overall	50.9	55.7	43.2	60.6	50.6	71.9
Overall	15-24 years	40.2	46.8	43.7	40.0	34.0	39.1
	24-29 years	17.0	14.8	20.7	13.7	12.8	13.8
	30-39 years	18.2	20.2	19.7	20.1	24.4	18.5
	40-49 years	13.2	9.5	11.3	12.5	13.1	12.9
	> = 50 years	11.4	8.7	4.6	13.6	15.7	15.7
	Overall	100.0	100.0	100.0	100.0	100.0	100.0
		560	663	391	809	312	1073

(1) For Madagascar, the analysis does not distinguish between marginal self-employed persons and self-employed persons with capital.

Source: Pilot employment studies in households in the capitals of: Burkina Faso, 1992; Cameroon, 1990-91; Côte d'Ivoire, 1986-87; Guinea, 1991-92; Madagascar, 1989; Mali, 1991.

Table L: Regression coefficients of probit structural equations of labour supply of households members [1]

Country	Burkina Faso		Cameroon		Côte d'Ivoire	
Independant variable	β	Sig T[2]	β	Sig T[2]	β	Sig T[2]
Education[3]						
Primary	0.46824	**0.06**	-	-	0.37956	**0.06**
Secondary first cycle, general	-	-	-1.55580[9]	**0.00**	-	-
Secondary second cycle, general	1.08660[8]	**0.08**	-1.55552	**0.00**	0.05916[10]	0.86
Secondary first cycle, technical	-	-	-1.12627	**0.00**	-	-
Secondary second cycle, technical	-	-	-1.67445	**0.00**	-	-
Higher	1.99340	**0.03**	-2.48798	**0.00**	-0.50063	0.65
Training[4]						
Apprenticeship in enterprises	1.51758	**0.00**	-0.02945	0.89	0.79641	**0.00**
Vocational centre/various	1.38024	**0.00**	0.23370	0.19	0.34675	0.14
Higher training	-	-	-	-	-0.55283	0.33
Diploma[5]						
Elementary (CEPE)	-	-	-0.01903	0.90	0.05344	0.79
Secondary first cycle	-	-	-0.16161	0.60	0.29345	0.40
Secondary second cycle	-	-	-0.30004	0.55	-	-
Higher	-	-	-0.37652	0.57	1.21684[12]	**0.06**
Apprenticeship	-	-	0.09349	0.73	1.04730	**0.00**
Other technical diploma	-	-	-	-	1.65384	**0.00**
Demography						
Age	0.36850	**0.00**	0.05791	0.45	0.33570	**0.00**
(Age)[2]	-0.00443	**0.00**	-0.00142	**0.08**	-0.00409	**0.00**
Period of residence in the capital	0.00477	0.96	-0.00727	0.51	-0.02337	0.18
(Period res. capital)[2]	0.00041	**0.03**	-0.00005	0.83	0.00005	0.89
Nationality[6]	-	-	-	-	0.02722	0.86
Family background						
Number of adult women	0.05926	**0.01**	-0.00204	0.93	-0.09530	**0.01**
Number of children < =7 years	0.00118	0.95	0.01666	0.57	-0.00459	0.88
Single men[7]	-0.63624	**0.00**	-0.37218	**0.03**	-0.12928	0.53
Married women[7]	-2.09319	**0.00**	-0.58439	**0.01**	-2.19319	**0.00**
Single women[7]	-1.10033	**0.00**	-0.48553	**0.04**	-0.13080	0.56
% parents educated	-0.00226	0.50	-0.00047	0.76	0.00236	0.55
% parents with training	0.01021	**0.03**	-0.00194	0.48	-0.00493	0.16
% parents employees	0.00095	0.79	-0.00616	0.89	-0.00013	0.98
% parents self-employed	-0.00553	**0.01**	-0.00768	0.86	-0.00310	0.35
Attributed income	-1.04224	**0.02**	1.91383	**0.00**	-0.99133	0.12
Constant	-4.32633	**0.00**	-2.60251	0.55	6.05597	0.24
Log likelihood	**-622.144**		**-512.669**		**-443.294**	
CHI²/Sig CHI²	**265.011**	**0.0000**	**514.616**	**0.0000**	**265.112**	**0.0000**
Correctly classified cases/N	**73.4%**	**1216**	**82.5%**	**1378**	**80.5%**	**1035**

Table L (contd.): Regression coefficients of probit structural equations of labour supply of households members[1]

Country	Guinea		Madagascar		Mali	
Independant variable	β	Sig T[2]	β	Sig T[2]	β	Sig T[2]
Education[3]						
Primary	0.19602	0.15	-	-	-0.06271[15]	0.60
Secondary first cycle, general	-0.14095	0.50	-	-	-	-
Secondary second cycle, general	-0.10647	0.62	-0.80321[9]	0.30	0.57706	**0.02**
Secondary first cycle, technical	0.11068	0.83	-	-	-	-
Secondary second cycle, technical	0.21609	0.68	-	-	-	-
Higher	-0.01180	0.98	-0.48380	0.13	-0.38759	0.21
Training[4]						
Apprenticeship in enterprises	2.44126	**0.00**	1.27980	**0.04**	0.80605	**0.00**
Vocational centre/various	1.88536	**0.00**	1.04988	0.11	1.15615	**0.00**
Higher training	-	-	-	-	-	-
Diploma[5]						
Elementary (CEPE)	-0.38150	0.29	1.00354	0.49	-0.16824	0.13
Secondary first cycle	-	-	-	-	0.17119	0.28
Secondary second cycle	1.31537[13]	**0.00**	-	-	0.29682[12]	0.15
Higher	1.56470	**0.00**	1.99645[14]	0.43	-	-
Apprenticeship	-0.47026	0.23	-0.99652	0.25	-0.50927	**0.09**
Other technical diploma	-	-	-	-	-	-
Demography						
Age	0.21061	**0.00**	0.37115	0.43	0.09134	**0.00**
(Age)^2	-0.00252	**0.00**	-0.00413	0.41	-0.00132	**0.00**
Period of residence in the capital	0.01494	0.17	-0.02940	0.71	0.02019	**0.01**
(Period res. capital)^2	-0.00038	**0.05**	0.00043	0.72	-0.00036	**0.02**
Nationality[6]	-	-	-	-	-	-
Family background						
Number of adult women	-0.00571	0.70	-0.18895	**0.04**	0.00621	0.65
Number of children < =7 years	0.03530	0.10	-0.15045	0.19	-0.00009	0.99
Single men[7]	-0.68354	**0.00**	-0.59253	**0.00**	-0.22963	0.14
Married women[7]	-0.97381	**0.00**	-1.19412	**0.00**	-0.64473	**0.09**
Single women[7]	-0.99723	**0.00**	-1.52136	**0.01**	-0.45604	**0.10**
% parents educated	0.00428	0.12	-0.00521	**0.10**	0.00129	0.54
% parents with training	-0.00140	0.58	0.00371	0.29	-0.00123	0.39
% parents employees	-0.00884	**0.00**	0.00250	0.42	-0.00159	0.71
% parents self-employed	-0.00718	**0.00**	0.00307	1.19	-0.00290	0.48
Attibuted income	-0.5616	0.48	-1.36012	0.62	1.2444	**0.02**
Constant	-1.95281	**0.04**	7.04441	0.66	3.72492	**0.00**
Log likelihood	**-866.456**		**-298.964**		**-1038.446**	
CHI²/Sig CHI²	**674.542**	**0.0000**	**148.260**	**0.0000**	**733.924**	**0.0000**
Correctly classified cases/N	**81.1%**	**2081**	**73.9%**	**597**	**76.4%**	**2205**

(1) The dependent variable is the labour supply (1 = yes, 0 = no); (2) Two-tailed probability that the coefficient is equal to zero; Wald statistic with probit; (3) Base = without education; (4) Base = without training; (5) Base = without diploma; (6) Base = non-nationals; (7) Base = head of household; (8) Secondary overall; (9) Base = without education/primary; (10) Secondary first cycle; (11) Secondary second cycle/higher; (12) Baccalaureat and other diplomas; (13) First and second cycles; (14) General diploma; (15) Basic.

Source: Pilot employment surveys in households in the capitals of: Burkina Faso, 1992; Cameroon, 1990-91; Côte d'Ivoire, 1986-87; Guinea, 1991-92; Madagascar, 1989; Mali, 1991.

Table M: Regression coefficients of logistic equations of labour supply of married women[1]

Country	Burkina Faso		Cameroon		Côte d'Ivoire	
Independante variable	β	Sig T^2	β	Sig T^2	β	Sig T^2
Education[3]						
Without education	-4.1078	**0.00**	-2.2335	**0.00**	-1.7155	**0.01**
Primary	-3.5938	**0.00**	-1.7187	**0.00**	-1.9747[10]	**0.00**
Secondary first cycle, general	-1.9554	0.09	-1.2116	0.05	-	-
Secondary second cycle, general	-0.6520	0.63	0.2452	0.75	-	-
Secondary first cycle, technical	-	-	-0.1614	0.81	-	-
Secondary second cycle, technical	-	-	-0.2434	0.73	-	-
Training[4]						
Without training	-0.9791	0.24	-2.1090	**0.00**	-0.0872	0.89
Apprenticeship enterprises	3.2139	**0.02**	-0.7581	0.35	0.8790	0.31
Age						
Age	0.1469	**0.03**	0.4030	**0.00**	0.3090	**0.03**
$(Age)^2$	-0.0017	**0.06**	-0.0050	**0.00**	-0.0049	**0.02**
Children $< = 7$ years[5]						
Without children	-0.2710	0.57	-0.0044	0.99	1.0963	**0.01**
One or two	0.0762	0.81	-0.8383	**0.01**	0.8940	**0.02**
Women $> = 15$ years[6]						
One woman	-0.8293	**0.02**	0.3695	0.37	-0.9484	**0.02**
Two women	-0.8444	**0.02**	-0.1082	0.96	-0.5699	0.17
Unemployment other members[7]						
Rate $= 0$	1.6946	**0.00**	-0.2315	0.50	-0.2253	0.52
Rate $< 50\%$	2.0917	**0.00**	-0.3668	0.60	-8.0403	0.72
Nationality[8]	-	-	-	-	-0.697	0.12
Status head of household[9]						
Irrégular	-0.1599	0.86	-0.2033	0.80	-6.4088	0.72
Marginal self-employed	0.9376	**0.07**	-0.0166	0.98	0.9872	**0.09**
Self-employed with capital	-0.0844	0.88	0.1186	0.85	3.4017	**0.00**
Protected emplyee	-0.3714	0.51	-0.0476	0.91	0.9070	**0.07**
Non-protected employee	0.5074	0.30	-0.9204	**0.06**	1.3715	**0.01**
Income other members	0.0097	**0.06**	0.0026	0.3	-0.00000053	0.62
Constant	0.1083	0.95	-4.0465	**0.03**	-4.081	**0.10**
-2 log likekihood	**336.097**		**298.646**		**270..85**	
CHI²/Sig CHI²	**125.476**	**0.0000**	**86.614**	**0.0000**	**72.526**	**0.0000**
Correctly classified cases/N	**76.7%**	**334**	**77.0%**	**278**	**74.3%**	**257**

Table M (contd.):   Regression coefficients of logistic equations of labour supply of married women[1]

Country	Guinea		Madagascar		Mali	
Independante variable	β	Sig T^2	β	Sig T^2	β	Sig T^2
Education[3]						
Without education	-3.6360	**0.00**	-		-2.8024	**0.04**
Primary	-3.6899	**0.00**	-0.2837[11]	0.69	-2.2408[16]	0.11
Secondary first cycle, general	-3.1729	**0.04**	-	-	-	-
Secondary second cycle, general	-2.5486	**0.03**	0.5549	0.40	-0.5563	0.69
Secondary first cycle, technical	-1.1139	0.37	-	-	-	-
Secondary second cycle, technical	0.2528	0.86	-	-	-	-
Training[4]	-1.6159	**0.05**	-1.8564[12]	**0.00**	-2.5955	**0.00**
Without training	0.7060	0.47	-	-	-1.5544	**0.09**
Apprenticeship enterprises						
Age						
Age	0.1713	**0.00**	0.0680	0.52	0.0594	0.38
$(Age)^2$	-0.0020	**0.00**	-0.0005	0.72	-0.0007	0.39
Children $<= 7$ years[5]						
Without children	-1.0752	**0.00**	0.0606[13]	0.90	-0.1341	0.72
One or two	-0.3910	**0.09**	-	-	0.0260	0.94
Women $>= 15$ years[6]						
One woman	-0.237	0.94	-0.2778	0.61	-1.5082	**0.02**
Two women	0.0138	0.96	0.3270	0.57	-0.6824	0.16
Unemployment other members[7]	0.0401	0.90	-0.2868[14]	0.62	0.3342	0.40
Rate = 0	0.0318	0.84	-	-	0.9159	**0.07**
Rate < 50%						
Nationality[8]	-	-	-	-	-	-
Status head of household[9]						
Irrégular	0.4971	0.19	-	-	0.2850	0.67
Marginal self-employed	0.2592	0.43	-0.8702[15]	0.23	0.3103	0.59
Self-employed with capital	0.5442	0.15	-	-	0.3188	0.47
Protected emplyee	-0.4078	0.20	-0.9568	0.14	0.7841	**0.03**
Non-protected employee	0.8664	**0.02**	-1.0202	0.13	0.3884	0.39
Income other members	-0.0069	**0.05**	-0.00000081	0.8	0.0001	**0.05**
Constant	1.4245	0.41	0.8843	0.71	1.5635	0.45
-2 log likekihood	**594.474**		**169.645**		**369.309**	
CHI²/Sig CHI²	**117.473**	**0.0000**	**30.527**	**0.0040**	**132.040**	**0.0000**
Correctly classified cases/N	**69.7%**	**522**	**70.1%**	**147**	**86.7%**	**496**

(1) The dependent variable is the labour supply; (2) Two-tailed probability that the coefficient is equal to zero, Wald statistic with Logit; (3) Base = higher; (4) Base = apprenticeship in enterprises or other modern training according to the countries; (5) Base = ⟩ 2 children unless otherwise indicated; (6) Base = more than two women unless otherwise indicated; (7) Unemployment rate of other members of household except head; Base = rate ⟩ = 50% unless otherwise indicated; (8) Base = non-nationals; (9) Base = unemployed, inactive; (10) Base = secondary/superior; (11) Without education/primary; (12) Base = apprenticeship or other training; (13) Base = zero; (14) Base = positive unemployment rate; (15) Irregular/self-employed; (16) Basic.
Source: Pilot employment surveys in households in the capitals of: Burkina Faso, 1992; Cameroon, 1990-91; Côte d'Ivoire, 1986-87; Guinea, 1991-92; Madagascar, 1989; Mali, 1991..

Table N: Access to capital by self-employed workers - present employment (%)[1]

Country Parameter		Burkina Faso	Cameroon	Côte d'Ivoire	Guinea	Mali
Irregular	Family/household	54.1	31.6	50.0	25.6	35.3
	Savings	31.2	35.0	0.0	72.6	45.2
	Small loans	11.8	3.9	0.0	0.0	12.0
	Bank/State	0.0	2.6	0.0	0.0	1.6
	Other cases[2]	2.9	26.9	50.0	1.8	5.9
Marginal self-	Family/household	43.5	45.5	78.0	38.5	23.8
employed	Savings	42.3	36.3	0.0	49.1	43.4
	Small loans	8.0	2.5	2.6	1.3	19.4
	Bank/State	0.0	0.0	0.0	1.0	0.0
	Other cases[2]	6.2	15.7	19.4	10.1	13.4
Self-employed	Family/household	23.3	28.4	64.3	31.6	20.2
with capital	Savings	55.0	47.0	0.0	51.8	74.6
	Small loans	5.0	0.0	0.0	2.4	5.0
	Bank/State	10.0	10.3	0.0	0.0	0.0
	Other cases[2]	6.7	14.3	37.7	14.2	0.0
Overall	Family/household	40.2	37.2	76.2	35.1	28.2
	Savings	43.9	38.5	0.0	53.1	49.2
	Small loans	7.7	2.3	2.2	1.4	13.3
	Bank/State	2.3	3.3	0.0	0.6	0.9
	Other cases[2]	5.9	18.7	21.6	9.8	1.2
	N	137	131	181	180	81

(1) Madagascar is excluded because of the poor quality of data; (2) Tontine, inheritance et miscellaneous.

Source: Pilot employment surveys in households in the capitals of: Burkina Faso, 1992; Cameroon, 1990-91; Côte d'Ivoire, 1986-87; Guinea, 1991-92; Madagascar, 1989; Mali, 1991.

Table O: Occupational transition matrix - Burkina Faso, Cameroon, Côte d'Ivoire and Mali[1]

First job Status		Irregular	Self-employed[2]	Protected employee	Non-prot. employee	Apprentice family help	Overall (N)(%)
Irregular	Burkina Faso	5.6	16.7	0.0	11.1	66.7	18
		25.0	16.7	0.0	4.3	14.1	10.2
	Cameroon	6.3	12.5	31.5	37.5	12.5	16
		25.0	9.5	12.5	6.7	33.3	10.0
	Côte d'Ivoire	6.3	6.3	25.0	62.5	0.0	16
		6.3	1.0	4.2	8.7	0.0	3.9
	Mali	9.1	9.1	18.2	9.1	54.5	11
		25.0	33.3	9.1	3.6	40.0	15.3
Marginal self-employed	Burkina Faso	4.9	2.4	0.0	7.3	85.4	41
		50.0	5.6	0.0	6.4	41.2	23.3
	Cameroon	0.0	23.8	19.0	57.1	0.0	21
		0.0	23.8	10.0	13.5	0.0	13.1
	Côte d'Ivoire	2.0	56.8	2.7	14.2	24.3	148
		18.8	80.8	4.2	18.3	46.8	36.4
	Mali	0.0	8.3	8.3	41.7	41.7	12
		0.0	33.3	4.5	17.9	33.3	16.7
Self-employed with capital	Burkina Faso	0.0	38.1	4.8	14.3	42.9	21
		0.0	44.4	4.5	6.4	10.6	11.9
	Cameroon	0.0	26.1	30.4	34.8	8.7	23
		0.0	28.6	17.5	9.0	33.3	14.4
	Côte d'Ivoire	0.0	30.8	15.4	38.5	15.4	13
		0.0	3.8	2.1	4.3	2.6	3.2
	Mali	9.1	9.1	27.3	36.4	18.2	11
		25.0	33.3	13.6	14.3	13.3	15.3
Protected employee	Burkina Faso	0.0	6.7	40.0	31.1	22.2	45
		0.0	16.7	81.8	28.8	11.8	25.6
	Cameroon	1.8	5.5	43.6	49.1	0.0	55
		25.0	14.3	60.0	30.3	0.0	34.4
	Côte d'Ivoire	6.5	2.9	54.7	23.7	12.2	139
		56.3	3.8	80.0	28.7	22.1	34.2
	Mali	5.8	0.0	77.8	16.7	0.0	18
		25.0	0.0	63.6	10.7	0.0	25.0
Non-protected employee	Burkina Faso	2.0	5.9	5.9	49.0	37.3	51
		25.0	16.7	13.6	53.2	22.4	29.0
	Cameroon	4.4	11.1	0.0	80.0	4.4	45
		50.0	23.8	0.0	40.4	33.3	28.1
	Côte d'Ivoire	3.3	12.1	9.9	50.5	24.2	91
		18.8	10.6	9.5	40.0	28.6	22.4
	Mali	5.0	0.0	10.0	75.0	10.0	20
		25.0	0.0	9.1	53.6	13.3	27.8
Overall (N) (%)	Burkina Faso	4	18	22	47	85	176
		2.3	10.2	12.5	26.7	48.3	100.0
	Cameroon	4	21	40	89	6	160
		2.5	13.1	25.0	55.6	3.8	100.0
	Côte d'Ivoire	16	104	95	115	77	407
		3.9	25.6	23.3	28.3	18.9	100.0
	Mali	4	3	22	28	15	72
		5.6	4.2	30.6	38.9	20.8	100.0

(1) Persons with a job and whose first job is different from their current employment. For each country, the first percentage refers to line percentages; the second refers to column percentages.
(2) Given the size of the samples, the first job makes no distinction between marginal workers and self-employed workers with capital.

Source: Pilot employment surveys in households in the capitals of: Burkina Faso, 1992; Cameroon, 1990-91; Côte d'Ivoire, 1986-87; Guinea, 1991-92; Madagascar, 1989; Mali, 1991.

2. Structural adjustment and the labour market in French-speaking Africa

I. Introduction[*]

Since independence, the public sector has been the principal source of development in the Francophone African countries. The colonial heritage, the desire to control the creation of wealth to ensure a better redistribution amongst the governing elites and the need to construct an institutional infrastructure led most African States to develop a large public sector, both productive and non-productive. Up until the end of the 1970s, this growth process, which was set within a basically favourable international context and allowed an increasing number of young graduates to be absorbed into the labour market, did not seem to hinder the development opportunities of many African countries. However, from the beginning of the 1980s, the economic transition process in these countries slowed down considerably. The decline in production, the growth of unemployment and inflation and the increasing current account imbalance were symptomatic of the general deterioration of economic activity in Africa. Between 1980 and 1990, the GDP annual growth rate was 2.1 per cent, which with population growth of 3.1 per cent per year during the same period, meant a drop in the standard of living.[1] The vulnerability of the African economies accentuated the effects of the financial imbalance and compromised any attempts to soften the effects of adjustment through recourse to external resources.

The destabilization of the African economies, compounded by administrative and institutional weakness in managing the crisis, explains the

---

[*] This paper has benefited from the comments by J.B. Figueiredo of the IILS.

[1] In the countries to which this study refers, the annual GDP growth rates rose as follows during the 1980s: Burkina Faso 4.3 per cent; Benin, Cameroon, 2.8 per cent; Côte d'Ivoire 0.5 per cent; Madagascar 1.1 per cent; Mali 4 per cent; Senegal 3 per cent; Togo 1.6 per cent; Zaire 1.8 per cent. No data are available for Guinea. Some data from the World Bank indicate that the per capita GNP of this country fell annually by 0.3 per cent between 1987 and 1989, and then rose by 2.2 per cent per year during the period 1988-1990. Thus the per capita GDP of sub-Saharan Africa increased by only 0.2 per cent per year during the period 1965-1990.

introduction at the beginning of the 1980s of structural adjustment programmes with the assistance of the International Monetary Fund and the World Bank. These programmes called into question state intervention at the economic and social levels through economic regulation and structural normalization and tried to establish a social order based on market forces. This macro-economic rebalancing affected in particular the scope and role of the public sector. Although the content of the structural adjustment programmes varied from country to country and changed over time, some common denominators can be clearly identified:[2] the reduction in overall demand in the light of the foreign debt situation and the level of production; the boosting of supply through price reform and the reallocation of resources to the private sector.

A few examples from the countries covered by this study will highlight the main ideas. From the beginning of the 1980s, Cote d'Ivoire attempted to remedy structural rigidities and supply problems, by introducing four successive structural adjustment programmes (1981, 1983, 1986 and 1990). In Cameroon, the structural weaknesses of the economy appeared at a later date – towards 1985 – although the government had to adopt a vast structural adjustment programme in 1989 to deal with the economic crisis. In Senegal, new agricultural and industrial policies introduced respectively in 1984 and 1986 also illustrated the trend towards state withdrawal, which is still continuing. In Mali, the Government launched a stabilization programme in 1982 to reduce the budgetary deficit. Despite the reduction of some of the imbalance, the pace of reform slowed down in 1986. In 1987 a new economic reform programme was adopted for the period 1988-92, along with an economic initiation programme in cooperation with the government of the United States. In Madagascar, an initial adjustment programme was introduced in 1982; however, the need to step up state withdrawal led to the adoption of several stand-by agreements in the second half of the 1980s. From the mid-1980s Guinea also undertook a programme of economic reform in cooperation with international institutions for the restructuring of the banking system, the promotion of the private sector and the reduction in public service staff. Finally, from the beginning of 1991, the structural adjustment programme adopted in Burkina Faso has sought to stabilize the employment level in the public administration and restructure the para-public sector.

Three aspects of the State's withdrawal are particularly important in labour market terms.[3] First, the public production sector requires profound

---

[2] Helleiner [1986].

[3] For a more detailed analysis, see Lachaud [1989].

institutional changes as it imposes high opportunity costs on the economy and accentuates internal and external imbalances. State withdrawal from the public sector has taken the 'following main forms. Some enterprises have been dissolved, in particular in the agricultural sector.[4] Public enterprises have been privatized, either in their capital – totally or partially – or their management; in the same way, in many African countries the State has reduced its participation in a number of companies. Finally, the desire to improve the economic performance of public enterprises has in many cases led to their rehabilitation or restructuring. State withdrawal from the public sector is in fact a relatively complex matter. The tendency has been to maintain or increase public production in strategic sectors – mining, energy and water, transport and telecommunications, export-based agriculture – by structural reforms and recourse to private management, while in non-strategic sectors, the tax contribution argument has led to pure and simple liquidation.[5] In most French-speaking African countries, the structure of the public production system has undergone profound changes. For example, some data confirm the decline of the public production system in Côte d'Ivoire during the period 1979-89. Whereas in 1979 employees in the public and para-public modern sector in Côte d'Ivoire worked in 61 public establishments, 93 state companies, 138 companies with 100 per cent public capital, and 228 companies with less than 100 per cent public capital, in 1989 the workforce in the public production sector was employed in two public establishments, four companies with 100 per cent public capital and 128 other companies with public capital.[6]

Second, the reduction of the budgetary deficit implies the rationalization of public expenditure. Various obligatory measures – the elimination of fictitious or unauthorized jobs; the redefinition of posts and skills; the monitoring of remuneration payments, in particular in teaching; the early retirement of non-skilled workers; the reduction of recruitment and the introduction of entrance competitions in the public service and

---

[4] In particular the Offices for the marketing of agricultural products. But liquidations have also affected industry and distribution.

[5] However, the application of this criterion has not always led to reducing the weight of the public sector. For example, in Zaire, at the beginning of the 1980s, several public administrative bodies were set up to increase the efficiency of macro-economic management or the mobilization of resources.

[6] In Côte d'Ivoire in the 1980s, many state companies became national public establishments. It should be noted that the structure of the public production sector has been identified indirectly. The above comparison excludes municipalities – not taken into account in 1975 – research institutes and multinational public bodies, with the two last categories being relatively stable.

universities – as well as others of an incentive kind, such as programmes for
the voluntary departure of public service staff[7] – were introduced to help
reduce the number of public officials. Furthermore, the rationalization of
the public service also included a freeze on salary increases and the
reduction of nominal salaries in the public service;[8] between 1980 and 1987
the share of public salaries in public expenditure in Africa fell by one
seventh.

Third, the institutional context of labour relations underwent
progressive changes during the 1980s. Many countries – in particular
Cameroon, Côte d'Ivoire, Senegal and Mali – amended their labour
legislation to make it more liberal. Labour relations in public enterprises
have either tended to be more influenced by the labour code and acquired
greater autonomy, particularly as regards recruitment, promotion and
remuneration – as in Mali, for example – or become more closely linked to
the public service statute.[9] In the public service, the blocking of salaries
significantly changed the framework of relations established by the public
service statute.

The introduction of structural adjustment programmes has modified the
dynamics of social systems, creating open disputes or hidden pockets of
resistance. The incidence and distribution of the social cost of the new
economic policies may encourage the development of internal conflicts
which are hardly conducive to speeding up the economic transition. The
new macro-economic context significantly extended the scope and depth of
poverty and labour market vulnerability, particularly in urban areas.
However, up to the mid- 1980s, it was believed that the social costs of
adjustment were inevitable or that they could be attenuated by the nature of
the structural policies[10] or the methods by which the social system
operated.[11] It was for this reason that from 1986 – prior to the joint initiative
of the World Bank, the United Nations Development Programme and the
African Development Bank concerning the social dimension of the
adjustment – the International Institute for Labour Studies of the

---

[7] For example in Mali at the end of the 1980s.

[8] The rationalization of public expenditure implies the reduction of wage differentials
between the public and private sectors, with the former being considered too high as
compared with the latter.

[9] Thus in Côte d'Ivoire state companies became national public establishments; now this
change of status resulted in stricter management control and the bringing of salaries into line
with those in the public service.

[10] For example the increase in producer prices.

[11] In particular increasing attention was given to the urban informal sector.

International Labour Organization began to study the effects on the labour market of the state withdrawal in a number of French-speaking countries of Africa. Given the difficulty of capturing the complexity of the social costs of adjustment, it appeared advisable, during the initial stage, to concentrate on those aspects of state withdrawal which were likely to accentuate significantly labour market imbalances, in particular the effects of the restructuring of public enterprises on employment and income. Although making use of the main results obtained from the preliminary studies,[12] this article tries to identify other labour market related aspects of structural adjustment, with special reference to labour market flexibility, the timeliness of wage policies in the public service and the role of institutions in the adjustment process.

The analysis is based on relatively varied statistical sources. First, on the basis of available data, macro-economic studies try to make a preliminary analysis of the impact of the structural adjustment programmes on employment and income distribution, in particular in urban areas.[13] Second, specific studies were carried out in two countries to provide a better understanding of the labour market integration processes following restructuring. An initial study was undertaken in Senegal in 1986,[14] and an empirical analysis was carried out in the same year in Côte d'Ivoire.[15] In each case the field of study was both substantially different and complementary. The research in Senegal covered a set of situations inherent in the restructuring policy: unemployment, maintenance in employment, reclassification, etc. On the other hand, the Côte d'Ivoire study covered only persons who had been retained in their jobs. Third, macro-economic

---

[12] See Lachaud [1989].

[13] Research of this kind has been carried out in the following countries: Benin (Adjai [1987]), Cameroon (Ambélie, Tabi Abodo [1987]), Côte d'Ivoire (Kouadio Bénié [1987a]), Mali [Traoré 1988]) and Zaire (Lachaud [1986]).

[14] This investigation examined labour in four restructured and/or liquidated state companies – SONAR, SEIB, SOMIVAC and SOSEPRA. Almost 2 per cent of staff in the enterprises before restructuring were surveyed in the agriculture, industry and handicrafts sectors. However, the sample of labour in the enterprises concerned was 5.6 per cent. The study was carried out in collaboration with the Ecole Nationale Supérieure Universitaire de Technologie of Dakar. The sample comprised 110 persons distributed amongst the 4 enterprises. See Lachaud [1987].

[15] The sample comprised 634 persons from three enterprises in the agricultural and public works sectors, which were put under state control and/or privatized, SOGB, SODEFOR and FODEXI. The size of the sample was 12.1 per cent of the workforce after restructuring. See Kouadio Bénié [1987b]. This research was carried out in collaboration with the National Vocational Training Office (ONFP) of Côte d'Ivoire. However, some of these data were used and processed by the present author.

statistics on the labour market for the years 1979 and 1989 allowed a study to be made of certain aspects of labour market flexibility in the modern sector in Côte d'Ivoire.[16] Fourth, with the aim of exploring the relationship between the structure of the labour market and urban poverty, a series of household pilot surveys has been carried out, between 1986 and 1991 in several African capitals.[17] Among other results, these data shed light on the effects of state withdrawal on the labour market.

This chapter, which tries to identify the labour market adjustment processes which are inherent to the application of the new economic policies, is divided into three parts. The first part focuses on adjustments in jobs and unemployment resulting from state withdrawal. The second part examines the flexibility of real wages and labour market distortions. In the third part, an examination of institutional adjustments on the labour market assesses the efficiency of the institutional changes linked to structural adjustment.

II. Structural adjustment, employment and unemployment

1. Structural adjustment and employment

In most African countries labour absorption has fallen in relative terms in recent years. In French-speaking Africa, the GDP growth rate in the 1970s exceeded that of the active population in almost three countries out of four, whereas in the following decades this was the case in only one-third of the countries.[18] For sub-Saharan countries as a whole, the GDP increased at an annual rate of 2.9 per cent and 2.1 per cent respectively in the 1970s and 1980s, whereas during the same periods, the active population increased respectively by 2.1 per cent and 2.5 per cent. This imbalance also became more marked in urban areas during the previous decade. One of the ways

---

[16] These are surveys of employees in the modern sector in Côte d'Ivoire, carried out in 1979 and 1989 by the National Vocational Training Office. The data were analyzed by the present author.

[17] Abidjan (Côte d'Ivoire), 1986-1987; Antananarivo (Madagascar, 1989); Yaoundé (Cameroon), 1990-1991; Conakry (Guinea), 1991; Bamako (Mali), 1991; Dakar (Senegal), 1991; Ouagadougou (Burkina Faso), 1991. These different investigations were carried out within the framework of the Network for labour market analysis in Africa (Ramta), on the initiative of the International Institute for Labour Studies of the ILO in Geneva. See Lachaud [1993b].

[18] Calculations made for 17 French-speaking African countries – excluding Guinea – based on: World Bank [1981]; World Bank [1992].

in which this decline in the urban labour absorption became evident was in the drop in employment in the public modern sector.[19] The institutional changes described earlier shed some light on this process.

The new macro-economic policies have significantly affected the evolution of public employment, as can be seen from the following two examples.[20] In Côte d'Ivoire, the liquidation of certain public enterprises during the period 1980-84 resulted in the lay-off of 10,679 persons, i.e. 10.5 per cent of the staff. According to available data, the rate of change of staff in public enterprises fell from –3.2 per cent in 1980 to –15.5 per cent in 1983.[21] In the same way, data from surveys of employees in the modern sector show that between 1979 and 1989, employment in public establishments in Côte d'Ivoire dropped by 26.4 per cent –3.1 per cent a year – whereas in enterprises in which the state participation is between 50 and 100 per cent, employment has stagnated in relative terms –0.3 per cent a year (figure 1).[22] Furthermore, the drop in staff is particularly evident in manufacturing, energy and construction. In Mali, public enterprises cut their staff by 25 per cent between 1979 and 1985. The Government also introduced a vast structural adjustment programme for the period 1988-1992 which included the reorganization of public enterprises and rural development operations, with incentives being given for voluntary departure from the public service. These three aspects of the new macro-economic policy led to a staff reduction of around 11 per cent in the public sector.[23]

---

[19] Adjustment can be made by other means; reduction in migration, growth of informal employment, reduction of real wages or unemployment. See below.

[20] In fact this situation has prevailed in most French-speaking African countries. For example, in Zaire, staff in the public service fell by 3 per cent a year between 1978 and 1985.

[21] Koudaio Bénié [1987a].

[22] Two observations must be made on this result. First, the comparability of the two surveys is not reliable. In 1989, the institutional conditions for the collection of data were unsatisfactory since the ONFP was in liquidation. Second, it should be noted that total employment and employment in large private enterprises also fell between 1979 and 1989 by 23 per cent and 26.4 per cent respectively. Similarly, according to these two surveys, the share of public employment – public enterprises and enterprises with public participation of between 50 and 100 per cent – increased from 40.3 per cent to 43 per cent between 1979 and 1989. Furthermore, the relative share of employment in public establishments, other public enterprises and private enterprises in 1979 was 28.6 per cent, 11.7 per cent and 59.7 per cent respectively; in 1989, the respective percentages were 27.3 per cent, 15.6 per cent and 57 per cent. This means that employment in the public production sector fell a little less quickly than in private enterprises.

[23] Staff in public enterprises was cut by at least 30 per cent – around 4,000 persons.

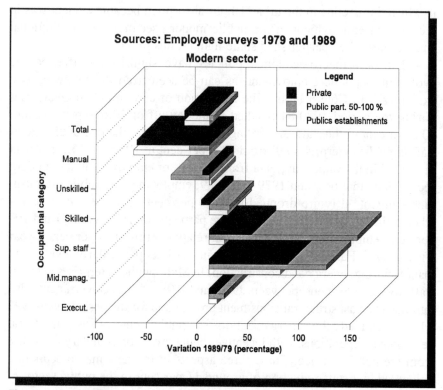

Figure 1: Evolution of wage employement in enterprises in the modern sector in Côte d'Ivoire, 1979-89

However, an analysis of the evolution of employment at the macro-economic level does not reveal the heterogeneity of the adjustment processes. The re-allocation of public funds increases the complexity of the imbalances on the labour market. Some indications of these imbalances may be mentioned. First, the data presented above encompass the negative and positive effects of internal and external shocks. The evolution of employment in public enterprises is in fact influenced by both internal and external factors. For example, in Zaire, the mining sector plays a major role in terms of jobs, in particular through Gécamines. During the first half of the 1980s, employment in this sector remained virtually stable, in part due to the drop in copper prices. It was calculated that if employment in Gécamines had increased at a rate of 2.1 per cent – instead of remaining stable – the number of employees in public enterprises as a whole, in the strict sense of the term, would not have changed between 1978 and 1986. In the same way, aggregate data may mask major transformations on the labour market. The liquidation of public enterprises may be accompanied by a reclassification of part of the labour force, which most of the time means a significantly different labour status. Privatization of management or capital has complex effects on the labour market. Although it is true that privatization implies the immediate lay off of almost all employees, since the new management or owners prefer to start off with a new work force, it may also have a positive effect on the labour market.[24]

Second, labour market imbalances seem to affect the various categories of labour in different ways. Two statistical data seem to corroborate this observation. First, at the macro-economic level, and despite statistical uncertainties, figure 1 above shows that the contraction of unskilled labour in public establishments in Côte d'Ivoire was most evident in the 1980s. Second, at the micro-economic level, the study of the four enterprises which were restructured and/or privatized in Senegal in 1986 shows that unskilled or poorly skilled occupational categories were the first victims of the restructuring, since their relative share in the contractual work force is the highest. In these four enterprises, with account being taken of re-classifications – of mainly managerial staff – in the public service, job maintenance was proportionally twice as high for managerial staff as for skilled employees.[25] Since the former are generally graduates of higher education, it can be concluded that persons with more access to the educational system are proportionally less vulnerable.

Third, specific imbalances resulting from the restructuring of public enterprises may spread out in both time and space. Thus the structural adjustment policy has had a significant effect on employment in the private sector. The reduction in overall demand, which can be ascribed to budgetary restrictions, the dismantling of public enterprises and the blocking or re-alignment of salaries of public officials has led to the partial or total closure of some enterprises in the private sector. Figure 1 shows the extent of job reduction in the private sector in Côte d'Ivoire between 1979 and 1989. These statistics are also confirmed by the fact that the number of lay offs in the private modern sector with prior authorization by the Ministry of Labour and the Ivoirization of Managerial Staff rose steadily between 1979

---

[24] Thus in Zaire, the Zairean Public Transport Office (OTCZ) had a workforce which in the middle of the 1970s was around 3,500 persons. Since the economic crisis increased the shortage of foreign currency, the impossibility of obtaining spare parts and the poor management of the enterprise resulted in a drop in activity and a reduction in employment to 300 persons in 1983. The management of this enterprise was privatized on 2 February 1984 and resulted in the dismissal of all the staff. However, the resumption of activity resulted in the re-recruitment of 50 of the most skilled former workers and in July 1986 the workforce totalled 870 persons. The proposed acquisition of additional buses brought the workforce up to 1,100 at the end of 1986.

[25] Dismissed workers are generally those with less education, less seniority in the enterprise and a lower level of internal mobility. See Lachaud [1989].

and 1984.[26] The imbalance between the graduate supply and demand, which is already very marked, may well worsen in coming years. For example, in Mali, the supply of graduates in the period 1988-1992 totalled 20,947 persons, whereas the economic system as a whole could produce only 5,000 new workplaces. In Benin, the surplus number of graduates was put at more than 20,000 in 1990, i.e. more than 40 per cent of the number holding such diplomas. Signs of this imbalance are evident in all the sub-Saharan countries: the blocking of recruitment in the public service, the introduction of entrance competitions in universities and the public service, the raising of qualifications required for access to specific posts, a reduction in the amount and number of scholarships and a drastic reduction in the salaries of new university teachers.

Fourth, some aspects of the social cost of adjustment can be better grasped if the analysis is taken beyond the individual level of employment. The different pilot employment surveys recently carried out within the RAMTA framework show that in the public sector – production and non-production – of seven African countries, the proportion of heads of households is two and a half times higher that in the private wage-earning sector.[27] The fact that these public sector employees provide between 50 and 80 per cent of income for households which, depending on the country, include an average of 6 to 13 persons is an indication of the social problem of some of the state withdrawal policies. On the other hand, the Senegal study shows that 41.2 per cent of persons laid off were from households in which there was at least another active person. But this result is a relative one when account is taken of sex. Indeed, more than two-thirds of the men laid off were the only breadwinners of their households, whereas this was the case with women in only one out of five households. This result should be set aside another aspect, namely that proportionally less women have found another job. The non-reintegration of women on the labour market is, all other things being equal, less dramatic in terms of employment and income since, theoretically, there may be compensation through redistribution processes. Two other elements, taken from the Senegal study, highlight the complexity of the phenomenon. First, the large majority of persons who are reclassified in the public service are from households with

---

[26] The number of authorizations and the total number of persons dismissed have progressively increased. The latter rose from 3,397 in 1979 to 7,074 in 1984. Host dismissals concerned Ivorian and foreign subordinate staff, even though managerial staff were progressively affected during the period. Furthermore, it should be noted that the "total cessation of activities" and the "reduction in activities" were the two main reasons invoked to justify the dismissal of employees.

[27] The proportions are comparable for married women. See Lachaud [1993a].

at least two active persons. Secondly, it is amongst those who have been laid off that the proportion of additional revenue is the highest.

In such circumstances, it may be useful to identify the speed of labour market adjustments. The Senegal study is one of the few to date which facilitates such an analysis. The 1986 survey highlights the degree of overall adjustments in the labour market. The most remarkable result is that 57.4 per cent of people laid off had found a new job at the time of the survey. Of course, individual situations on the labour market depend on the time when persons have lost their jobs. Those who had found new jobs had been laid off for more than one year, whereas those not exercising any economic activity and who were looking for employment had lost their jobs approximately six months before. Although these data can be fully appreciated only if account is taken of certain qualitative aspects of the labour market – type of job, level of income, etc. – they are an indicator of the degree of tension existing on the labour market.[28]

It is clear that the restructuring of public enterprises has resulted in serious imbalances in the labour market and interrupted the occupational careers of many people. But the adjustments which have occurred within the social system explain the relative absence of any major shock. In Senegal, more than half the employees laid off for less than two years previously had found jobs, and more than half of those looking for a job were from households with at least another active member – although with a number of children well below average – and a high proportion of those looking for a job – employed or not employed – had additional sources of income. If these mechanisms have probably had a real influence in most French-speaking African countries, in other countries – Zaire, for example – the dysfunctioning of the economic system has reduced the possibilities for income distribution through the labour market. The underground economy is one way of maintaining the protection of some and limiting the vulnerability of others. In both cases, it becomes a major component of the social process and is a source of flexibility and stability.

2.   Labour market mobility and informalization

Although labour market transformations are inherent to the development process, state withdrawal seems to have had a significant effect.

First, an examination of external mobility – the reinsertion of workers laid off as a result of restructuring and/or liquidation – from data collected in the Senegal survey suggests a number of observations.[29] Mobility between

---

[28] However, 43.6 per cent of those who found a new job were looking for another job.

[29] Data on other countries, although much less precise, collaborates some of these

categories, even if accentuated by the imprecise nature of the classifications, remains important and may have two major consequences: an acceleration of "bumping" and of less favourable age-income profiles. Indeed, it is clear that many supervisors and, to a lesser extent, middle management staff at present hold jobs which are below their skill levels. However, labour market re-integration would appear to have been easier for managerial staff. This is particularly true for middle management staff and supervisors, of whom almost 70 per cent have found new jobs, whereas a much higher proportion of manual workers and temporary employees remain without any economic activity. Secondly, the restructuring of the public sector leads to mobility from wage employment towards self-employment, particularly in the informal sector.[30] Of course, the latter remains of minority importance since it is a source of employment for only 22 per cent of persons who have lost their jobs and found new ones. But this result is worth noting, especially since there is an enormous difference by sex in the method of labour market integration; 42.9 per cent of women are now working in the informal sector, compared to only 17.6 per cent of men. Thus the informal sector plays an important role in the balancing of the social system. The fact that it also plays a secondary role is not surprising. Modern sector/informal sector mobility depends on a number of complex and interdependent factors, both on the supply and demand sides: the role of human and technical capital, the nature of institutions, the dynamics of the overall economic system, etc.[31] Furthermore, it must be stressed that most members of the informal sector work in trade and transport. But although the obstacles to entry in these sectors, particularly in terms of human capital, may not be very difficult to overcome, the relative saturation of these activities may mortgage opportunities for the future growth of income. Thus labour market re-integration must be examined not only in terms of present employment, but in terms of income growth and future career prospects.[32] These observations

---

elements.

[30] The informal sector is made up of units of production, services and commerce whose management method differs from that of the modern sector (in particular the absence of standardized accounts).

[31] See Lachaud [1987]. It should also be noted that persons who have found another job in the informal sector are from households made up of less members exercising an activity. Of course, this result is logical, since those who are at present in the informal sector are 29 years old on average, whereas those who have become integrated into the modern sector are almost 38. But this result can also be explained in a different way: the more urgent need to find a means of subsistence increases the opportunity cost of looking for a job in the modern sector.

[32] A similar observation must be made in the case of Mali. As a result of the

on this type of labour market mobility appear to be corroborated by other data. An analysis of occupational careers over a period of twenty years on the basis of data from the different household pilot employment surveys noted earlier, shows that the proportion of vulnerable jobs – irregular and marginal self-employed workers – seems to have increased in the urban areas of Africa. An analysis of the data on this cohort of employed persons[33] reveals that over the last twenty years, the net percentage gains of irregular and marginal self-employed persons taken together – compared with protected and non-protected employees – have been 13.9 per cent, 10.8 per cent, 5.2 per cent and 25.4 per cent respectively for Burkina Faso, Cameroon, Côte d'Ivoire and Mali.[34] Of course, this kind of mobility may be the result of free choice. Self-employment is far from having the residual character which it is often said to have and it may actually reflect a certain upward mobility. But this kind of mobility can probably also be explained by state withdrawal. It should be remembered that according to the different surveys, between 10 per cent and 30 per cent of job losses are due to the liquidation, restructuring and privatization of public enterprises.[35] Although the labour market ensures the occupational promotion of some persons, adjustments in terms of increasing vulnerability are likely. Finally, labour market reintegration tends to reproduce a certain logic inherent in the structure and functioning of the market. Persons who moved into the informal sector had little education and had in most cases acquired their skills outside the modern sector or had previously exercised a secondary informal activity. Furthermore, the precarious nature of the labour market reintegration of temporary employees of public enterprises is also evident, with 42.9 per cent being without a job and 42.9 per cent self-employed.

---

programme of voluntary departures from the public service in the second half of the 1980s, with support from the Government of the United States, many persons took up a commerce-related activity.

[33] With no account being taken of apprentices – first job – or self-employed persons with capital – present employment.

[34] Furthermore, it is interesting to note that this is independent of the level of development of the country. Thus in Cameroon, amongst present marginal self-employed persons, 19 per cent and 57.1 per cent have entered the labour market as protected workers and non-protected workers respectively. In the same way, between one-fifth and one-third of present irregular workers in Abidjan, Bamako and Yaoundé had their first employment as protected wage earners. Lachaud [1993b].

[35] Mention should be made of another factor in this context. In the modern sector – excluding the public service – of Côte d'Ivoire, between 1979 and 1989, the number of enterprises with ten or less employees fell from 54.2 per cent to 49.1 per cent; however, in the meantime the proportion of employees in these enterprises increased from 5.2 per cent to 7.1 per cent.

Thus structural adjustment seems to accentuate the precarious labour market situation of vulnerable workers. This result is significant in as far as in the modern industrial sector in Senegal, the share of temporary workers is estimated to be 40 per cent of permanent workers. Furthermore, although the employment of permanent workers hardly increased between 1980 and 1985, precarious employment, on the other hand, seems to have risen during this period. This tendency might well be accentuated by recent changes in the institutional context: the possibility of renewing fixed term contracts and the abolition of the monopoly of the Manpower Office.[36] Of course, the procedures governing access to employment account for some aspects of these labour market adjustments.[37]

Second, when public enterprises are not liquidated, their restructuring more often than not implies a modification of the internal labour market structure. Although this aspect is not easy to capture at the statistical level, the survey carried out in Côte d'Ivoire in 1986 does shed some light on this process.[38] An examination of labour mobility at the inter-occupational category level, currently used in enterprises which have been put under state control or privatized, shows that 27.7 per cent of persons changed category. Some workers seem to have been "downgraded" – 4 per cent – whereas others – 23.7 per cent – moved up the occupational hierarchy. In particular, there has been a relative reduction in the category of manual workers and an increase in the number of skilled workers and supervisors. However, this approach remains very inadequate, since it is unable to apprehend the evolution in the structure of labour as a whole over the period under review.[39] This is because the mobility being captured is that of labour which has been kept on in restructured enterprises. But the overall workforce of enterprises to which the data refer has changed significantly following the introduction of restructuring measures.[40] In these circumstances, recruitment and/or dismissal have modified the structure of labour in a different way from that which is apprehended. Unfortunately, the surveys carried out in enterprises provide little information on this point.[41] An examination of the

---

[36] These results are based on a recent study in Senegal of 80 enterprises in the industrial modern sector. Terrell, Svejnar [1989].

[37] See the last part of this paper.

[38] Kouadio Bénié [1987b].

[39] Between the time of restructuring and the time of the survey.

[40] Between 1980 and 1985, the SOGB workforce (privatized management) increased from 2,830 to 4,421 persons, and that of Forexi (privatization) fell from 441 to 156 persons. Data on SODEFOR are not available.

[41] The trend towards an increase in skills seems logical, although it depends on a

factors which influence the upward mobility rate of workers kept on in public enterprises in Côte d'Ivoire shows that a change of occupational category has little relationship with change in the status of the enterprise. Upward mobility depends above all on seniority in the enterprise and the existence of training. The fact that a worker is promoted following restructuring has not systematically resulted in a change of occupational category. Taken alone, reclassification in the public service seems to have had a negative effect on the upward mobility rate. However, the reclassification occurred later – in 1985 – which explains the lesser mobility of persons affected by this change in status. Thus for persons kept on in restructured enterprises, occupational mobility hardly seems to be affected in the short term. However, this result does not mean the absence of any changes in career profiles, in particular from the point of view of income.

3. Unemployment and structural adjustment

In sub-Saharan Africa, in recent years, urban unemployment has been a major adjustment on the labour market. Between 1975 and 1990, the rate of urban unemployment is estimated to have doubled, from 10 to around 20 per cent.[42] According to more recent data on some French-speaking countries, at the beginning of the 1990s, between one-fifth and one-quarter of the population aged 15 or above were unemployed in five countries out of six, and between 20 and 40 per cent of secondary household members were unemployed.[43] Although it is relatively difficult to determine exactly the real influence of the new economic policies on the overall level of unemployment,[44] two types of data suggest that the implementation of the structural adjustment programmes has had a profound effect on the level of unemployment.

First, some statistical elements give a picture of the situation in French-speaking countries. In Mali, when the first economic stabilization programme was introduced in 1982, the rate of unemployment in the

---

number of factors, in particular the branch of activity. Furthermore, the evolution of the structure of skills probably modifies the relative weight of vulnerable work. According to branches of activity, the increase in the level of employment may be accompanied by the recruitment of occasional labour, in a larger proportion than before the change in status of the enterprise.

[42] Vandemoortele [1991].

[43] Lachaud [1993b].

[44] Furthermore, in French-speaking Africa, the apprehension of unemployment and its evolution is particularly difficult due to statistical reasons.

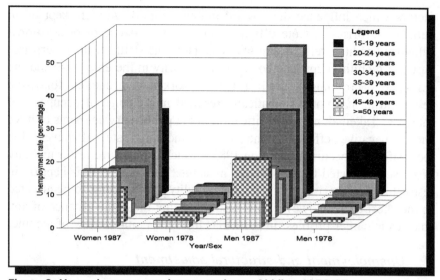

Figure 2: Unemployment rate by age and sex, Abidjan 1978-87

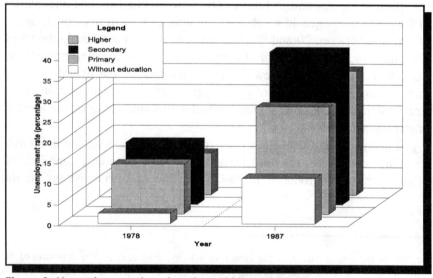

Figure 3: Unemployment by education, Abidjan 1978-87

capital[45] – Bamako – rose from 8.1 per cent in 1976 to 16.9 per cent in 1991. In the same way, in Côte d'Ivoire, the rate of unemployment in Abidjan increased threefold at the beginning of the 1980s – 7.7 per cent in 1978 and 22.8 per cent in 1986-87.[46] Figures 2 and 3 illustrate two features. Above all unemployment amongst young people (15-24 years) seems to have increased. In 1978, 15.5 per cent of men aged between 15 and 19 were unemployed; this proportion rose to 38.2 per cent in 1986-87. In the 20-24 year old age group, the unemployment rate amongst men even increased fourfold, although this phenomenon is much more accentuated amongst young women where in the 15-24 year age group unemployment rates increased tenfold. Second, an analysis by level of education shows that the unemployment rate differential was particularly marked amongst persons without schooling or who have a level of education beyond the primary level. The differential for 1978 and 1986-87 was one to three for these two categories, but only one to two for persons with primary education. In fact this situation is not specific to Côte d'Ivoire. The various pilot employment studies recently carried out in six French-speaking countries confirm the scope of unemployment amongst young persons and graduates in the African capitals. In four countries out of six, between one-third and one-half of people aged between 15 and 29 are unemployed; in the two other countries, the proportion is one-quarter. Furthermore, if the unemployment rate of people without schooling is on average only 10 per cent, it rises to between 25 and 40 per cent in the case of those who have no secondary ·education. A different picture of the adjustment process in terms of unemployment appears when account is taken of marginal unemployment. In two-thirds of the countries concerned, between one-fifth and almost half of secondary women members are potentially active workers. If in some countries – Mali, Guinea – this result may in part be ascribed to traditional structures which restrict the participation of women in the labour market, it might well be that the economic crisis has significantly accentuated worker discouragement. Furthermore, various studies show clearly that difficulty of access to a first job is the main reason for urban unemployment. In five out of six countries, at least 70 per cent of unemployed persons are looking for their first job.[47] Even in Guinea where the effect of restructuring

---

[45] Active population age 10 years or above. During this period, the unemployment rate of men and women increased respectively from 7 per cent to 17 per cent and from 15.4 per cent to 16.1 per cent. In 1988, unemployment in Bamako was already 16 per cent.

[46] In 1978, the unemployment rate for men and women was respectively 8.1 per cent and 6.6 per cent; in 1986-1987, the rates were 25.1 per cent and 19.3 per cent respectively.

[47] Unemployed persons without occupational experience were between 23 and 26 years old, whereas those who had lost their job were on average between 30 and 40 years old.

and the liquidation of public enterprises on job loss has been more marked than anywhere else, the proportion of unemployed people looking for their first job is around 60 per cent. The young structure of the population and the gulf between their aspirations and job opportunities to a large extent explain the situation. This phenomenon has probably become more accentuated since the early 1980s when recruitment in the public service was restricted, and above all from the second half of the 1980s, when public recruitment was frozen in many African countries. However, the role of the restructuring of the public production sector should not be under-estimated in the growth of urban unemployment in Africa. In Guinea, almost 40 per cent of job losses are probably due to the liquidation, restructuring and privatization of public enterprises, compared with 34.4 per cent, 6.3 per cent, 18 per cent and 13.7 per cent respectively in Mali, Côte d'Ivoire, Cameroon and Burkina Faso.[48]

Second, theoretical analysis also suggests the possibility of growth in unemployment along with the implementation of structural adjustment programmes. The orthodox model admits the existence of transitional unemployment simultaneously with the sectoral reallocation of resources. The reduction of activity in the non-tradeables sector may be more rapid than the expansion of production in the tradeables sector, in particular if the latter requires new investments. Thus as a result of the drop in total production, production factors will not be used; however, this transitional employment will gradually fall with the expansion of activities in the tradeables sector, which are much more labour-intensive than those in the non-tradeables sector[49]. Furthermore, it is possible that the main balance mechanisms are not linked to the reallocation of resources along the production frontier, but inherent in the changes to the aggregate product and the distribution of income. In this case, unemployment may result from a reduction in aggregate demand following the drop in real wages.[50] The imperfection of some markets may have repercussions on other markets. For example, surplus supply in the labour market forces households to reduce the demand for goods, which indirectly affects the product market and the level of unemployment. In other words, the actual labour demand will be affected by the rationing of enterprises on the product market.[51] In the African context, the structuralist arguments probably explain to some

---

[48] Lachaud [1993b].

[49] World Bank [1990]. This result remains true even if the hypothesis of wage rigidity is relaxed; however, transitional unemployment is less high.

[50] Taylor (1988).

[51] Cuddington et al. (1984).

extent the present incidence of urban unemployment. For example, in Côte d'Ivoire, it is unlikely that the reduction of wage employment in the private sector during the 1980s – Figure 1 – is linked only to a process of reallocation of resources.

Although these arguments are of a general kind, the adjustments at work in the labour market are also the result of specific processes. First of all, let us consider the unemployment of graduates. It is true that whatever efforts are made to reduce the demand for education, adjustment policies exert powerful additional effects in terms of graduate unemployment and accentuate the phenomenon of "bumping", especially at the lower levels.[52] However, the new economic policies tend to modify the process governing the allocation of graduates on the labour market and may well have a subtraction effect by improving the employment outlook of graduates of the educational system. Indeed, access to higher ranking jobs in the public service has often been linked to criteria other than academic diplomas, such as seniority or personal relations. Thus in Zaire many officials without higher education diplomas have managed to obtain posts which are theoretically beyond their skill levels. Conversely, a large number of officials classified as senior managerial staff are in fact assigned to subordinate or even merely executory tasks. Very often ushers or drivers without any additional training obtain positions of command, as heads of division. In these circumstances, the rationalization of the public service introduced in most African countries could lead to a better matching of employment and training, which would increase the possibilities for absorbing young graduates. In the same way, the policies for the reclassification of public enterprise staff into the public service could have a comparable effect. Finally, this reallocation policy could also reduce the loss of attraction by graduates towards the public service as a result of the wage distortion between private and public sectors. However, recent adjustments of salaries in the public service do not seem to have strengthened the link between salaries and productivity.

The role of unemployment in the labour market integration process is not homogeneous. Despite the limited nature of the data, the survey on Senegal provides some useful guidelines in this respect.[53] First, whereas

---

[52] In Mali, in a single year 1986, only 746 graduates were able to find a job out of a total number of 5,800 persons. According to some estimates (Traoré [1988]), the surplus of skilled job vacancies in the period 1988-1992 was around 16,000, out of a wage population of around 130,000 persons.

[53] In this respect it must be emphasized that the maximum duration between the survey of the first dismissals in enterprises in the sample is 20 months. In this context, the data available in correlation with the reduced size of the sample are necessarily limited.

labour market integration was preceded by a period of unemployment of more than 8 months for two-thirds of the people concerned, integration into the informal sector was more rarely preceded by a period of inactivity. In fact, amongst those working in the informal sector, 25 per cent had a period of unemployment, whereas the proportion is 75 per cent in the modern sector. This result is not surprising insofar as the previous qualifications of some individuals and/or the exercise of a secondary activity have led to a rapid initiation of an occupation. Furthermore, those with a period of unemployment had practically no additional activities, whereas persons who obtained employment directly after their dismissal had exercised such activities in 28.6 per cent of cases. This means that the additional activities exercised during the course of salaried employment in public enterprises have in some cases become people's main activities and have provided them with direct access to employment. On the other hand, those who had only their salary had to carry out informal jobs during their period of unemployment and have tended to retain them when they have found new employment. This pattern is not unique but it could help explain the absence of any major social shock accompanying structural adjustment. Secondly, the level of human capital exercises an influence both on the frequency of unemployment and its duration. Thus people without any technical training remained inactive for more than 12 months, whereas graduates of higher education had to wait less than 6 months before finding a new job. This is particularly clear for those holding a BTS/DUT/DEC certificate,[54] even if a proportion similar to that of other labour categories has experienced a period of unemployment. Furthermore, those who received technical training in a vocational training centre leading to a CAP certificate[55] have become more rapidly integrated into the labour market if they hold a diploma.[56] Thirdly, the role of the family and personal relations increases the complexity of the labour market integration processes. Although this question will be examined later, it should be noted here that the speed of the labour market adjustment is, all other things being equal, determined by the role of social institutions. Thus the survey on Senegal shows that there is a very clear difference – which is statistically significant – in the role of personal relations for those

---

[54] Higher technician's certificate; university diploma in technology; certificate of studies in accountancy.

[55] Certificate of occupational proficiency.

[56] A variance analysis shows that the level of technical training accounts for 60 per cent in the variation of the log of the duration of unemployment. Furthermore, the fact of not having any technical training increases by 50 per cent the duration of unemployment as compared with the main average, whereas qualifications acquired in higher education reduce it by 49 per cent.

who obtained employment directly after their dismissal and those who experienced a period of unemployment before finding a new job.

III. Structural adjustment and labour market distortions

According to the orthodox approach, although transitional unemployment may result from the resource reallocation process, the imperfection of labour markets could also be the cause of the increase of unemployment during structural adjustment. In this connection two distortions are frequently mentioned:[57] the rigidity of real wages and labour market segmentation in the public and modern private sectors.

1. Real wages and labour market flexibility

The existence of labour market flexibility in the developing countries is frequently mentioned and is probably a reality. For example, in the African context, it was recently claimed that real wages had on average fallen by 30 per cent between 1980 and 1986.[58] In the same way, another recent study on 12 developing countries, including three in sub-Saharan Africa – Ghana, Côte d'Ivoire and Kenya – concluded that labour markets are relatively flexible during the adjustment process.[59] Although in the African context the availability of appropriate data is the main difficulty[60] in apprehending the evolution of real wages, most studies on this subject fail to take into account two elements. On the one hand, the variation in the composition of labour affects the structure of wages of all individuals or groups. For example, in Côte d'Ivoire, macro-economic statistics show that the share of the managerial workforce considerably increased between 1979 and 1989, whereas during the same period the category of labourers fell substantially (Table A in the appendix).[61] If no account were taken of this

---

[57] The distortions concerning labour market institutions will be examined in the next section.

[58] Vandermoortele [1991].

[59] Horton, Kanbur, Mazumdar [1991]. See also the bibliography provided by: Levy, Newman [1989].

[60] Sectoral coverage – modern, informal; private, public – of wages; additional wage components; comparability over time, etc. In general, salaries in the public service are the best known and the pay services can provide appropriate data.

[61] For example, the share of occupational categories in the modern production sector which are higher than or equal to those of supervisors increased from 15.8 per cent in 1979 to 25.8 per cent in 1989; during the same period, the share of labourers fell from 29.5 per

evolution in the composition of labour, real wages in the modern production sector would have increased – slightly – in this country by 2.4 per cent in the 1980s. Now the calculation of real wages, using the weights for labour categories of the base year – 1979 – indicates that the latter fell by 18.4 per cent in ten years. On the other hand, an estimation of real wages depends on the price index used. In the above example, the nominal wage deflator was the consumer price index in Abidjan calculated from IMF statistics. However, if the implicit GDP deflator had been used,[62] real wages in Côte d'Ivoire would have fallen by only 0.9 per cent between 1979 and 1989. Furthermore, the question of the price index is essential to determining sectoral relative real labour costs – the ratio between the nominal wage in a sector and the producer price index in the same sector – and the purchasing power in terms of consumption – the ratio between the nominal wage divided by the consumer price index, with the latter being a weighted average of sectoral price indices. In particular, the resource allocation process inherent in the orthodox model takes account of the flexibility of the relative real cost of labour between the tradeables and non-tradeables sectors.

Levy and Newman have recently tried to apprehend the evolution of real wages in Cote d'Ivoire between 1979 and 1984, by taking into account changes in the structure of labour.[63] Their analysis examines the evolution of wages of workers who retained their jobs and of newly recruited workers,[64] and concludes that the fall in employment in Côte d'Ivoire can be attributed to the rigidity of the labour market. However, Levy and Newman's approach involves two uncertainties. First, the populations of workers of 1984 and 1979 are not exactly homogeneous, although the method for evaluating real wages used is based upon this hypothesis.[65]

---

cent to 14.4 per cent. Although the comparability of the two surveys of employees may be debatable, this evolution reflects a logical development in the structure of labour.

[62] It reflects the annual movements of prices of all goods and services produced in an economy.

[63] Levy, Newman (1989).

[64] Five last years.

[65] The two authors recognize this fact: "While in 1984 the total population of workers was made up of only those who had kept their jobs and new recruits, this was not the case in 1979. Workers who were recruited before 1974 and who had lost their job between 1979 and 1984 were not included in the estimate. Furthermore, a number of workers who had been re-recruited in 1979 were counted amongst workers who had kept their jobs. This means that the weighted average of real wage variations of workers who had kept their jobs and new recruits is not exactly equal to that which would be obtained for workers as a whole". Levy, Newman [1989], p. 26.

Second, the sensitivity of the estimation of real wages vis-a-vis the price index used is not mentioned.

This paper tries to overcome these two difficulties and apprehend the evolution of real wages in the modern production sector in Côte d'Ivoire in the period 1979-89. Although this sector accounts for only around 10 per cent of employment in this country, such an investigation seems to be justified for several reasons. First, the period 1979-1989 saw the implementation of three structural adjustment programmes which helped compound the recessions of 1983-84 and 1987-1988.[66] According to data from surveys of wage earners in the modern production sector, employment in this sector fell by 23 per cent between 1979 and 1989. Second, the wage policies of the public authorities apply above all to this sector, and wage rigidities are supposed to be greater here. Finally, the evolution of wages in the modern production sector influences remunerations in the informal sector and probably expectations concerning the search for employment. As in the study by Levy and Newman, the identification of real wages in this study tries to distinguish between the effects of the variation in the level of variables influencing wages and the variation of their effects on the latter. Furthermore, it is important to identify the real remunerations of newly recruited workers, since their earnings are a measure of the marginal cost of labour for the enterprise and one of the means of reducing wage costs is to reduce the wages of new recruits. However, the method of analysis used in this research differs significantly from that of the two authors mentioned above. Initially, the objective was to estimate the equations [1] and [2] which express, for a sector j, the potential wage of a worker, in 1979 and 1989 respectively. L_{oj} and L_{tj} are the vectors of the variables which determine wages,[67] β_{oj} and β_{tj} represent the vector of coefficients, W_{oj} and W_{tj} represent wages, and the random terms are indicated by u_{oj} and u_{tj}.

[1] $Ln(W_{oj}) = L_{oj}\beta_{oj} + u_{oj}$

[2] $Ln(W_{tj}) = L_{tj}8\beta_{tj} + u_{tj}$

Subsequently, after testing the stability of the coefficients of the j sectors – Chow's test – the wage differentials between 1989 and 1979 were broken

---

[66] In the three development policy statements, 1981, 1983 and 1986 – the adjustment policies lay special emphasis on financial stabilization through a reduction in public investment and expenditure. During the period 1980-1989, the GDP increased by only 1.2 per cent per year; it fell by 2.5 per cent, 2 per cent, 2.7 per cent and 3.7 per cent respectively in 1983, 1984, 1987 and 1988. World Bank [1991], [1989].

[67] The list of these variables is explained in Tables B to E in the annex.

down into two elements: (i) a difference due to the variation in the level of the variables (L); (ii) a difference due to the structure of remunerations (ϕ).[68] The breakdown, generally carried out with reference to the sample average, is expressed by the equation [3] where $\hat{Y}_{oj}$ and $\hat{Y}_{tj}$ refer to the average of the logarithm of wages.

[3] $\hat{Y}_{tj} - \hat{Y}_{oj} = 0.5(\phi_{tj} + \phi_{oj})(\bar{L}_{tj} - \bar{L}_{oj}) + 0.5(\bar{L}_{tj} + \bar{L}_{oj})(\phi_{tj} - \phi_{oj})$

Finally, if α_j represents the weighting coefficient inherent in the differences between the level of the variables (L) of the j sector estimated on the basis of [3] and p_i the price index i, the variation of real wages between 1989 and 1979, D_j, was calculated by the equation [4], in which W_{oj} = average nominal wage of 1979 in the sector j; W_{tj} = average nominal wage of 1989 of the sector j.

[4] $D_j = \{[(W_{tj} - W_{oj})(1 - \alpha_j) + W_{oj}]P_i - W_{oj}\}/W_{oj}$

Several observations can be made on the results of this model. First, the regression equations[69] (Tables B, C, D and E in the appendix) highlight a number of preliminary elements which indicate changes related to structural adjustment. First, there is a compression in the general level of wages between 1979 and 1989, with the differentials in the constant terms being all negative (Table F in the annex). The general drop in the level of remunerations is particularly evident in the case of new recruits in the private sector. Furthermore, the marginal yield rates of education, vocational and technical training and diplomas, which explain most of the earnings variance,[70] seem to have dropped between 1979 and 1989,[71] although the age-earnings profiles became relatively less flat for young recruits irrespective of the sector – public/private, and tradeables/non-tradeables. Second, earnings obtained in the para-public sector have fallen relatively; all other things being equal, the fact of working in the para-public sector in 1989 resulted in a reduction in the log of wages of 29.7 per cent against 11 per cent in 1979. All other things being equal, the advantage of working in Abidjan became somewhat less important, especially for

---

[68] In fact the wage differential attributable to the structure of incomes may be divided into two elements: (i) a difference due to the base wage (constant term), and; (ii) a difference due to the yield of characteristics (the other ϕ).

[69] The numbers refer to the total population of the surveys and not a sample of this population.

[70] See the variations of F at the end of each table.

[71] In the public sector, the coefficient of the diploma even became negative (Table D).

Table 1: Net variation of real wages in Côte d'Ivoire, 1979-89

Parameters Sector/status of enterprise	Percentage variation			
	Consumer price index[2]		Implicit GDP deflator[3]	
	1989/79[1]	Yearly	1989/79[1]	Yearly
All employees	-29.6	-3.5	-14.5	-1.5
Tradeables sector[4]	-25.5	-2.9	-9.5	-1.0
Non-tradeables sector[5]	-30.0	-3.5	-15.5	-1.6
Para-public sector[6]	-36.0	-4.4	-22.3	-2.5
Private sector	-24.4	-2.8	-8.2	-0.9
New recruits[7]	-45.5	-5.8	-33.4	-3.9
Tradeables sector[4]	-35.6	-4.3	-21.7	-2.4
Non-tradeables sector[5]	-36.2	-4.4	-22.5	-2.5
Para-public sector[6]	-43.9	-5.6	-31.9	-3.8
Private sector	-38.3	-4.7	-25.0	-2.8

(1) See equation (4) for the calculation of real wages; (2) 1989-89: + 74.7 per cent [IMF (1992)];
(3) Estimated at + 43.8 per cent for the period 1979-89 (World Bank [1991] and author's estimate);
(4) Agriculture: branches 1 to 5; Manufacturing sector: branches 6 to 21; (5) Energy, construction: branches 22 to 23; Services, branches 24 to 33; (6) State participation greater than 50 per cent; (7) Recruitment during the last three years.
Source: Labour surveys of 1979 and 1989 (ONFP): Table F.

persons employed in the para-public sector (Table D). This could indicate a reduction in income differences between Abidjan and the rest of the country. In addition, the relative wage advantage of women was maintained in the private sector, although it disappeared in the public sector. In the same way, the relative advantage of Ivorians as compared with non-Ivorians increased substantially, as well as their proportion in the labour market. Although Côte d'Ivoire is still a country of immigration, the international migratory movement characteristic of the bordering countries probably slowed during the 1980s as a result of the economic crisis.[72] Finally, although enterprise size seems to play a small role in the earnings variance, the very marked reduction in the average size of enterprises in the public sector led to an inversion of the sign of the coefficient of this variable. Indeed, in 1980, enterprise size in the para-public sector had a positive effect on wage.

Second, labour market flexibility in the modern production sector in Côte d'Ivoire seems to have supported the adjustment process and it is impossible to attribute the drop in employment to the rigidity of real wages. Table 1 shows that the average real wage dropped significantly during the

---

[72] Structural changes in bordering countries also contributed to reducing the volume of the migration movement. For example, the reintegration of Mali into the CFA franc zone in 1985 reduced the exchange advantage of Malians.

period 1979-89. Depending on the deflator used, the reduction is between 27.6 per cent and 14.5 per cent;[73] that is, the variation in real remuneration for workers with the same characteristics. Furthermore, a reduction in real wages of 3.5 per cent per year between 1979 and 1989 is approximately equal to the annual drop in per capita GDP during the same period. However, there are important differences. First, the drop in wages is much greater for new recruits. This means that with account being taken of major movements in enterprises and labour, the payment of real wages which are lower in relative terms for newly recruited persons may be an important means of reducing labour costs. The phenomenon of "bumping" would probably seem to be one of the factors involved. Second, the drop in real wages has been much more marked in the para-public sector than in the private sector, irrespective of the population considered. This result is logical given the institutional changes mentioned above. Third, the evolution in relative wages seems in part to reflect the expectations of the orthodox model. According to the latter, in the short term the reallocation of resources should lead to an increase in employment in the tradeables sector and a reduction of employment in the non-tradeables sector. However, as a correlative to the hypothesis of full employment on the labour market, this twofold movement of labour is possible only if the real wage expressed in product terms – nominal wage divided by producer price – decreases in the tradeables sector – incentive to use more labour – and increases in the non-tradeables sector – incentive to use less labour. The results of this research reveal a drop in real wages in both the tradeables and non-tradeables sectors. Between 1979 and 1989, the drop in wage employment was greater in the former (–37.7 per cent)[74] than in the latter (–14.3 per cent).[75] The fact that employment fell sharply in the manufacturing sector and, on the other hand, increased significantly in the services sector, is not very encouraging in developmental terms. However, this mixed result may be due to uncertainties of a conceptual – distinction between the tradeables and non-tradeables sectors – and statistical kind – comparability of surveys of employees of 1979 and 1989 and the use of a single consumer price index instead of sectoral producer price indices.

---

[73] Levy and Newman estimate that, all other things being equal, the drop in real wages between 1979 and 1984 was 25 per cent both for employees as a whole and for new recruits in the modern sector in Côte d'Ivoire.

[74] –20.0 per cent and –43.7 per cent respectively in agriculture and manufacturing.

[75] –78.9 per cent and +21.8 per cent respectively in energy and construction and services.

This analysis provides sufficient evidence to support the hypothesis of labour market flexibility.[76] In Côte d'Ivoire, during the years 1979-89 – the sharp drop in employment and the growth of unemployment, accompanied by a significant reduction in real wages, suggest that changes in the overall product and income distribution have had powerful effects on the labour market.

2. Labour market segmentation in the modern sector[77]

The implementation of structural adjustment programmes from the early 1980s led to increasing doubts about the efficiency of the public sector in general and the labour market related to it in particular. The very large budgetary weight of salaries in the public sector, which are largely dependent on mechanisms external to the market, and the existence of economic rent gave rise to the idea that, for institutional reasons, salaries in the public sector – in the wide sense of the term – were too high as compared with those in the private sector. In these circumstances, the modern sector of the labour market is segmented since workers with the same profile receive remunerations which are not independent of their localization. This kind of reasoning played a central role in the establishment of policies inherent to structural adjustment programmes in Africa. One of the important features of the rationalization of public expenditure implies the reduction of wage differentials between the public and private sectors, the former being considered too high as compared with the latter. Thus, between 1980 and 1987, the share of public employees' salaries in total public expenditure in sub-Saharan Africa fell by one-seventh;[78] at the beginning of the 1990s, these economic policy guidelines

---

[76] Furthermore, the 1986 survey on the three public enterprises which were brought under state control and/or privatized shows that for persons kept on in their jobs, real wages – including bonuses and benefits – fell in two-thirds of cases. For most employees, the reduction in real wages was less than 50 per cent; however, the scope of the drop in real remuneration is greater as the occupational category increases. Furthermore, a multiple classification analysis shows that the type of change in status of enterprises, education and occupational mobility explain the drop in real remuneration. For example, all other things being equal, the percentage of persons with lower real wages increased by 6 per cent as compared with the main average in enterprises brought under state control and by 13 per cent in enterprises where the capital was privatized. See Lachaud [1989] for the results in nominal terms; the results in real terms, indicated above, have not been published. It should also be noted that the drop in real wages is not the only element of labour market flexibility. See also developments concerning labour market institutions.

[77] This section is based on: Lachaud [1993a].

[78] Vandemoortelle [1991].

were still being largely followed.[79]

After more than a decade of structural adjustment in Africa, it may in fact appear surprising that one of the fundamental justifications for the policies mentioned above – the existence of a wage differential between the public and private sectors – was not given greater attention.[80] On the one hand, few statistical studies have been carried out in Africa on this question and those which do exist generally cover a specific country[81] or are unreliable in their methodology.[82] On the other hand, as noted above, the sharp drop in real wages in most African countries, in particular those of employees in the public sector, has probably contributed to reducing the alleged difference between the public and private sectors – even taking into account additional wage components. This question is examined in this section on the basis of a comparative analysis. Seven countries were included in the research: Burkina Faso, Cameroon, Côte d'Ivoire, Guinea, Madagascar, Mali and Senegal; furthermore, for one of them – Côte d'Ivoire – a comparison over time was also made. Two statistical sources were used. First, the most important data underlying the comparative analysis between countries were obtained from a series of household pilot employment surveys carried out between 1986 and 1991 in several African capitals – Abidjan, 1986-87; Antananarivo, 1989; Yaoundé, 1990-91; Conakry, 1991; Bamako, 1991; Dakar, 1991; Ouagadougou, 1991 – on the initiative of the International Institute for Labour Studies. In each case, the random samples covered 300 households.[83] Second, the data from the labour surveys of employees in the modern production sector in Côte d'Ivoire in 1979 and 1989 provide a comparative analysis over time.

Table G in the appendix presents some statistics on employment and wages in the public and private sectors of countries covered by this research. In the African capitals wage employment plays a predominant role, accounting for between one-third and two-thirds of urban employ-

---

[79] The many examples include that of Côte d'Ivoire which in July 1992 reduced the salaries of new teachers in higher education by 50 per cent.

[80] This view is shared by Standing [1991].

[81] See Van der Gaag, Stelcner, Vijverberg [1989]; Glewwe [1991].

[82] Lindauer, Sabot [1983].

[83] These surveys set out to examine the links between the structure of the labour market and urban poverty. Thus although the objective was not to evaluate wage differences between the sectors, such an analysis can be made from the available data. In fact the use of these data in the present context may help strengthen the solidity of the comparative analysis. In fact all the surveys were relatively homogeneous as regards sampling, statistical support and concepts used. However, it is true that restricted size of the samples is a factor limiting the present analysis.

ment.[84] Despite the state withdrawal during the 1980s, the weight of the public sector is still considerable: between one-quarter and one-third of employment in the different capitals. The private sector is not defined vis-a-vis the "modern sector", since it comprises all employees in the different capitals; hence the so-called "private sector" includes a number of wage earners on the fringe of the "informal sector". Table G also shows that in the seven countries considered, nominal salaries in the public sector are higher than those of the private sector.[85] The differences seem to be higher in the case of intermediate income countries – 62 to 100 per cent: Cameroon, Côte d'Ivoire, Senegal – than for the less advanced countries – 30 per cent: Madagascar, Guinea, Mali. However, as regards Burkina Faso – a low income country – the relative size of public sector salaries is comparable to that of intermediate income countries.[86] The data tend to show that salary dispersion in the public sector is less than in the private sector, possibly influenced by the heterogeneous nature of the status of workers in the private sector. It is important to recall that no distinction is made between the public service and public enterprises. In fact, the different pilot surveys show that except in Burkina Faso there is little difference between the average salaries in these two components of the public sector.[87]

This assessment of the wage differences between the public and private sectors remains imperfect as no account is taken of the characteristics of workers in the process determining remuneration. Table I in the annex highlights major differences between employees in the public sector and those in the private sector. In these circumstances, it seems indispensable to adopt a more appropriate approach. Despite the uncertainties and controversy generated by the human capital theory,[88] the estimation of earnings functions is a pragmatic method which allows the inclusion of the major implications of the models of optimal human capital within a simple analytical framework. This analysis takes into account three possible

---

[84] The date on Senegal must be examined with prudence.

[85] All the T-Tests are significant to 0.01 (2-tail probability).

[86] One of the factors contributing to the situation seems to be the relative importance of benefits in kind. Indeed, it is in the countries where nominal wage differences between the public/private sectors are the highest that the relative importance of benefits in kind of employees in the public sector as compared with those in the private sector is greatest; at the same time, the share of related wage components is highest in countries where remuneration differentials are the greatest.

[87] Table H in the annex shows the T-Test and tends to indicate that the hypothesis of the equality of the wage averages of the two populations – public service and public enterprises – must be accepted.

[88] Willis [1986].

activities and two labour markets.[89] Workers may be either employees in the private sector, employees in the public sector or belong to a residual category comprising independent workers and non-employed persons. On the other hand, labour markets are made up of the private sector and the public sector. For the reasons given above, the public sector comprises both the public administration and public enterprises.[90] This model generates two binary choices. First, persons are divided into salaried workers (public and private) and those in the above-mentioned residual category. Second, the first category is sub-divided between those who work in the private sector and those who work in the public sector. The model can be expressed as follows:

[5] $Ln(W_u) = L_u\beta_u + U_u$

[6] $Ln(W_i) = L_i\beta_i + U_i$

[7] $I_1{}^* = Z_1\alpha_1 + \epsilon_1$

[8] $I_2{}^* = Z_2\alpha_2 + \epsilon_2$

Equations [5] and [6] express the potential wage of a worker respectively in the public sector and the private sector. L_u and L_i are the vectors of the variables which determine wages, β_u and β_i represent vector coefficients, W_u and W_i represent wages and the random terms are indicated by U_u and U_i. The Z are vectors of exogenous variables which may encompass some or all the variables inherent to L: Z_1 and Z_2 comprise the characteristics associated with the probability of being respectively an employee and an employee in the public sector. Equation [8] represents the equation of selecting salaried employment as compared with the residual status – non-salaried – and the equation [7] the selection equation of employees in the public sector as compared with employees in the private sector. The $I_1{}^*$ and $I_2{}^*$ are non-observable variables associated with observable indicators which take the value of 1 if the non-observed valued are higher than or equal to 0 and 0 if they are negative. In the present case, I_2 is observed for all the population; $I_2{}^* \geq 0$ if the person is an employee. On the other hand I_1 is observed if $I_2{}^* \geq 0$.[91] From a practical point of view, the

---

[89] See for example: Glewwe [1991].

[90] We have already pointed out that this approach was justified in as far as salaries in the public service and in public enterprises appear to be very similar. See Lindauer, Sabot [1983] and Terrell [1991] for a disaggregation of the public sector.

[91] Thus, Wu is determined if $I_1{}^* \geq 0$ and $I_2{}^* \geq 0$; in the same way, Wi is observed if $I_2{}^* \geq 0$

following estimation strategy was used. First, the probit estimation of equation [8] provides an estimation of the Mills inverse ratio, $\text{Lambda}0(s_0)$. This coefficient captures the probability of being included in the sample as an employee (public or private). This the dependent variable of this probit model takes the value 1 if the person is an employee and 0 in the opposite case. The independent variables used were age, period of schooling, length of training, size of household, sex and matrimonial status. Second, a second probit model made it possible to estimate equation [7]. In this case, the dependent variable takes the value 1 if the person is an employee in the public sector and 0 in the opposite case – employee in the private sector. The $\text{Lambda}1(s_1)$ and $\text{Lambda}2(s_2)$ coefficients, which capture the probability of being an employee respectively in the public sector or the private sector, were estimated.[92] Third, equations [9] and [10] were estimated by the least squares method.

$$[9] \quad L_n(W_u) = \phi_u L_u + \sigma_u S_0 + \Omega_u S_1 + \pi_u$$

$$[10] \quad L_n(W_i) = \phi_i L_i + \sigma_i S_0 + \Omega_i S_1 + \pi_i$$

where $E(\pi) = 0$ for u, i.

Finally, wage differentials between private and public sectors can be decomposed into three sources:[93] (i) a difference due to personal characteristics (L); (ii) a difference due to the structure of remunerations (ϕ), and; (iii) the selectivity bias (σ, Ω). The decomposition, generally evaluated at the sample means (indicated by bars), is :

$$[11] \quad \hat{Y}_u - \hat{Y}_i = 0.5(\phi_u + \phi_i)(\bar{L}_u - \bar{L}_i) + 0.5(\bar{L}_u + \bar{L}_i)(\phi_u - \phi_i) + \sigma_u \bar{s}_0 + \Omega_u \bar{s}_1 - \sigma_i \bar{s}_0 + \Omega_i \bar{s}_2$$

where $\hat{Y}_u$ and $\hat{Y}_i$ refer to the logarithm of wages and $\bar{s}$ the average of S.[94]

---

and $I_1 < 0$.

[92] $\text{Lambda}1 = f(\phi)F(\phi)$ and $\text{Lambda}2 = f(\phi)/[1-F(\phi)]$. See Hechman [1976]; Lee [1979].

[93] See Oaxaca [1973]; Idson, Feaster [1990]; Terrell [1991].

[94] In practice, the coefficient of the constant term is generally associated to the other ϕ coefficients of the earnings function, in order to identify the wage differential inherent in the structure of remunerations. According to the human capital theory, the constant term can be ascribed to the basic earnings, in the absence of any characteristics related to human capital. Consequently, the wage differential attributable to the earnings structure can be divided into two elements: (i) a difference due to basic salary or rent (constant term) and (ii) difference which can be attributed to the yields of the characteristics of human capital (the

Several comments can be made on the regression coefficients of the earnings functions for the full model which are presented in table J in the appendix[95] First, there is a large difference between the public and private sectors in French-speaking Africa. The analysis suggests that the level of education is a more important determinant than diplomas in the public sector; the reverse seems to be the case in the private sector.[96] Modern vocational training increases earnings in the private sector only in Côte d'Ivoire, with apprenticeship also seeming to play a larger role. In fact, age and vocational experience most determine earnings in the private sector.[97] The results also show that remunerations are higher for men in the private sector; in four countries out of seven, the sex coefficient is positive and statistically significant. Second, the selectivity bias seems to be observed in five countries – Burkina Faso, Cameroon, Guinea, Madagascar and Mali – both for employees in the public sector and in the private sector.[98] Normally, if it is accepted that persons choose employment status to maximize their potential earnings, the coefficient would have to be positive. In the present case, Lambda0 is negative in the five countries – Burkina Faso, Cameroon, Guinea, Madagascar, Mali – where it is significant, for the public sector as well as for the private sector. A negative coefficient means that non observable factorst increase the probability to participate to the labour market as a wage-earner and also contribute to the likelihood that a person will earn a below average wage. A negative coefficient could imply

---

other ϕ). We have followed the approach used by Terrell [1991].

[95] The multiple classification analysis, the economic estimation without selection bias and the probit functions do not appear in this paper. See our basic paper: Lachaud [1993a].

[96] In five countries out of seven – Burkina Faso, Cameroon, Côte d'Ivoire, Guinea and Senegal – the coefficients of education, in particular at the higher level, play an important role in determining earnings in the public sector. Furthermore, the marginal yields increase with level of education. However, in the private sector, education has a positive impact in only three countries – Burkina Faso, Côte d'Ivoire and Madagascar. As regards diplomas, in particular at the secondary level, they are positively related to earnings in the private sector in three countries – Côte d'Ivoire, Guinea and Senegal – and also with earnings in the public sector in three countries – Cameroon, Madagascar and Senegal.

[97] The age-related variable is significant in four countries out of seven in the private sector and only in two countries out of seven in the public sector. In the same way, job experience has a positive influence on earnings in the private sector in four countries; in the public sector this positive impact appears in only two countries.

[98] The Lambda coefficients represent the covariance between the terms respecting errors – perturbations – in the equations of choice and the terms respecting errors in the earnings equations. Thus the Lambda0 coefficient captures the probability of being included in a sample as an employee, whilst the Lambda1 and Lambda2 coefficients capture the probability of being an employee respectively in the public sector and the private sector.

Table 2: Breakdown of wage differentials between the public and private sectors in French-speaking Africa

Parameters	Compari-son of wages[1]	Total gross diffe-rence	Characte-ristics (L)		Earnings function				
Country			Value	%	Constant	Other ϕ	Lambda	Overall bonus[2] %	%
Burkina Faso	$\hat{Y}_u - \hat{Y}_i$	0.7987	0.5373	67.3	5.5806	-5.1901	-0.1291	20.5	32.7
Cameroon	$\hat{Y}_u - \hat{Y}_i$	0.5477	0.1915	35.0	-4.1718	3.6968	0.8312	38.4	65.0
Côte d'Ivoire	$\hat{Y}_u - \hat{Y}_i$	0.7904	0.6849	86.7	3.5482	-3.1261	-0.3166	12.6	13.3
Guinea	$\hat{Y}_u - \hat{Y}_i$	0.2121	0.2463	116.1	-0.5763	0.4751	0.0670	-4.7	-16.1
Madagascar	$\hat{Y}_u - \hat{Y}_i$	0.2294	0.3310	144.3	4.9906	-4.9699	-0.1223	-13.4	-44.1
Mali	$\hat{Y}_u - \hat{Y}_i$	0.3138	-0.0165	-14.8	-0.7736	1.1187	0.0152	34.8	114.8
Senegal	$\hat{Y}_u - \hat{Y}_i$	0.8684	0.7054	81.2	-0.6829	1.2266	-0.3807	19.0	18.8

(1) log $\hat{Y}_u$ = average of the log of salaries in the public sector; log $\hat{Y}_i$ = average of log of wages in the private sector; (2) the calculation was as follows. For example, for Cameroon, Table 1 shows a difference in average wages of 17.5 CFA francs. The contribution of human capital to this difference is (17.5x0.35) = 6.125 CFA francs. The balance is therefore 17.5-6.125 = 11.375 CFA francs, i.e. 11.375/29.6 = 39.6 per cent (29.6 FCFA is the average wage in the private sector).

the existence of barriers to entry or a skewed process of selection of the labour market; for example, the most productive people[99] are not selected as employees. Furthermore, only the Lambda1 coefficient is significant and positive only in the case of Madagascar.[100]

Table 2 shows the breakdown of wage differences between the public and private sectors for seven French-speaking African countries. Several comments can be made on this breakdown based on equation [11]. First, in four countries out of seven – Côte d'Ivoire, Guinea, Madagascar and Senegal – more than 80 per cent of the difference between wages in the public and private sectors can be explained by personal differences, in particular human capital – in five countries out of seven this factor accounts for more than two-thirds of the wage differential.[101] An analysis of the part

[99] The earnings obtained are an indicator of productivity.

[100] This reflects a positive covariance between factors omitted in the equation of choice [7] and factors omitted in the earnings equation [5]. In other words, non-observed characteristics which increase the probability of a person working in the public sector also help increase the salary of that person.

[101] This result to a large extent confirms the observations made on the basis of the multi-variate analysis without selection bias. Furthermore, in the case of Cameroon, Burkina Faso

which can be ascribed to the earnings function produces different results. In three countries – Burkina Faso, Côte d'Ivoire, Madagascar – the size of the constant term reflects the existence of a rent, which is largely offset by the lower profitability of human capital in the public sector. But the constant terms for the two other countries – Guinea, Senegal – where characteristcs play a major role are negative. For Burkina Faso, Côte d'Ivoire, Madagascar and Senegal, the selection bias reduces the wage differential between the public and private sectors. This means that if the non-observable characteristics were randomly distributed by sectors, the wage differential would be much higher than at present. As regards two countries – Cameroon, Mali – individual characteristics play a lesser role, the constant terms are negative, whereas the contribution of the other coefficients is largely positive; thus the human capital yield in the public sector is higher than in the private sector. But the overall bonus of employment in the public sector is rather high. Table 2 also shows overall bonuses (in percentage terms) workers obtain by belonging to the public sector. These bonuses are important in only two countries, Cameroon and Mali, where they account account for more than one-third of the wage differential. However, in two other countries – Burkina Faso, Senegal – the overall bonuses are around 20 per cent. Thus, in Cameroon the sectoral wage differential is 59.1 per cent (Table G), of which 35 per cent is due to individual characteristics. With account being taken of the latter, the average salary in the public sector is still more than 11 CFA francs higher per week (38.4 per cent) than the average wage in the private sector.

This analysis thus highlights a number of situations. First, in almost three-quarters of the countries in the sample – two intermediate income countries, Côte d'Ivoire and Senegal; three low income countries, Burkina Faso, Guinea and Madagascar – most of the wage differential between the public and private sectors is due to individual characteristics. The remainder is in three cases due to a basic bonus on wages and in two cases to greater profitability of human capital in the public sector. Second, in the two other countries – Cameroon, Mali – the higher yield of human capital in the public sector and to a lesser extent the selection bias explain sectoral earning differentials. Third, as a correlative, the fact that in four countries out of seven the basic bonus on salaries in the public sector – a constant term – is non-existent and that the contribution of the other coefficients is largely positive, suggests that in these countries the general level of salaries has dropped in the public sector whereas the age earnings profiles have

_____

and Senegal, the variance analysis highlighted the extent to which sectoral organization contributed to wage differentials.

remained high. The overall bonuses are in fact high in only two countries. These results seem consistent if account is taken of the wage policies recently introduced with the structural adjustment programmes in Africa.

These conclusions can be taken further by examining the evolution in sectoral wage differentials during the adjustment process. Because of the absence of data, this was done for only one country – Côte d'Ivoire – for the period 1978-89, using different statistical sources.[102] However, in order to ensure coherence with previously analyzed data, account was taken of only the case of Abidjan. The coefficients of the regression equations of the earnings functions, presented in Table K in the appendix, show that in 1979 there were increasing yields according to the level of education, both in the para-public and private sectors, although these yields were higher in the latter. In 1989, this trend was apparently inverted. For each level of education, the coefficients for the public sector were higher than those of the private sector. At the same time, whereas diplomas continued to be valued in the private sector, the reverse was true in the para-public sector, where the coefficients for diplomas became negative. There was also a significant reduction in the age coefficient for the public sector between 1979 and 1989, whereas the situation remained stable in the private sector. Occupational experience in employment increased its role in the determination of earnings during the 1980s, irrespective of the sector considered. Finally, the importance of the selection bias seems to have increased between 1979 and 1989. Thus in Côte d'Ivoire, at the end of the 1980s, persons who chose the private sector had non-observable characteristics, influencing wages in the private sector, which were higher than average. On the other hand, the reverse was true in the para-public sector for the same period.

Table 3 shows the breakdown of wage differentials in the para-public and private sectors in Côte d'Ivoire for 1979 and 1989. The wage differential is relatively small and fell during the 1980s. In 1979, the wage differential was 8.8 per cent in favour of the para-public sector; the figure was only 4.8 per cent in 1989. This evolution is largely due to the policies inherent in the structural adjustment process.

---

[102] Surveys of employees in the modern sector in Côte d'Ivoire in 1979 and 1989 were used, although analysis was handicapped by a number of factors: (i) the data exclude the public service; (ii) only the "modern" sector is taken into account; (iii) the salary is the gross monthly remuneration and excludes bonuses, allowances and benefits in kind; (iv) the size of the samples is different; the data refer to two samples of 10 per cent of establishments randomly selected from the 1979 and 1989 surveys; (v) use of data from establishment surveys also limits analytical possibilities compared with the economic model previously used; in particular, the equation of choice [8] is no longer applicable.

Table 3: Breakdown of wage differentials between the para-public and private sectors in Côte d'Ivoire, Abidjan, 1979-89

Parameters	Compa-rison of wages[1]	Total gross difference	Characte-ristics (L)		Earnings function				
Country			Value	%	Constant	Other ϕ	Lambda	%	Overall bonus[2] %
1979	$\hat{Y}_u - \hat{Y}_i$	0.0849	0.0563	66.3	0.6799	-0.5179	-0.1334	65.0	3.0
1989	$\hat{Y}_u - \hat{Y}_i$	0.0479	0.0383	80.0	-1.1444	1.6703	-0.5163	13.3	1.0

(1) log $\hat{Y}_u$ = average of the log of salaries in the public sector; log $\hat{Y}_i$ = average of log of wages in the private sector; (2) the calculation was as in table 2.

Individual characteristics explain most of the wage differentials and the importance of this factor increased throughout the 1980s. The structure of the coefficients of earnings functions also reveals major changes. In 1979, the basic bonus was to the advantage of the wage differential, whereas the profitability of human capital was higher in the private sector, as noted earlier. On the other hand, in 1989, the reverse was true. With account being taken of the wage policy inherent in the structural adjustment process in Côte d'Ivoire, the general level of remunerations – the basic bonus fell relatively in the public sector, although the age-earnings profile in the sector became less flat. Whether this change encourages a more equitable distribution of income in the para-public sector is unsure. Finally, the last column of Table 3 shows the global bonuses in percentage terms accruing to workers simply because they belong to the para-public sector. These bonuses are extremely low given the narrowness of the sectoral differential.

IV. Structural adjustment and labour market institutions

The functioning of the labour market cannot be analised independently of the institutional context.[103] The hypothesis of the orthodox model is that

---

[103] See Rodgers [1991] for a summary of this question. According to Rodgers, institutions which affect the structure and functioning of the labour market concern mainly: (i) the nature of employment contracts; (ii) the machinery for supervising these contracts; (iii) the method of organization of the labour force; (iv) the method of organization of employers; (v) institutions proper to the labour market itself; (vi) the type of wages paid; (vii) the process of fixing wages; (viii) training institutions; (ix) the organization of jobs within enterprises; (x) the structure of production conntrol; (xi) the rules governing self employment; (xii) social security regulations; (xiii) quality of life standards; (xiv) the organization of labour supply within and outside the household. When the rules are codified by law, reference is made to

labour market institutions handicap the structural adjustment process. An examination of the truth of this argument implies a two-fold relativization. First, in the absence of any informal labour market institutions, the social impact of adjustment would have been considerable. Second, the effectiveness of the formal institutional changes advocated by the orthodox model remains uncertain.

1. Informal labour market institutions and social adjustment

Despite the severity of the social crisis in Africa, the adjustment process was implemented throughout the 1980s without any major social upheaval. Of course, aspirations for greater democracy have revealed new dynamics within the social systems which generated open conflict or led to hidden pockets of resistance. But, fundamentally, social and intellectual structures and the African way of life have cushioned the social impact of the economic crisis.[104] In western societies, would workers remain indifferent to wage reductions of around 50 per cent?

A review of the some of the basic characteristics of African society will provide a better understanding of the role of certain labour market institutions in the adjustment process: (i) submission to the divine order: nature is the master of human destiny; (ii) refusal of logical time: the past can only repeat itself and concern about the future is perfunctory – there is no dynamic perception of the future, hence the weakness of voluntarist policies;[105] (iii) absence of any separation between state power and supernatural forces: the legitimization of power by the "powers of magic" helps reinforce individual passiveness; (iv) the individual is deeply rooted in the community: vertically, an individual is rooted in his family, in his primordial ancestry, horizontally he is rooted in his group and society; this situation helps limit individual autonomy, which is however necessary to any affirmation of political, economic and social action; (v) the cult of celebration – conviviality which may explain some bureaucratic inefficiency – and the refusal of open conflict – hence to the aspiration towards an often

---

the formal character of institutions; on the other hand, when the rules and standards of behaviour are based on traditional society, and applied within the framework of the latter, the institutions are of an informal nature.

[104] This does not mean that the need is not recognized for an interior cultural revolution which although preserving a certain cultural identity would prevent African societies from adopting an autarkic particularism.. See for example: Etounga-Manguelle [1990].

[105] There is no need to ask questions about the future, which depends on God; the emphasis is placed on the present, where the past plays a small role.

unachievable ideal;[106] (vi) the feeble importance attached to production and consumption relations: the relationship with other people or with the gods often takes priority over relations with things or wealth. Without any doubt, in the context of the new economic policies, many aspects of traditional society have cushioned the social effects of adjustment in Africa, as can be seen from the following examples.

First, access to employment. Some recent studies have shown that access to salaried employment was due in between 25 and 40 per cent of cases to the use of family or ethnic relations. In poor households, approximately twice as many persons use traditional social relations to obtain a job as compared with persons from affluent households. Access to employment through social institutions is positively correlated to labour market vulnerability.[107] The data from the survey carried out in Senegal in 1986 on the staff of four restructured or privatized public enterprises reflects this situation. On the one hand, as noted above, the role of personal relations in access to employment had been much more important for those who had gained access to employment after dismissal, and as compared with workers who had been unemployed for a time before finding a new job. On the other hand, the search for employment in the case of workers affected by state withdrawal is essentially carried out through personal relations. In these circumstances, the role of informal social institutions is to accelerate the adjustment processes on the labour market. In fact, the survey on Dakar shows that the length of unemployment is shorter in households with more than one breadwinner than in households where there is only one active person – 9.4 months in the former and 6.5 months in the second – whereas the reverse might have been expected.

Second, the distribution of income. In Africa household employment surveys show that the head of the household makes the largest contribution to group income – 50 to 80 per cent – but that the role of secondary workers, particularly in countries dominated by traditional social structures – is essential. This means that the well-being of an average household is the result of multiple sources of labour. In the context of state withdrawal, the solidarity of traditional society is a means of limiting the social impact of adjustment in terms of unemployment or the informalization of work. For example, the survey on Senegal showed that 41.2 per cent of workers dismissed as a result of the restructuring or privatization of public enterprises were from households in which there was at least one other active person. The downward revision of salary expectations is greater for

---

[106] National unity, for example.

[107] Lachaud [1993b].

persons from households in which there is only one breadwinner.[108] In the same way, the role of the extended family is apparent as a means of subsistence of unemployed persons. Figure 4 shows that for 70 to 80 per cent of unemployed persons in the African capitals, the income redistribution within the household or through friendship is the only means of subsistence of unemployed persons.[109] Furthermore, the economic crisis in Africa also implies an intensification of income redistribution between urban and rural areas. Although unemployment has led to an increase in transfers from the rural sector to the urban sector, the reverse is also true. For example, in Côte d'Ivoire, the drop in income in the cocoa producing area of the east of the country has led active persons in the urban area to help the rural inhabitants of this region, in particular as regards expenditure on health.

Third, institutions of traditional societies play a major role in training. Access to apprenticeship, since the role of the State is relatively marginal, depends essentially on family connections for the transmission of technical skills and financing. The pilot employment surveys to which reference is made above showed that the absence of apprenticeship increased probability of unemployment and reduced the labour supply both for men and women. The reduction or stabilization of state expenditure on education has attenuated the excess demand for training, part of which however has been met through recourse to traditional social relations. However, it is likely that if the imbalances worsen, a mechanism of rationing by price or quantity would weaken the inertia of traditional African structures and the cost of this type of training would represent an increasing burden which would be more and more difficult for poor households to bear. All other things being equal, the role of informal labour market institutions in African society is to provide an additional degree of freedom to the pace of economic reform. Undoubtedly, this favourable institutional environment has sometimes led to a preference for "shock treatment" over the "gradualism" of economic reform.

---

[108] Other factors also contribute to this: the absence of technical training; the female sex; a long period of unemployment. Lachaud [1989].

[109] The exercise of a small trade is not very common, which shows, contrary to what is sometimes claimed, that employment is a reality of African urban areas.

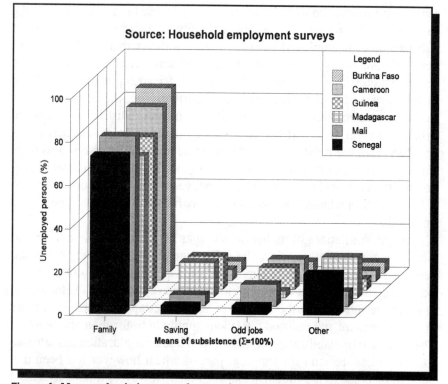

Figure 4: Means of subsistence of unemployed persons in African capitals in the early 1990s

2.   Structural adjustment and the efficiency of formal labour market institutions[110]

The institutional labour market context in French-speaking Africa is relatively homogenous: the trade union movement is weak and industrial relations are organized by the Labour Code and other legal provisions. The modern private sector is subject to a more or less rigid system of regulation. In the public sector, the institutional framework of labour relations is fixed either by the public service statutes – in the administration – or by a specific Act – in public enterprises. For its part the informal sector operates on the bases of competition and traditions. The idea is that the rigidity of the rules of the game and the standards of behaviour which structure the essential aspects of the way the labour market operates – labour legislation, wage policies – restricts the efficiency of the latter and suggests that changes

---

[110] This section is based essentially on: Lachaud [1991].

should be made to the institutional context of the labour market.[111] Several aspects of this process can be highlighted by reference to some examples in Cote d'Ivoire, Mali and Togo,

A. Changes in the institutional context of the labour market

The abolition of the monopoly of the Manpower Offices should be considered first. In Africa, the gulf between the actual recruitment processes and the role played by the Manpower Offices in these processes is increasing. For example, in Mali, only 20 to 30 per cent of enterprises notify the Office of Manpower and Employment (ONMOE) of their job vacancies. Many heads of enterprises or officials of the employers' association say this is mainly due to a lack of interest in this procedure as the resources available to ONMOE are inadequate to match job applications and job vacancies.[112] This situation would in part explain the high rate of rejection by employers of proposed applications and the number of unfilled job vacancies.[113] However, the small role played by ONMOE in providing information on the labour market can also be seen in attitudes concerning job applications. The household pilot employment surveys carried out in Bamako in 1988 and 1991 show that less than 10 per cent of unemployed persons use the ONMOE services.[114] Furthermore, an analysis of the labour recruitment methods in the modern sector clearly confirms the marginal-ization of the ONMOE.[115] Thus the ONMOE no longer has a monopoly of recruitment and justifies with difficulty its continued existence at the legal

---

[111] This analysis will be restricted to an examination of the institutional context of the modern sector.

[112] Manual processing, absence of standard national classification, virtual absence of any possibility of testing the training of persons, lack of coordination between the placement and registration division and the information and employment promotion division. In these circumstances, a matching of job vacancies and job applications may become only approximate if the official omits or adds information on the occupational characteristics of persons, and may take up an enormous amount of time.

[113] 27.3 per cent, 6.5 per cent, 0.6 per cent and 3.4 per cent respectively, in 1986, 1987, 1988 and 1989.

[114] The number of graduates applying to the unit responsible for the promotion of young graduates, which has been set up in the ONMOE, is not any higher: 9 per cent. This proportion appears to be relatively weak bearing in mind that 3,315 graduates were registered with this unit at the end of the 1989 exercise.

[115] On the basis of 1987 labour reports, 19.2 per cent of persons were recruited through the public service – the proportion is even lower amongst executive staff (7.9 per cent) and women (13.0 per cent); in the same way, the general survey of workers subject to the provisions of the 1984 Labour Code shows that 22 per cent of persons were recruited through the ONMOE.

level. Private recruitment offices already exist, in particular in the case of security enterprises. In these circumstances, the obligatory notifi-cation procedure and the maintenance of the ONMOE monopoly in recruit-ment have been relaxed. In the case of Togo, the repeal of section 161 of the Labour Code respecting the monopoly of the employment services is due to the same reasons,[116] while in Côte d'Ivoire, the Manpower Office (OMOCI), whose monopoly ended in 1992, has been substantially reorganized.[117] In Senegal, the elimination of the recruitment monopoly has been accompanied by more opportunities for the renewal of fixed term contracts.

A second element is the amendment of regulations governing dismissals and the right to strike. In the French-speaking African countries, the suspension and resiliation of employment contracts are subordinated to two requirements of a dissuasive nature: advance notice and advance request addressed to the labour inspector in the event of dismissal. In Côte d'Ivoire, the new legislative provisions introduced in 1992 have tried to establish new procedures governing dismissal. In order to step up the procedure for dismissal on economic grounds, which was considered long and costly for enterprises in difficulties, the prior authorization requirement has been abolished. In other countries, such as Togo, when this procedure was provided for only by an inter-occupational collective agreement, the new Act has not maintained the administrative authorization requirement, and the labour inspector plays merely an advisory role. Although prior authorization of collective dismissals is justified, in some cases, for individual dismissals, its continued application is more debatable, since the employer at all events may obtain the judicial resiliation of contract. In the event of dispute, a dismissed worker may appeal to the Labour Court. The bases for such an argument in the case of Mali are as follows. The maintenance of prior authorization for dismissal may have a negative influence on the produc-tivity of an enterprise. Available data show that individual dismissals and disputes account for 90 per cent of the working time of labour inspectors: each inspector dealing with an average of between 4 or 5 cases a day, which leaves little time for inspections in enterprises.[118] If the prior authorization

---

[116] Silete-Adogli [1992].

[117] Four missions have now been entrusted to the new structure: the placement of target groups; the registration of job applications and vacancies in order to centralize data; supervision of market regularity and the policy of assistance to unemployed persons; the establishment of a recruitment assistance policy. Furthermore structures have been set up to promote a more effective management of the labour market: National Committee on Employment; National Employment Fund; Employment Observatory. Kouadio Bénié [1992].

[118] Thus in the final quarter of 1989, at the labour inspection in Bamako, there were 289

requirement were abolished, individual disputes would scarcely take up more than an estimated 40 per cent of the working time of labour inspectors. Their extra availability could be used for additional visits to enterprises, with a view to improving working conditions and in particular the quality of industrial relations which are important to the efficiency of the enterprises.[119]

The institutional changes advocated include restrictions on the scope of the right to strike. In Côte d'Ivoire the new Act promuglated in 1992 increases the complexity of the use of strike action in cases of collective disputes which may arise in the public production sector; the three levels of conciliation for which provision is made in the 1992 Act restrict the risks of strike by the 28 trade unions of officials.[120] In fact, this evolution is probably indicative of deep seated changes in the industrial relations system and some studies have shown that the state withdrawal has sometimes been accompanied by a decline in trade union participation.[121]

Third, the role of the State in wage policy has been considered excessive.[122] Whereas in the English-speaking African countries the State leaves it to employers and trade unions to fix the minimum wage,[123] in French-speaking Africa the public authorities have considerable influence in this sphere. In the case of Mali, two observations clearly illustrate this situation. First, the State plays an essential role both in fixing the SMIG and the level of market wages. Wages in the modern private sector seem to be determined in part by decisions by the public authorities in this sphere. On the one hand, enterprises incorporate into the wage structure the various

---

requests for dismissals, of which 254 concerned individual disputes; of these, 185 were taken to conciliation and 179 to the Labour court. 243 requests for dismissals were granted and 46 were refused.

[119] Provided additional resources are available. It should be noted that many employers and employees are not familiar with the Labour Code. The dissemination of information appears indispensable both socially and economically and it might be useful to encourage labour inspectors to establish a system of labour market information. Such a measure may help reduce the number of disputes.

[120] Kouadio Bénié [1992]. In Togo, the new Bill makes provision for the regulation of the exercise of the right to strike.

[121] In Senegal, for example. See Lachaud [1989]. It is true that in many African countries trade unions, which have close ties with the political power, have participated in the implementation of adjustment policies.

[122] But state decisions on wages may be justified for budgetary reasons or as a means of eliminating certain labour market distortions: blocking of wages; harmonization of remunerations in the public sector.

[123] Except if there is a breakdown in collective bargaining machinery and/or when wages are low.

increases proposed by the public authority; on the other, the absence of any wage initiative by the State seems to lead to the virtual immobility of remuneration levels. The situation at the beginning of 1990 was indicative of this situation in as far as wages in the private modern sector had been virtually blocked since 1986. Now the Government intervenes in the fixing of wages by occupational category only in the absence of a collective agreement, which is not the case here. In this context, the SMIG seems to play an important role since its variations are to a large extent reflected in other remunerations. However, the SMIG rose twice as fast as other remunerations between 1976 and 1986. If this view is correct, it would mean a reduction in wage differences by occupational categories as well as a substantial reduction in real wages. The logical conclusion of this analysis is that minimum wage legislation would lead to a distortion on the labour market. However, the low level of the real minimum wage also suggests that such an argument is excessive. Even if the SMIG seems to be on average lower than the market wage for unskilled labour, its coverage would have to be determined. If wages have increased more rapidly than would have been possible through only market mechanisms,[124] this is not due to collective bargaining but rather to a quasi-unilateral decision by the State. Workers' trade union officials particularly emphasize this point. The Higher Labour Council, which must normally "study the elements used as a basis for determining mimumum wages, with account being taken of economic conditions and their effect on the means of existence of workers" has not met for a long time.[125]

Fourth, in structural adjustment programmes, the need to control state expenditure has led to a rationalization of employment in the public service. In Mali, this economic policy line has taken several forms. First, there is the preparation of the organizational charts of the public services.[126] The

---

[124] This would be socially desirable given the low levels of remuneration.

[125] It is true that the problem of low remuneration is not easy to resolve in the present economic circumstances; the systematic raising of low wages reduces advancement based on skills and may in the end have an affect on productivity, whereas a major increase may be detrimental to profits. However, the long period which has elapsed since collective agreements were concluded suggests that their content should be re-examined. This is perhaps the occasion to relaunch collective bargaining either within the Higher Labour Council or within an ad hoc Tripartite Commission. The Labour Code makes provision for a "joint commission".

[126] In Mali this strategy is regulated by three basic texts. First, Ordinance No. 79-9/CMLN of 19 January 1979 to establish the basic principles for the establishment, organization, management and control of the public services. Second, Decree No. 179/PG-RM of 23 July 1985 to fix the conditions and procedures for the preparation and management of organizational charts. Finally, Decree No. 204/PG-RM of 21 August 1985 to establish the

organizational chart is defined as a chart which establishes for each structure, on a five year basis, the permanent posts or positions which are necessary to the smooth running of the public services.[127] This reform which was designed to define the necessary staff levels for each administration, skill levels and place of work, came into effect at the end of 1985 and applies to both the public service and in public enterprises. At present, the scope of this reform is difficult to assess. A priori, the reduction of recruitment is part of this strategy[128] and recruitment in the public service has been reduced since the early 1980s. The virtual freezing of recruitment in 1981 and of entry competitions in the public service in 1983 – with a progressive reduction in the number of posts offered – is one of the results of the Ordinance of 26 September 1977, mentioned above. Finally, a programme for the voluntary departure of workers from the public service was introduced with support from USAID. This programme is based on two objectives: (i) to reduce the volume of the wage bill in the state budget by encouraging officials to leave on a voluntary basis, to allow resources to be reallocated for the purchase of material and state investment; (ii) to promote the private sector by establishing mechanisms to facilitate access by departing workers to bank credit through the financing of their private enterprise projects. The purpose of this programme was designed to encourage the voluntary retirement of 600 officials over two years (1986-1987). In Côte d'Ivoire, the 1992 Act allowed officials who had been granted voluntary departure to receive early payment of a part of their pensions.

---

methods of management and control of the structures of the public services. In Côte d'Ivoire some of these aspects are contained in Act No. 92-569 of 1992.

[127] The objective is: (i) to establish a reference framework for the preparation of the state budget with a view to controlling staff levels and posts to be filled; (ii) to require an objective justification for the establishment of posts or jobs in the light of the real needs of the services; (iii) to enable a comparison to be made between available human resources and medium term needs with a view to drawing up vocational training and further training plans for officials; (iv) to encourage a matching of posts and structures to the tasks entrusted to the administrations.

[128] However, the organizational charts should be designed to: (i) develop vocational training to allow existing staff to be trained for new tasks or transfers required by the restructuring of certain posts; (ii) recruit new officials to fill posts which it has not been possible to fill through the training of existing staff; (iii) restructure surplus staff or staff unsuited to needs. In fact, no forward planning employment programme, with special reference to vocational training, seems to have been established in the public service. For example, 21 posts in the public service were not filled in 1988 because of a lack of applicants. In these circumstances, it might be appropriate to carry out an in-depth analysis of the establishment of organizational charts.

Fifth, the restructuring of the public production sector has required the establishment of a clear legal framework to regulate the organization, functioning, management and control of public enterprises.[129] An analysis of the new provisions in Mali respecting the status of staff in public enterprises seems to indicate important changes which might significantly modify personnel policy in these enterprises and strengthen the development of internal markets: greater autonomy of public enterprises, linking of remuneration to productivity, stricter control of promotions and the strengthening of social consensus. The new Act of 1989 now extends to public industrial and commercial establishments and stipulates that "establishment agreements may be concluded in each enterprise, national company or public establishment of an industrial or commercial nature with a view to adapting the provisions of this Act to the particular conditions of the enterprise". As regards recruitment, section 7 abolishes the virtual obligation to recruit at the end of the trial period. Furthermore, section 10 suppresses the obligation of filling by competition a post which has been provisionally filled by a worker for a specified period. In the same way, section 11 of the former Act, which made it obligatory to report any change in classification and remunerations to the trade union committee and the labour inspector, has been suppressed. The breaking of employment contracts is made more specific: but section 14 of the new Act incorporates section 38 of the amended Labour Code. This provision states that the suspension of labour contracts is subject to the agreement of the labour inspector. Section 17 of the 1989 Act stipulated the conditions governing the classification of workers. As before, any disputes must be placed before the Classification Committee; however, the text stipulates that "decisions are taken by a majority of votes by members of the Committee. The reasons, therefore, must always be given. When one of the parties does not accept this decision, the matter is placed before the respective Labour Court. However, the criteria governing reclassification will take account of the employment held and vocational skills". The new Act seems to make important changes regarding remunerations. Section 18 now authorizes the management of the enterprise to link remuneration with productivity. In the same way, section 19 stipulates that "benefits in kind shall be fixed by establishment agreements in the light of the specific characteristics of each

---

[129] In this connection, Act No. 87-51/AN-RM of 10 August 1987 to establish the fundamental principles of the organization and functioning of public establishments of an industrial and commercial nature (EPIC) and state companies was adopted and introduced. At the same time, Act No. 89-85/AN-RM of 1 November 1989 was repealed and replaced Act No. 81-10/AN-RM of 3 March 1981 to establish statutes for staff in state companies and enterprises and Malian staff in mixed economy enterprises.

enterprise". In this connection, the draft decree prepared in application of the Act of November 1989, established a salary increase of 20 per cent for staff in categories E, D and C;[130] and a 10 per cent increase for staff in categories B, A and for other staff. This measure could increase incentives and limit the phenomenon of holding two jobs. The procedure regarding promotions has also been amended. In particular, for category A, advancement is determined exclusively by training, instead of an occupational competition as before. Furthermore, "the forms of advancement within a category shall be fixed by establishment agreement" (section 23). Under this provision, the General Director is no longer authorized to decide such advancements.[131]

B. The uncertain efficiency of the new institutional content of the labour market

The foregoing analysis, which suggests that major institutional changes are required to reduce or eliminate labour market distortions – in particular in urban areas – calls for a number of observations.

First, the analytical orientation proposed defines institutions as rules and standards of behaviour to restrict the freedom of individual persons.[132] This means that the "rules of the game" determine the context in which markets operate and influences their efficiency as well as the distribution processes. In other words, whereas the traditional neoclassic model considers institutions as exogenous, the recent prolongations of the neoclassic analysis endogenize the institutional factors within a more global model. In particular, the transaction costs approach stresses the idea that market deficiencies explain the existence of economic institutions and that institutional changes must be designed to minimize transaction costs.[133] But the performances of institutions are defined in terms of individual and utilitarian objectives which are the basis of neoclassic economy. In the developing countries, in general, and in the sub-Saharan countries of Africa, in particular, it is not sure that this kind of analysis takes sufficient account of factors other than the pursuit of personal interest to explain the economic and social behaviour of

---

[130] i.e. the least skilled categories.

[131] The other provisions of the Act of 1989 include the broadening of trade union activities and the establishment of staff delegates. Sections 42-52 are designed to promote consensus within the enterprise.

[132] Another approach to institutions is simply in term of "organizations". Van Arkadie [1989].

[133] Nabli, Nugent [1989]. For a summary of these question see also: Eggertsson [1990].

individuals.[134] As noted above, personal, family or ethnic relations play an important role in the process of access to employment. Furthermore, this analysis implicitly supposes the continued optimality of institutions in as far as it applies to the social choice of institutions the mechanics of the process of competitive balance.[135] The existence of imperfect information may generate sub-optimal situations, even in the case of private contractual agreements. The development of private labour offices as a socially effective institutional change is unsure. Particular mechanisms may well reinforce the stability of the institutional changes which generate further dysfunctionings. Finally, this analytical option implicitly involves the question of the "identification" of institutional changes.[136] Are the new labour market institutions induced by the supply side – the pressure exerted by entrepreneurs in the modern sector – or by the demand side – population and technology changes? In the African context, changes in the labour market institutions are to a very large extent influenced by supply side aspects.

Second, labour market institutions encompass both formal and informal elements. Whereas the former are explicitly covered by regulatory provisions, the latter may reflect informal conventions not codified by the law but which deeply influence its application. This means that the "rules of the game" may have the same formal structure whilst at the same time generating different individual behaviour dependent on the informal environment. The basic features of African society, and in particular the methods by which persons are rooted in that society, should not be forgotten. Let us take for example the decision to suppress the authorization for dismissal. In many situations, this change of regulation would probably not affect the welfare of individuals at the overall level. In fact, in the previous situation, effective dismissal depended to a large extent on the power relations system established within the social system. These informal influences may continue to play an important role, despite the adoption of new regulations. The same observation is true for the new Act which is supposed to regulate personnel policy in public enterprises. Thus the decision to establish a new industrial relations model based on formal rules taken from the experience of industrialized countries may be thwarted by the specific nature of the local context. The role of institutions in the development process is not always recognized and current analyses which tend to emphasize this phenomenon should be encouraged. But it must also be recognized that some orientations seem to be paradoxical. Whereas the basic

---

[134] Van Arkadie [1989].

[135] Bardhan [1989].

[136] Bardhan [1989].

idea is to reduce transaction costs, the simple transposition of the rules of the game to another environment may help reduce the market efficiency. In the case of the suppression of the authorization of dismissal, for example, the lesser administrative activity of the labour inspectors may theoretically lead to improved occupational information in enterprises. In fact, the effectiveness of this institutional change implies relations of complementarity between "institutions". On the one hand the State must support this substitution of activities and have the means available to do so; on the other hand, the production system must be able to cooperate. The development of the informal sector is in part linked to the desire to escape from the relationship between power and the formal economy; thus the institutional changes inherent in the labour market will have limited effects on the economic system as a whole. In other words, the interference of informal elements is a handicap to the presumed efficiency of new institutions. This situation must be emphasized in the African context since there is an enormous lag between the law and the methods of its application.

Third, without challenging the existence of labour market dysfunctionings, does the situation of underemployed persons depend on the elimination of such rigidities? Some approaches have already shown that if the labour demand in the sector in which these distortions occur is relatively inelastic, and if the share of this sector in the total population is weak, the elimination of these distortions has only a slight impact on the marginal productivity of the low productivity sector. Excess supply is eliminated through a reduction of the labour supply rather than an increase in employment[137]. This means that if the increase of income in the low productivity sector is an important objective, policies other than the elimination of such dysfunctionings are required. In the case of Mali, it is important to emphasize that modern employment is virtually non-existent in the rural sector and that in urban areas it covers only 30 per cent of the active population.[138] Furthermore, attention must be given to the qualitative evaluation of distortions since the policies recommended in this sphere may have major social consequences.

Fourth, in the developing countries in general and in Africa in particular, institutional changes must be apprehended within the institutional context as a whole. Focusing on certain institutions, irrespective of their role in the overall development process and the present or potential links between them and other institutions, may weaken the effectiveness of anticipated changes. On the path towards development, institutions maintain various kinds of

---

[137] Squire [1981].

[138] Lachaud (1990).

relations which may be defined in terms of complementarity, indifference or competition. For example, the basic idea underlying the promotion of new formal labour institutions – in particular those which might increase flexibility – is the improved effectiveness of the production system, and thus more employment. However, many institutional reforms may help achieve this objective and those concerning the labour market may, given the present development level, be socially costly and economically ineffective. In many African countries, the constraint on investment, in particular foreign investment, is not only related to local economic conditions – the size of the market, infrastructure, etc. – but to the effective existence of specific formal institutions. The "privatization" of the state machinery makes any judicial settlement of economic disputes impossible, which in turn is largely responsible for the displacement of investment outside the continent and in the end the reduction of employment. In this context, what can be expected from a reform of formal labour market institutions? Thus without calling into question the timeliness of certain institutional changes in the labour market, it is likely that the conditions in which they are carried out will limit their actual effectiveness.

Conclusion

In French-speaking Africa in the 1980s the state withdrawal from the labour market had a considerable impact. This study has examined some of the elements which might be used to pursue the matter in greater detail.

First, new economic policies have significantly affected the growth of pubic employment. In Côte d'Ivoire, between 1979 and 1989, total employment in the modern production sector fell by 23 per cent, whereas the drop was 26.4 per cent in public establishments. Furthermore, in most countries labour market imbalances seem to have affected unskilled labour in particular. In addition the decline in public employment had a significant social effect in that the proportion of heads of households – who account for between 50 and 80 per cent of the group income – is between one and a half and two times higher in this sector than in the private wage earning sector.

Second, an examination of labour mobility on the labour market reveals a process of informalization. For example, in the case of Senegal, 22 per cent of persons who had lost their jobs following the restructuring of public enterprises now carry on an activity in the informal sector. This kind of mobility has been facilitated by the previous exercise of a secondary activity and the existence of apprenticeship. More generally, household employment surveys carried out at the end of the 1980s and the early 1990s tend to show an increase in vulnerable jobs in the urban areas of Africa. This greater labour market vulnerability has sometimes been the result of a process of deskilling within enterprises.

Third, the growth of unemployment along with the implementation of structural adjustment programmes, although accepted by the orthodox model, might result in preference being given to structuralist arguments, in particular the reduction of aggregate demand following the drop in real wages. However, analysis shows that adjustments in terms of unemployment are far from being homogeneous. Thus mobility towards the internal informal sector, the existence of technical training and the role of social relations considerably influence the speed of labour market adjustments.

Fourth, assessing the development of real wages implies that account is taken of the variation in the composition of labour and that specific attention is given to the price index used. On the basis of data on Côte d'Ivoire, the variations in real wages over the period 1979-1989 have been measured. Assuming no change in the characteristics of persons and enterprises, the average real wage of workers as a whole fell by 26.9 per cent, whereas the drop was 45.2 per cent for newly recruited workers – within the last three years. In these circumstances, labour market flexibility in the modern production sector in Côte d'Ivoire seems to have supported the adjustment process and it is impossible to attribute the drop in employment to the rigidity of real wages.

Fifth, whereas one of the important aspects of the rationalization of public expenditure implies a reduction in wage differentials between the public and private sectors, with the level of the former being considered too high in comparison with the latter, this paper suggests that this point of view might not be appropriate in many African countries. In five countries out of the seven studied – Côte d'Ivoire, Senegal, Burkina Faso, Guinea and Madagascar – most of the wage differences between the public and private sectors can be ascribed to personal characteristics. The rest is in three cases related to a basic bonus on wages and in two cases to the greater profitability of human capital in the public sector. In the two other countries – Cameroon and Mali – the higher yield on human capital in the public sector and to a lesser extent the selection bias explain the differences in sectoral earnings. Furthermore, the fact that in four countries out of seven the basic bonus on wages in the public sector is non-existent and the fact that the contribution of the other coefficients is largely positive suggests that for these countries the general level of salaries has fallen in the public sector whereas the age-earnings profiles have remained high. Overall bonuses are in fact high only in two countries. Finally, wage differences between the public and private production sectors in Côte d'Ivoire fell between 1979 and 1989. These results are consistent with the wage policy guidelines recently introduced within the framework of structural adjustment programmes in Africa. They tend to show that labour market distortions in the modern sector are less important than is usually thought and that the pursuit of policies to reduce wages in the public sector is not justifiable either economically or socially.

Sixth, an analysis of labour market institutions in the African context modifies the orthodox model in two ways. First, African mental and social structures and habits have cushioned the social impact of the economic crisis. For example, family or ethnic solidarity has made adjustment easier in terms of unemployment, which gives an additional margin of manoeuvre for the implementation of structural adjustment. Secondly, the social effectiveness of institutional changes on the labour market is probably much more complex to apprehend in the African context than is suggested by the orthodox model. There are deep doubts concerning the effectiveness of the recommended institutional changes: the performance of institutions vis-a-vis individual objectives; the homogeneous nature of the rules of the game which nevertheless structure individual behaviour in different ways depending on the informal environment; the dependency of the effectiveness of institutional changes on the complementarity of institutions.

Bibliographical references

Adjaï, L.D. 1987. *La restructuration du secteur public et para-public et les effets sur le marché du travail au Bénin*, Geneva, mimeo, International Institute for Labour Studies.

Ambelie, L.., Tabi Abodo, A. 1987. *La restructuration du secteur public et para-public et les effets sur le marché du travail au Cameroun*, Geneva, mimeo, International Institute for Labour Studies.

Bardhan, P. 1989. "The new institutional economics and development theory: a brief critical assessment", *World development*, Vol. 17, No. 9, September.

Cuddington, J.T.P., Johansson, P., Löfgren, K.G. 1984. *Disequilibrium macroeconomics in open economics*, Oxford, Basil Blackwell.

Diallo, I., 1987. *Etude sur le désengagement de l'Etat, Problématique, modalités et répercussions: le cas du Sénégal*, Dakar, Ministry of Labour.

Eggertsson, T. 1990. *Economic behaviour and institutions*, Cambridge, Cambridge University Press.

Etounga-Manguelle, D. 1991. *L'Afrique a-t-elle besoin d'un programme d'ajustement culturel?*. Ivry-sur-Seine, Editions nouvelles du sud.

Glewwe, P. 1991. *Schooling, skills and the returns to government investment in education: an exploration using data from Ghana,* Washington, LSMS WP No. 76, World Bank.

Heckman, J. 1976. "The common structure of statistical models of truncation, sample selection and limited dependant variable and a simple estimator for such models", *Annals of economic and social measurement*, Vol. 5, No. 4.

Helleiner, G.K. 1986. *Africa and the International Monetary Fund*, Washington, International Monetary Fund.

Horton, S., Kanbur, R., Mazumdar, D. 1991. "Labour markets in an era of adjustment: evidence from 12 developing countries", *International Labour Review*, Vol. 130, No. 5-6.

Idson, T., Feaster, D. 1990. "A selectivity model of employer-size wage differentials", *Journal of Labor Economics*, Vol. 8, No. 1.

International Monetary Fund 1992. *International financial statistics*, Washington.

Kouadio Bénié, M. 1987a. *La restructuration du secteur public et para-public et les effets sur le marché du travail en Côte d'Ivoire*, Geneva, mimeo, International Institute for Labour Studies.

—. 1987b. *Les entreprises publiques restructurées et le marché du travail: le cas du Côte d'Ivoire*, Geneva, mimeo, International Institute for Labour Studies.

—. 1992. *L'ajustement structurel et les institutions du marché du travail en Côte d'Ivoire*, Geneva, mimeo, International Institute for Labour Studies.

Lachaud, J.-P. 1986. *La restructuration du secteur public et para-public et les effets sur le marché du travail au Zaïre*, Geneva, mimeo, International Institute for Labour Studies.

—. 1987. *Restructuration des entreprises publiques et ajustements sur le marché du travail au Sénégal: des possibilités à la mesure des espérances*, Geneva, Discussion Paper Series No. 4, International Institute for Labour Studies.

—. 1989. *Le désengagement de l'Etat et les ajustements sur le marché du travail en Afrique francophone*, Geneva, Research Series, No. 96, International Institute for Labour Studies.

—. 1990. Le marché du travail au Mali: analyse et politiques, Washington, International management and development group, Ltd.

—. 1991. *L'ajustement structurel et les institutions du marché du travail au Mali: quelques éléments d'analyse*, Geneva, mimeo, Ramta meeting, 2-3 May, Yaoundé, International Institute for Labour Studies.

—. 1993a. *Les écarts de salaires entre les secteurs public et privé en Afrique francophone: analyse comparative*, Geneva, dicussion papers No. 53, International Institute for Labour Studies.

—. 1993b. *Pauvreté et marché du travail en Afrique au sud du Sahara: analyse comparative*, Geneva, Discussion Paper Series No. 55, International Institute for Labour Studies.

Lee, L.-F. 1979. "Unionism and wage rates: a simultaneous equations model with qualitative and limited dependant variables" *International economic review*, Vol. 19, No. 2.

Levy, V., Newman, J.L. 1989. "Wage rigidity: Micro and macro evidence on labor market adjustment in the modern sector", *World Bank economic review*, No. 3(1), Washington.

Lindauer, D., Sabot, R.H. 1983. "The public/private wage differential in a poor urban economy", *Journal of development economics*, Vol. 12.

Nabli, M.K., Nugent, J.B. (eds) 1989. *The new institutional economics and development. Theory and applications to Tunisia*, New York, North-Holland.

Oaxaca, R. 1973. "Male-female wage differentials in urban labor markets", *International economic review*, No. 14

Rodgers, G. 1991. *Labour institutions and economic development*, Geneva, discussion papers No. 41, International Institute for Labour Studies

Silete-Adogli, D.V. 1992. *Les institutions du marché du travail à l'ère des ajustements et du processes de démocratisation, le cas du Togo*, Geneva, mimeo, International Institute for Labour Studies.

Squire, L. 1981. *Employment policy in developing countries*, Washington, World Bank.

Standing, G. 1991. "Structural adjustment and labour market policies: towards social adjustment", in Standing, G., Tokman, V. (eds): *Towards social adjustment, Labour market issues in structural adjustment*, Geneva, ILO.

Taylor, L. 1998. *Varieties of stabilisation experience*, Oxford, Clarendon Press.

Terrell, K. 1991. *A selectivity model of public-private wage differentials in Haiti*, Pittsburg, Working papers No. 268, University of Pittsburg.

Terrell, K., Svejnar, J. 1989. *The industrial labor market & economic performance in Senegal*, London, Westview Press.

Traoré, M. 1988. *La restructuration des entreprises publiques et para-publiques et le marché de l'emploi au Mali,* Geneva, mimeo, International Institute for Labour Studies.

Van Arkadie, B. 1989. "The role of institutions in development", *Proceedings of the World Bank annual conference on development economics*, Washington, World Bank.

Van der Gaag, J., Stelcner, M., Vijverberg, W. 1989. *Public-private sector wage comparisons and moonlighting in developing countries*, Washington, LSMS WP No. 52, World Bank.

Vandermoortelle, J. 1991. Labour market informalisation in sub-saharan Africa", in Standing, G., Tockman, V. (eds): *Toward social adjustment*, Geneva, ILO.

Willis, R. 1986. "Wage determinants: a survey and reinterpretation of human capital earnings functions", in Ashenfelter, O., et al. (eds), *Handbooks of labor economics*, New York, Elsevier science publishers BV

World Bank. 1981. *World Development report 1992*, Washington.

—. 1989. *Social Development in Africa report*, Statistical tables, Washington.

—. 1990. *Making adjustment work for the poor, A framework for policy reform in Africa*, Washington.

—. 1991. *World Development report 1992*, Washington.

—. 1992. *World Development report 1992*, Washington.

Appendices

Table A: Changes in real wages. Côte d'Ivoire, 1979-89

Year	1979 (W$_0$)				1989[1] (W$_t$)				(W$_t$-W$_0$)/ W$_0$
Parameter	Mean[2]	SD	N	%	Mean[2]	SD	N	%	(%)
Occupational category									
Management	426.8	388.9	2430	1.1	312.0	388.6	4050	2.2	-26.9
Senior executive	352.4	234.1	9014	4.2	314.4	289.0	8516	4.7	-10.8
Middle executive	181.3	118.0	6642	3.1	137.6	119.2	11735	6.5	-24.1
Supervisory staff	109.8	69.0	15622	7.4	94.7	66.2	22479	12.4	-13.8
Skilled workers	56.8	56.2	40462	19.1	52.5	37.9	39924	22.0	-7.8
Non-skilled workers	39.3	96.2	75229	35.4	30.4	19.8	68490	37.7	-22.7
Labourers	26.7	123.7	62640	29.5	17.2	37.5	26099	14.4	-35.6
Apprentices	19.7	12.3	411	0.2	16.9	10.4	461	0.3	-14.2
Total	**66.2**	**139.6**	**212450**	**100.0**	**67.8**	**122.2**	**181754**	**100.0**	**+2.4**
Total - weighting 1979	-	-	-	-	54.0	-	-	-	**-18.4**[6]
Sex									
Male	63.9	141.2	201599	5.1	66.1	125.0	160899	88.5	+3.4
Female	108.6	95.0	10885	94.9	80.5	96.9	20858	11.5	-25.9
Status of enterprises									
Para-public[3]	57.1	139.5	85726	40.3	50.1	67.7	75695	41.6	-12.3
Private	72.4	139.3	126758	59.7	80.3	148.1	106062	58.4	+10.9
Size of enterprises									
0-10	81.8	273.0	6979	3.3	70.3	102.3	8934	4.9	-14.1
11-99	89.7	151.0	33465	15.8	79.1	147.9	44914	24.7	-11.8
100-499	69.8	160.1	61536	28.9	69.3	125.3	48413	26.6	-0.7
≥500	56.2	106.3	110504	52.0	60.1	104.5	79496	43.7	+6.9
Sector									
Tradeables[4]	**48.8**	**104.9**	**82807**	**39.0**	**50.5**	**108.5**	**58208**	**32.0**	**+3.5**
Agriculture	39.2	110.2	25498	12.0	26.5	76.4	21762	12.0	-32.4
Manufacturing	53.1	102.2	57309	27.0	64.9	121.6	36446	20.0	+22.2
Non-tradeables[5]	**77.4**	**156.8**	**129677**	**61.0**	**75.9**	**127.4**	**123549**	**68.0**	**-1.9**
Energie, construction	63.7	114.3	42009	19.8	95.2	124.1	11116	6.1	+49.4
Services	83.9	173.1	87668	41.3	73.9	127.5	112433	61.9	-11.9
Géographical zone									
Abidjan	72.0	140.2	45002	21.2	77.8	136.9	129683	71.3	+8.1
Hors Abidjan	44.6	135.1	167482	78.8	42.7	67.8	52074	28.7	-4.3

(1) Real wage: nominal wage deflated by consumer price index according to IMF statistics (IMF [1992]). Between 1979 and 1989, the consumer price index rose by 74.7 per cent; (2) Gross monthly wage in thousands of CFA francs; (3) State participation greater than 50 per cent; (4) Agriculture: branches 1 to 5; Manufacturing sector: branches 6 to 21;(5)Energy, construction: branches 22 to 23; Services: branches 24 to 33; (6) - 0.9 per cent if the index is the implicit GDP deflator.
Source: Based on data from manpower surveys of 1979 and 1989 (ONFP).

Table B: **Regression coefficients of the equations for all employees in the modern production sector in Cote d'Ivoire, 1979-1989[1]**

Year/sector	All employees			
	1979		1989	
Dependent variables	β	Mean	β	Mean
Group 1				
Years of education	0.09073	3.664	0.08560	5.543
	(252.89)*		(219.84)*	
Technical/vocational training[2]	0.36533	0.091	0.22055	0.145
	(71.62)*		(40.30)*	
Diploma[3]	0.12576	0.213	0.09207	0.318
	(31.656)*		(21.036)*	
Group 2				
Job experience	0.01755	5.803	0.04645	8.756
	(27.50)*		(64.21)*	
(Job experience)[2]/100	-0.00731	0.678	-0.09340	1.243
	(-2.77)*		(-34.82)*	
Age	0.06688	33.023	0.07561	36.235
	(66.99)*		(52.65)*	
(Age)[2]/100	-0.05957	11.712	-0.06295	13.831
	(-44.90)*		(-34.01)*	
Nationality[4]	0.07795	0.688	0.17353	0.738
	(29.21)*		(45.98)*	
Sex[5]	-0.11154	0.949	0.01669	0.885
	(-20.00)*		(3.36)*	
Group 3				
Department[6]	0.26628	0.788	0.21274	0.713
	(89.57)*		(60.24)*	
Status of enterprise[7]	-0.11698	0.403	-0.32756	0.416
	(-41.76)*		(-95.73)*	
Size of enterprise	-2.04E-05	1761.104	1.34E-05	1186.268
	(-37.22)*		(13.92)*	
Constant	1.66656		1.36493	
	(90.20)*		(51.91)*	
Variation F (sig)				
Group 1	*0.41804 (0.0000)*		*0.34366 (0.0000)*	
Group 2	*0.09404 (0.0000)*		*0.15515 (0.0000)*	
Group 3	*0.03214 (0.0000)*		*0.03854 (0.0000)*	
R[2]	0.54422		0.53734	
Adjusted R[2]	0.54420		0.53731	
F	21141.768		17589.888	
Sig F	0.0000		0.0000	
N	212484		181757	

Table B (contd.): Regression coefficients of the equations for employees in the modern production sector – tradeables and non-tradeables sectors – in Cote d'Ivoire, 1979-1989[1]

Year/sector	Tradeables[9]				Non-tradeables[10]			
Dependent variables	1979		1989		1979		1989	
	β	Mean	β	Mean	β	Mean	β	Mean
Group 1								
Years of education	0.08997 (138.70)*	2.788	0.07441 (92.09)*	3.796	0.08192 (200.49)*	4.223	0.08325 (191.09)*	6.367
Tech./voc. training[2]	0.50576 (51.00)*	0.059	0.46761 (35.84)*	0.078	0.33694 (60.38)*	0.111	0.18620 (31.84)*	0.177
Diploma[3]	0.13288 (19.56)*	0.159	0.22637 (23.77)*	0.164	0.10787 (23.58)*	0.248	0.01625 (3.37)*	0.390
Group 2								
Job experience	0.03734 (31.49)*	5.490	0.04421 (34.18)*	7.548	0.01172 (16.16)*	5.976	0.04644 (55.02)*	9.324
(Job exp.)²/100	-0.10033 (-18.57)*	0.574	-0.05188 (-10.27)*	0.999	0.01186 (4.10)*	0.736	-0.10054 (-32.71)*	1.358
Age	0.06007 (35.18)*	31.676	0.05225 (22.88)*	34.352	0.06041 (51.82)*	33.768	0.06786 (36.94)*	37.146
(Age)²/100	-0.04956 (-21.28)*	10.766	-0.03508 (-11.48)*	12.518	-0.05514 (-36.10)*	12.235	-0.05888 (-25.44)*	14.467
Nationality[4]	0.24049 (55.22)*	0.687	0.27853 (22.88)*	0.625	-0.07122 (-22.16)*	0.688	0.01376 (2.84)*	0.791
Sex[5]	-0.14662 (-12.84)*	0.972	0.19240 (17.73)*	0.953	-0.04772 (-7.91)*	0.934	-0.00298 (-0.43)	0.863
Group 3								
Department[6]	0.11077 (25.62)*	0.616	0.06279 (10.67)*	0.611	0.24585 (50.18)*	0.898	0.28731 (63.39)*	0.762
Status of enterprise[7]	-0.24359 (-54.81)*	0.366	-0.54061 (-79.39)*	0.236	-0.00379 (-1.09)	0.428	-0.22629 (-54.26)*	0.501
Size of enterprise	-1.80E-05 (-16.77)*	1438.610	2.33E-06 (0.46)	577.331	-4.45E-05 (-69.73)*	1967.036	-8.81E-06 (-8.78)*	1473.159
Constant	1.64404 (52.26)*		1.59737 (38.79)*		2.04257 (92.87)*		1.77699 (51.11)*	
Variation F (sig)								
Group 1	*0.39556 (0.0000)*		*0.34201 (0.0000)*		*0.42283 (0.0000)*		*0.31643 (0.0000)*	
Group 2	*0.10685 (0.0000)*		*0.21930 (0.0000)*		*0.09040 (0.0000)*		*0.11697 (0.0000)*	
Group 3	*0.04074 (0.0000)*		*0.04542 (0.0000)*		*0.02829 (0.0000)*		*0.04115 (0.0000)*	
R²	0.54315		0.60673		0.54152		0.47454	
Adjusted R²	0.54308		0.60665		0.54147		0.47449	
F	8202.840		7482.001		12762.259		9297.144	
Sig F	0.0000		0.0000		0.0000		0.0000	
N	82807		58208		129677		123549	
Chow[8] (F)	1521.33		747.98		-		-	
Sig Chow	0.0000		0.0000		-		-	

(1) The modern sector is composed of the para-public sector-State companies and companies in which the State has a participation (greater than 50 per cent) – and the private sector – the formal sector i.e. establishments which maintain accounts and which have a turnover of at least 12 million CFA francs a year. The dependent variable is the logarithm of the gross monthly wage. The t is between parentheses; * = statistically significant to 1 per cent; ** = statistically significant to more than 1 per cent; (2) base = no technical or vocational training; (3) base = without diploma; (4) base = non-Ivorians; (5) base = women; (6) base = outside Abidjan; (7) base = private sector; (8) the Chow test refers to equations of the tradeables and non-tradeables sectors; (9) Agriculture: branches 1 to 5: manufacturing sector: branches 6 to 21; (10) Energy, construction: branches 22 to 23; services: branches 24 to 33.
Source: based on data from manpower surveys of 1979 and 1989 (ONFP).

Table C: Regression coefficients of the equations of newly recruited employees in the modern production sector in Cote d'Ivoire, 1979-1989[1]

Year/sector	All newly recruited employees			
Dependent variables	1979		1989	
	β	Mean	β	Mean
Group 1				
Years of education	0.07989 (160.17)*	4.559	0.08424 (113.37)*	5.101
Techical/vocational training[2]	0.42073 (60.39)*	0.116	0.23879 (21.07)*	0.125
Diploma[3]	0.11082 (19.90)*	0.257	0.20860 (22.18)*	0.250
Group 2				
Age	0.06552 (46.39)*	29.661	0.06298 (24.95)*	30.909
(Age)^2/100	-0.05977 (-14.79)*	9.395	-0.03662 (-10.22)*	10.142
Nationality[4]	-0.06173 (-14.79)*	0.724	0.11120 (16.81)*	0.634
Sex[5]	-0.08699 (-11.73)*	0.931	0.07396 (7.94)*	0.877
Group 3				
Department[6]	0.21744 (46.72)*	0.803	0.24406 (37.33)*	0.651
Status enterprise[7]	-0.12817 (-29.11)*	0.386	-0.36461 (-50.72)*	0.368
Size of enterprise	-1.49E-07 (-0.16)	1648.074	3.03E-05 (12.09)*	778.536
Constant	1.92754 (76.70)*		1.51981 (35.10)*	
Variation F (sig)				
Group 1	*0.43501 (0.0000)*		*0.42432 (0.0000)*	
Group 2	*0.07079 (0.0000)*		*0.08743 (0.0000)*	
Group 3	*0.01928 (0.0000)*		*0.04066 (0.0000)*	
R^2	0.52508		0.55241	
Adjusted R^2	0.52503		0.55233	
F	9822.895		6648.688	
Sig F	0.0000		0.0000	
N	88856		53882	

Table C (contd.): **Regression coefficients of the equations of newly recruited employees in the tradeables and non-tradeables sectors in Cote d'Ivoire, 1979-1989[1]**

Year/sector	Tradeables[9]				Non-tradeables[10]			
Dependent variables	1979		1989		1979		1989	
	β	Mean	β	Mean	β	Mean	β	Mean
Group 1								
Year of education	0.07719 (81.29)*	3.759	0.07127 (48.69)*	3.036	0.07347 (131.02)*	4.987	0.07920 (95.97)*	6.536
Tech./ voc./training[2]	0.57154 (39.75)*	0.084	0.47444 (19.15)*	0.064	0.38165 (50.88)*	0.133	0.20785 (17.37)*	0.168
Diploma[3]	0.12064 (11.88)*	0.202	0.19717 (10.30)*	0.124	0.08911 (14.17)*	0.286	0.13880 (13.60)*	0.337
Group 2								
Age	0.06285 (24.67)*	28.350	0.04008 (10.82)*	29.434	0.05472 (33.65)*	30.361	0.05753 (17.24)*	32.073
(Age)[2]/100	-0.05518 (-14.69)*	8.577	-0.01705 (-3.11)*	9.218	-0.04906 (-21.47)*	9.832	-0.03513 (-7.67)*	10.871
Nationality[4]	0.08078 (10.55)*	0.748	0.21852 (20.80)*	0.480	-0.17862 (-37.09)*	0.711	-0.16375 (-18.75)*	0.741
Sex[5]	-0.13150 (-8.29)*	0.958	0.26765 (16.16)*	0.917	-0.02374 (-2.99)*	0.917	0.01234 (1.16)	0.849
Group 3								
Department[6]	0.06860 (9.80)*	0.619	0.13813 (14.54)*	0.582	0.21911 (30.35)*	0.902	0.31596 (36.60)*	0.700
Status enterprise[7]	-0.27433 (-37.76)*	0.364	-0.55296 (-50.33)*	0.299	0.02896 (5.36)	0.398	-0.18130 (-19.15)*	0.416
Size of enterprise	-1.06E-05 (-4.13)*	1057.970	-1.84E-04 (-16.59)	519.307	-3.12E-05 (-31.76)*	1964.118	-4.36E-06 (-1.68)	958.698
Constant	1.89673 (41.93)*		1.88541 (29.94)*		2.28681 (77.46)*		2.00434 (33.59)*	

Variation F (sig)				
Group 1		*0.37709 (0.0000)*	*0.44721 (0.0000)*	*0.38643 (0.0000)*
Group 2		*0.10119 (0.0000)*	*0.06776 (0.0000)*	*0.09139 (0.0000)*
Group 3		*0.07608 (0.0000)*	*0.01492 (0.0000)*	*0.04085 (0.0000)*
R²		**0.54436**	**0.52989**	**0.51867**
Adjusted R²		**0.54415**	**0.52981**	**0.51852**
F		**2746.878**	**6521.157**	**3424.371**
Sig F		**0.0000**	**0.0000**	**0.0000**
N		**22093**	**57865**	**31789**
Chow[8] (F)		**507.15**	**-**	**-**
Sig Chow		**0.0000**	**-**	**-**

(1) The modern sector is composed of the para-public sector – State companies and companies in which the State has a participation (greater than 50 per cent) – and the private sector – the formal sector i.e. establishments which maintain accounts and which have a turnover of at least 12 million CFA francs a year. The dependent variable is the logarithm of the gross monthly wage. The t is between parentheses; * = statistically significant to 1 per cent; ** = statistically significant to more than 1 per cent; (2) base = no technical or vocational training; (3) base = without diploma; (4) base = non-Ivorians; (5) base = women; (6) base = outside Abidjan; (7) base = private sector; (8) the Chow test refers to equations of the tradeables and non-tradeables sectors; (9) Agriculture: branches 1 to 5: manufacturing sector: branches 6 to 21; (10) Energy, construction: branches 22 to 23; services: branches 24 to 33.
Source: based on data from manpower surveys of 1979 and 1989 (ONFP).

Table D: Regression coefficients of the equations for all employees in the modern production sector in Côte d'Ivoire, 1979-1989[1]

Year/sector	All employees			
Dependent variables	1979		1989	
	β	Mean	β	Mean
Group 1				
Years of education	0.09030	3.664	0.08956	5.543
	(250.78)*		(225.70)*	
Technical/Vocational training[2]	0.36055	0.091	0.22780	0.145
	(70.41)*		(40.61)*	
Diploma[3]	0.12180	0.213	0.02386	0.318
	(30.545)*		(5.39)*	
Group 2				
Job experience	0.01687	5.803	0.04648	8.756
	(26.333*		(64.69)*	
$(\text{Job experience})^2/100$	-0.00662	0.678	-0.09367	1.243
	(-2.49)*		(-34.07)*	
Age	0.06676	33.023	0.07739	36.235
	(66.07)*		(35.01)*	
$(\text{Age})^2/100$	-0.05939	11.712	-0.06461	13.831
	(-44.58)*		(-34.06)*	
Nationality[4]	0.07026	0.688	0.13463	0.738
	(26.29)*		(33.01)*	
Sex[5]	-0.10554	0.949	0.03541	0.885
	(-18.85)*		(6.96)*	
Group 3				
Department[6]	0.28227	0.788	0.26645	0.713
	(95.35)*		(74.56)*	
Size of enterprise	-3.15E-05	1761.104	-1.86E-05	1186.268
	(-65.48)*		(-20.04)*	
Constant	1.63409		1.19733	
	(88.16)*		(44.53)*	
Variation F (sig)				
Group 1	*0.41804 (0.0000)*		*0.34366 (0.0000)*	
Group 2	*0.09404 (0.0000)*		*0.15515 (0.0000)*	
Group 3	*0.02840 (0.0000)*		*0.01520 (0.0000)*	
R^2	0.54048		0.51401	
Adjusted R^2	0.54046		0.51398	
F	22718.752		17474.599	
Sig F	0.0000		0.0000	
N	212484		181757	

Table D (contd.): **Regression coefficients of the equations for all employees in the para-public and private modern sectors in Côte d'Ivoire, 1979-1989[1]**

Year/sector	Para-public sector				Private sector			
Dependent variables	1979		1989		1979		1989	
	β	Mean	β	Mean	β	Mean	β	Mean
Group 1								
Years of education	0.08689 (162.89)*	3.584	0.06756 (117.925*	5.254	0.09305 (193.05)*	3.718	0.08964 (171.19)*	5.750
Tech./voc. training[2]	0.37441 (48.07)*	0.088	0.39356 (51.17)*	0.137	0.37326 (56.11)*	0.092	0.12383 (16.61)*	0.151
Diploma[3]	0.12950 (22.19)*	0.214	-0.03202 (-5.51)*	0.367	0.09351 (17.51)*	0.212	0.17792 (28.44)*	0.282
Group 2								
Job experience	0.01987 (22.30)*	6.109	0.05731 (54.44)*	9.252	0.01549 (17.25)*	5.599	0.04515 (46.13)*	8.402
(Job experience)^2/100	0.00273 (0.77)	0.749	-0.10318 (-27.33)*	1.340	-0.02109 (-5.47)*	0.631	-0.08797 (-24.21)*	1.174
Age	0.06028 (41.50)*	33.272	0.05769 (25.86)*	36.390	0.06744 (50.10)*	32.856	0.08239 (45.04)*	36.131
(Age)^2/100	-0.05592 (-29.17)*	11.886	-0.05275 (-18.22)*	13.923	-0.05768 (-32.11)*	11.595	-0.06885 (-29.35)*	13.770
Nationality[4]	0.24897 (58.25)*	0.741	0.55091 (89.23)*	0.809	-0.01671 (-4.88)*	0.652	0.00425 (0.88)	0.687
Sex[5]	-0.07007 (-8.04)*	0.953	0.07231 (10.91)*	0.878	-0.11570 (-16.11)*	0.946	-0.02511 (-3.60*)	0.890
Group 3								
Department[6]	0.37949 (89.39)*	0.733	0.21439 (45.47)*	0.651	0.19437 (46.63)	0.826	0.20653 (41.31)*	0.758
Size of enterprise	-2.74E-05 (-47.78)*	3223.890	2.64E-05 (23.09)	1878.959	2.12E-05 (13.54)*	771.827	-3.10E-05 (-18.31)*	691.904
Constant	1.48758 (52.26)*		1.19659 (29.67)*		1.73817 (69.87)*		1.36181 (40.42)*	
Variation F (sig)								
Group 1	*0.44432 (0.0000)*		*0.36790 (0.0000)*		*0.40713 (0.0000)*		*0.33534 (0.0000)*	
Group 2	*0.10927 (0.0000)*		*0.22652 (0.0000)*		*0.09554 (0.0000)*		*0.15395 (0.0000)*	
Group 3	*0.04282 (0.0000)*		*0.01761 (0.0000)*		*0.00888 (0.0000)*		*0.00925 (0.0000)*	
R^2	0.59640		0.61203		0.51156		0.49853	
Adjusted R^2	0.59635		0.61197		0.51151		0.49848	
F	11514.742		10853.752		12067.575		9584.467	
Sig F	0.0000		0.0000		0.0000		0.0000	
N	85726		75695		126758		106062	
Chow[7] (F)	476.82		1427.73		-		-	
Sig Chow	0.0000		0.0000		-		-	

(1) The modern sector is composed of the para-public sector-State companies and companies in which the State has a participation (greater than 50 per cent) – and the private sector – the formal sector i.e. establishments which maintain accounts and which have a turnover of at least 12 million CFA francs a year. The dependent variable is the logarithm of the gross monthly wage; the independant variable of the "Status of enterprise" (as in table A) is not taken into consideration. The t is between parentheses; * = statistically significant to 1 per cent; ** = statistically significant to more than 1 per cent; (2) base = no technical or vocational training; (3) base = without diploma; (4) base = non-Ivorians; (5) base = women; (6) base = outside Abidjan; (7) the Chow test refers to equations of the tradeables and non-tradeables sectors.

Source: based on data from manpower surveys of 1979 and 1989 (ONFP).

Table E: **Regression coefficients of the equations of newly recruited employees in the modern production sector in Côte d'Ivoire, 1979-1989[1]**

Year/sector	All newly recruited employee			
Dependent	1979		1989	
	β	Mean	β	Mean
Group 1				
Years of education	0.07992	4.559	0.08986	5.101
	(159.48)*		(119.50)*	
Technical/vocational training[2]	0.41179	0.116	0.23142	0.125
	(58.88)*		(19.95)*	
Diploma[3]	0.10739	0.257	0.15769	0.250
	(19.20)*		(16.47)*	
Group 2				
Age	0.06525	29.661	0.06570	30.909
	(45.97)*		(25.43)*	
(Age)²/100	-0.05929	9.395	-0.03801	10.142
	(-29.25)*		(-10.36)*	
Nationality[4]	-0.07006	0.724	0.10785	0.634
	(-16.74)*		(15.93)*	
Sex[5]	-0.07800	0.931	0.08792	0.877
	(-10.48)*		(9.23)*	
Group 3				
Department[6]	0.23471	0.803	0.29171	0.651
	(50.60)*		(44.04)*	
Size of enterprise	-1.40E-05	1648.074	-2.69E-05	778.536
	(-18.60)*		(-11.76)*	
Constant	1.89024		1.30411	
	(74.96)*		(29.57)*	
Variation F (sig)				
Group 1	*0.43501 (0.0000)*		*0.42432 (0.0000)*	
Group 2	*0.07079 (0.0000)*		*0.08743 (0.0000)*	
Group 3	*0.01475 (0.0000)*		*0.01929 (0.0000)*	
R²	0.52055		0.53103	
Adjusted R²	0.52050		0.53095	
F	10718.055		6777.974	
Sig F	0.0000		0.0000	
N	88856		53882	

Table E (contd.): **Regression coefficients of the equations of newly recruited employees in the para-public and private modern sectors in Côte d'Ivoire, 1979-1989[1]**

Year/sector	Para-public sector				Private sector			
Dependent variables	1979		1989		1979		1989	
	β	Mean	β	Mean	β	Mean	β	Mean
Group 1								
Years of education	0.07551 (101.55)*	4.286	0.06824 (54.46)*	3.619	0.08113 (123.76)*	4.730	0.08709 (95.48)*	5.963
Tech./voc. training[2]	0.47147 (43.41)*	0.108	0.36833 (18.28)*	0.090	0.40.829 (46.02)*	0.121	0.21248 (15.77)*	0.146
Diploma[3]	0.09310 (11.22)*	0.248	0.28161 (17.58)*	0.205	0.09122 (12.47)*	0.262	0.14737 (12.88)*	0.276
Group 2								
Age	0.05701 (29.29)*	29.815	0.04234 (9.388*	29.681	0.06541 (33.48)*	29.563	0.07404 (24.55)*	31.473
(Age)²/100	-0.05448 (-19.72)*	9.485	-0.02047 (-3.12)*	9.315	-0.05716 (-20.43)*	9.338	-0.05091 (-12.01)*	10.522
Nationality[4]	0.19746 (30.31)*	0.748	0.47938 (43.40)*	0.643	-0.19671 (-36.43)*	0.710	-0.07302 (-8.83)*	0.629
Sex[5]	-0.01457 (-1.24)	0.939	0.08561 (5.70)*	0.889	-0.10139 (-10.80)*	0.927	0.04564 (3.94)*	0.870
Group 3								
Department[6]	0.33836 (49.14)*	0.776	0.28360 (30.39)*	0.512	0.16356 (26.38)	0.820	0.25201 (28.20)*	0.732
Size of enterprise	-1.85E-06 (-1.98)**	3270.630	3.54E-05 (13.43)	1630.637	2.69E-05 (10.51)*	639.116	-6.13E-05 (-8.51)*	282.795
Constant	1.67032 (47.766*		1.38345 (18.314*		2.04370 (59.11)*		1.48615 (28.51)*	
Variation F (sig)								
Group 1	*0.46943 (0.0000)*		*0.44047 (0.0000)*		*0.41659 (0.0000)*		*0.38584 (0.0000)*	
Group 2	*0.05582 (0.0000)*		*0.09025 (0.0000)*		*0.09599 (0.0000)*		*0.10635 (0.0000)*	
Group 3	*0.03312 (0.0000)*		*0.02509 (0.0000)*		*0.00692 (0.0000)*		*0.01357 (0.0000)*	
R²	0.55837		0.55591		0.51950		0.50576	
Adjusted R²	0.55825		0.55571		0.51942		0.50563	
F	4813.717		2755.070		6555.507		3871.984	
Sig F	0.0000		0.0000		0.0000		0.0000	
N	34276		19808		54580		34064	
Chow[8] (F)	356.83		475.86		-		-	
Sig Chow	0.0000		0.0000		-		-	

(1) The modern sector is composed of the para-public sector-State companies and companies in which the State has a participation (greater than 50 per cent) – and the private sector – the formal sector i.e. establishments which maintain accounts and which have a turnover of at least 12 million CFA francs a year. The dependent variable is the logarithm of the gross monthly wage. The t is between parentheses; * = statistically significant to 1 per cent; ** = statistically significant to more than 1 per cent; (2) base = no technical or vocational training; (3) base = without diploma; (4) base = non-Ivorians; (5) base = women; (6) base = outside Abidjan; (7) the Chow test refers to equations of the tradeables and non-tradeables sectors.
Source: based on data from manpower surveys of 1979 and 1989 (ONFP).

Table F: Breakdown of wage differences in the modern production sector in Côte d'Ivoire in 1979 and 1989

Parameters Country	Wage comparison[1]	Total gross differential	Caracteristics (L) Value	%	Earnings fonction Constant	Other φ	%
All employees	$\log\hat{Y}_1-\log\hat{Y}_0$	0.4919	0.3485	70.9	-0.3016	0.4450	29.1
Tradeables	$\log\hat{Y}_1-\log\hat{Y}_0$	0.4195	0.2628	62.7	-0.0466	0.2032	37.3
Non-tradeables	$\log\hat{Y}_1-\log\hat{Y}_0$	0.4733	0.3259	68.9	-0.2655	0.4129	31.1
Para-public	$\log\hat{Y}_1-\log\hat{Y}_0$	0.4154	0.3236	77.9	-0.2909	0.3527	22.1
Private	$\log\hat{Y}_1-\log\hat{Y}_0$	0.5515	0.3634	65.9	-0.3763	0.5645	34.1
New recruits	$\log\hat{Y}_1-\log\hat{Y}_0$	0.0400	0.0449	112.4	-0.4077	0.4027	-12.4
Tradeables	$\log\hat{Y}_1-\log\hat{Y}_0$	-0.1064	-0.0168	15.8	-0.0113	-0.0782	84.2
Non-tradeables	$\log\hat{Y}_1-\log\hat{Y}_0$	0.1897	0.1436	75.7	-0.2824	0.3285	24.3
Para-public	$\log\hat{Y}_1-\log\hat{Y}_0$	-0.2670	-0.2104	78.8	-0.2868	0.2303	21.2
Private	$\log\hat{Y}_1-\log\hat{Y}_0$	0.2152	0.1826	84.9	-0.5575	0.5901	15.1

(1) $\log\hat{Y}_1$ = average of log of wages in 1989; $\log\hat{Y}_0$ = average of log of wages in 1979.
Source: based on data from manpower surveys of 1979 and 1989 (ONFP); tables B, C, D, E.

Table G: Descriptive statistics on wages and employment in the public and private sectors in French-speaking Africa[1]

Country/ sector	Burkina Faso		Cameroon		Côte d'Ivoire		Guinea		Madagascar		Mali		Senegal	
Parameter	Pub.	Priv.	Pub.	Priv.	Pub.	Priv.	Pub.	Priv.	Pub.	Priv.	Pub.	Priv.	Pub.	Priv.
Distribution														
Mean (000 CFA/sem.)	24.4[2]	15.0[2]	47.1[2]	29.6[2]	37.7[2]	19.4[2]	20.8[2]	16.1[2]	24.9[2,4]	19.1[2,4]	12.9[2]	9.9[2]	40.0[2]	19.9[2]
(SD)	(17.2)	(19.7)	(32.4)	(31.1)	(30.1)	(19.6)	(16.3)	(7.5)	(25.8)	(13.2)	(27.4)	(12.7)	(26.5)	(19.9)
25e percent.[3]	13.5	4.8	23.4	13.0	16.3	9.0	15.0	10.0	15.0	10.0	6.0	4.0	20.7	7.0
75e percent.[3]	30.0	14.0	62.0	33.0	45.0	23.7	23.0	20.0	26.0	22.6	13.0	10.0	53.5	25.0
Médian	20.0	8.0	39.5	21.0	35.0	12.5	17.5	14.0	20.0	15.0	9.0	6.0	31.0	10.0
Gap (%): $(W_u-W_i)/W_i$[5]	62.7		59.1		94.3		29.2		30.4		30.3		101.0	
Structure Bonuses, benefits (%)	5.7	1.4	6.1	7.9	6.8	9.2	12.7	4.3	5.1	7.3	6.3	5.1	12.3	10.3
Benefits in kinds (%)	3.8	2.1	6.4	2.8	13.8	2.1	6.7	0.2	2.1	4.2	0.8	9.0	15.7	5.3
Employment Capital (%)[6]	30.0	15.2	22.3	21.7	13.1	35.0	23.3	9.0	35.7	31.7	22.7	15.0	32.6	45.0
N	153	81	188	105	76	201	183	71	106	94	228	151	102	141

(1) The public sector includes the public service and public enterprises; the private sector does not make a distinction between the formal and informal sectors; (2) including bonuses, allowances, gratifications, social benefits and benefits in kind. The t test shows that the hypothesis of the equality of wage averages in the public and private sectors must be rejected; (3) weighted value of Xi and Xi + 1 by the formula $(1-f)Xi+fXi+1$ in which $(W+1)p$ is broken down into a whole part i and a fraction f; (4) thousands of FMG per week; (5) u and i refer respectively to the public sector and the private sector; (6) percentage of the urban active population.

Source: Household pilot employment surveys in the capitals of Burkina Faso, 1991; Cameroon, 1990-91; Cote d'Ivoire, 1986-87; Guinea, 1991; Madagascar, 1989; Mali, 1991; Senegal, 1991.

Table H: Comparison of salaries in the public service and public enterprises in French-speaking Africa: T-test[1]

Parameter	Sample						Variance	Test t[3]	
	Public service			· Public enterprises			(sig F)[2]	Value	Sig
Country	Mean	SD	N	Mean	SD	N			
Burkina Faso	22.1	13.3	105	29.5	22.9	48	0.000	-2.90	0.040
Cameroon	47.9	33.2	140	44.9	30.2	48	0.461	0.56	0.579
Côte d'Ivoire	39	28.0	55	34.4	35.5	21	0.167	0.53	0.554
Guinea	20.3	11.5	142	22.4	27.3	41	0.000	-0.48	0.636
Mali	13	28.8	201	12.2	12.6	27	0.000	0.28	0.782
Senegal	39.7	22.7	80	41.1	38.0	22	0.001	-0.17	0.867

(1) No distinction between the public service and public enterprises was made in Madagascar. Salaries are expressed in thousands of CFA francs per week; (2) If the significance level observed for the F test is low, the hypothesis that the population variances are identical must be rejected and the separate variance test must be used. Otherwise the weighted variance test – the calculation of t takes account of a variance which is a weighted average of individual variances – must be used; (3) t test of the separate variance or the weighted variance as the case may be (see note (2)).

Source: Household pilot employment surveys in the capitals of Burkina Faso, 1991; Cameroon, 1990-91; Côte d'Ivoire, 1986-87; Guinea, 1991; Madagascar, 1989; Mali, 1991; Senegal, 1991.

Table I: Descriptives statistics of samples[1,2]

Country/sector	Burkina Faso		Cameroon		Côte d'Ivoire	
Parameter	Public	Private	Public	Private	Public	Private
Mean of log of wage[3]	2.988	2.188	3.638	3.049	3.376	2.646
	(0.657)	(0.968)	(0.677)	(0.806)	(0.714)	(0.792)
Age[4]	36.6	30.8	37.5	32.9	36.5	31.9
	(7.5)	(8.5)	(8.3)	(8.6)	(8.5)	(8.2)
Résidence in the capital[5]	18.4	17.6	16.6	15.7	15.8	13.0
	(11.3)	(10.7)	(11.2)	(11.7)	(10.8)	(9.3)
Nationality[6]	98	96.3	100	97.3	86.8	68.3
Education						
Illiterate	13.2	32.2			9.2	24.2
Primary	15.0	24.7	11.0[9]	28.9	23.6	36.1
Secondary first cycle (general)	17.0	18.5	14.3	22.8	39.4[10]	30.6
Secondary second cycle (gen.)	14.3	8.6	16.9	14.2	26.3	12.8
Secondary first cycle (technical)	2.6	4.9	12.7	10.4	-	-
Secondary second cycle (tech.)	5.2	1.2	9.0	12.3	-	-
Higher	32.7	9.9	36.1	11.4	9.2	1.5
Training						
Without training	53.7	51.9	60.7	57.2	14.4	33.1
Apprenticeship	6.5	29.6	11.7	29.5	15.7	39.6
Vocational training	39.8	18.5	27.6	13.3	69.7	27.7
Diploma						
Elementary diploma	-	-	16.4	29.6	27.6	35.1
Secondary 1c. diploma	-	-	22.8	22.8	-	-
Secondary 2c. diploma	39.2[17]	16.0[17]	25.5	12.3	55.2[11]	25.7[11]
Higher diploma	-	-	34.5	11.4	60.5[12]	31.1[12]
Apprenticeship/other diploma	27.4[18]	11.1[18]	6.3	15.2	14.4	20.2
General experience[4]	18.9	16.8	16.7	18.4	19.1	17.6
	(10.6)	(10.3)	(9.3)	(9.5)	(11.3)	(10.1)
Job experience[4]	10.9	5.7	11.2	6.3	8.3	8.7
	(7.2)	(5.3)	(11.9)	(6.0)	(2.37)	(2.4)
Occupational category						
Management/senior executive	34.7	10.7	28.1	8.0	13.2	1.5
Middle executive/supervisor	31.7	13.1	30.2	12.5	46.1	10.4
Employee/skilled labourer	16.2	28.6	27.1	27.7	28.9	47.0
Employee/unskilled worker	13.2	22.6	12.5	31.3	9.2	33.2
Labourer	4.2	25.0	2.1	20.5	2.6	7.9
Size of household[7]	7.4	8.8	8.8	8,6	7.0	6.3
	(5.3)	(7.8)	(3.4)	(4.1)	(3.9)	(3.7)
Matrimonial status/sex						
Head of household	64.8	42.0	60.4	45.4	73.7	52.5
Unmarried male	10.4	43.2	9.4	37.0	7.8	30.1
Married female	19.6	9.9	26.0	7.4	14.4	7.4
Unmarried female	5.2	4.9	3.6	10.2	3.9	9.9
Situation of relatives[8]						
Parents educated (%)	20.1	17.7	43.6	42.0	15.8	7.4
Parents with training (%)	6.9	6.6	22.9	19.3	9.5	6.1
Parents employees (%)	27.6	20.6	30.6	23.9	11.2	7.8
Parents self-employed (%)	41.7	45.2	63.0	73.5	45.4	53.2
Sample (N)	153	81	188	102	76	202

Tableau I (contd.): Descriptives statistics of samples[1,2]

Country/sector	Guinea		Madagascar		Mali		Senegal	
Parameter	Public	Private	Public	Private	Public	Private	Public	Private
Mean of log of wage[3]	2.893	2.682	3.013	2.753	2.229	1.913	3.502	2.571
	(0.484)	(0.442)	(0.561)	(0.630)	(0.648)	(0.795)	(0.611)	(0.912)
Age[4]	39.2	33.5	41.4	38.8	38.2	29.9	37.9	35.5
	(8.3)	(9.8)	(8.7)	(11.9)	(9.7)	(9.8)	(8.7)	(13.3)
Résidence in the	24.1	21.3	26.9	31.7	24.4	21.3	31.0	26.2
capital[5]	(13.2)	(12.0)	(15.2)	(14.6)	(12.3)	(12.1)	(12.2)	(15.0)
Nationality[6]	100	0	100	100	97.8	98	96.1	97.2
Education								
Illiterate	7.6	28.1			13.1	33.7	7.8	32.4
Primary	5.4	12.6	9.4[14]	25.5	22.3[16]	41.7[16]	13.7	32.4
Second. first c. (gen)	12.5	21.1	-	-	-	-	-	-
Second. sec. c. (gen.)	14.2	14.0	67.9[15]	60.6	11.8	4.6	28.4	19.1
Second. first c. (tech.)	10.9	8.4	-	-	-	-	-	-
Second. sec. c. (tech.)	18.5	7.0	-	-	34.2	13.9	17.6	7.8
Higher	30.6	8.4	22.6	13.8	18.4	5.9	31.3	8.4
Formation								
Without training	59.0	26.7	50.9	67.0	40.7	46.3	28.4	71.1
Apprenticeship	13.1	53.5	15.1	9.6	6.1	23.8	0.0	7.4
Vocational training	28.9	18.3	33.9	23.4	45.1	18.5	70.6	20.4
Diplôme								
Elementary	1.1	0.0	12.2	23.4	33.7	51.6	19.6	19..0
Secondary 1c.	-	-	-	-	-	-	29.4	12.7
Secondary 2c.	28.4[13]	18.3[13]	85.8[11]	63.8[11]	48.7[13]	19.9[13]	16.7	3.5
Higher	34.4	7.0	14.1[12]	9.6[12]	17.9	5.3	32.3	8.4
Apprent./other	17.4	15.4	29.2	17.0	-	-	-	-
General experience[4]	19.2	17.1	22.1	21.5	19.7	16.3	19.0	22.8
	(10.6)	(12.0)	(9.6)	(13.6)	(12.5)	(11.4)	(13.7)	(14.6)
Job experience[4]	10.3	5.3	16.0	11.8	11.2	6.4	7.6	5.5
	(7.6)	(5.6)	(8.6)	(9.9)	(8.4)	(6.7)	(7.6)	(7.7)
Occupational category								
Manage./senior exe.	41.8	8.5	13.4	11.4	20.4	7.2	21.6	4.3
Middle executive/sup.	28.6	7.0	26.8	22.8	35.8	11.8	43.1	7.1
Empl./skilled labourer	17.6	47.9	40.2	25.3	23.5	30.1	16.7	18.4
Empl./unskilled worker	7.7	32.4	19.6	40.3	12.8	29.4	13.7	22.7
Labourer	4.4	4.2	-	-	7.5	21.6	4.9	47.5
Size of household[7]	12.3	13.4	5.3	5.0	12.8	12.8	6.6	8.7
	(5.3)	(5.4)	(1.6)	(1.9)	(4.8)	(4.6)	(3.9)	(5.0)
Matrimonial status/sex								
Head of household	50.8	26.8	60.3	60.6	39.4	12.6	70.6	45.1
Unmarried male	22.4	62.0	4.7	10.6	31.5	64.2	14.7	33.1
Married female	19.7	4.2	28.3	15.9	17.9	7.9	14.7	10.6
Unmarried female	7.1	7.0	6.6	12.7	10.9	15.2	0.0	11.3
Situation of relatives[8]								
Parents educated (%)	14.2	10.1	87.7	87.9	-	-	20.7	9.8
Parents w. training (%)	15.3	8.1	11.6	14.6	-	-	4.0	2.9
Parents employees (%)	27.1	18.5	53.5	51.2	-	-	34.6	19.2
Parents self-empl. (%)	48.8	49.5	44.3	46.5	-	-	61.0	74.0
Sample (N)	183	71	106	88	228	151	91	133

(1) The public sector includes administrations and State companies; the private sector does not make a difference between the formal and informal sectors; (2) Standard differentials between parentheses; (3) Thousands of CFA francs or FMG francs (Madagascar) per week -including bonuses, allowances, gratifications, etc. (4) Years; (5) Duration in years; (6) 1 = nationality of country, 0 = foreigners; (7) Average size weighted by the number of employees in the household; several employees may belong to the same household; (8) Percentages of relatives of the head and the main spouse of the household respectively with education (> primary), with training, employees and self-employed persons; (9) Without education/primary in the case of Cameroon; (10) Including technical secondary education; (11) Diploma ≥ general secondary education; (12) Diploma ≥ technical secondary education; (13) Secondary diploma of the first and second cycles; (14) Without education/primary; (15) Secondary; (16) Basic 1 + 2; (17) General diploma of any kind; (18) Technical diploma of any kind.
Source: Household pilot employment surveys in the capitals of Burkina Faso, 1991; Cameroon, 1990-91; Côte d'Ivoire, 1986-87; Guinea, 1991; Madagascar, 1989; Mali, 1991; Senegal, 1991.

Table J: Regression coefficients of the equations of salaries in the public and private sectors in French-speaking Africa[1]

Country/sector	Burkina Faso		Cameroon		Côte d'Ivoire	
Independent var.	Public	Private	Public	Private	Public	Private
Education[2]						
Primary	0.00493	0.38469	-	-	0.46648	-0.05781
	(0.024)	(1.653)**	-	-	(2.269)*	(-0.491)
Second. 1cg	0.39303	0.95978	0.25013[5]	0.03901	0.79554	0.17483
	1.692**	(3.159)*	(1.456)	(0.212)	(2.956)*	(1.279)
Second. 2cg	0.61497	1.20207	0.35928	-0.22593	1.06098[6]	0.27340
	(2.460)*	(2.988)*	(1.846)**	(-0.777)	(3.318)*	(1.455)
Second. 1ct	0.37269	0.86440	0.13356	0.16651	-	-
	(1.015)	(2.200)*	(0.714)	(0.660)	-	-
Second. 2ct	0.52080	1.66479	0.31373	0.03382	-	-
	(1.744)*	(2.296)*	(1.437)	(0.119)	-	-
Higher	0.73197	1.98856	0.60398	0.64314	1.07355	1.58720
	(2.736)*	(4.687)*	(2.515)*	(1.268)	(2.827)*	(4.515)*
Training[3]						
Apprenticeship	0.09138	-0.17550	0.06360	0.37858	0.00241	0.30926
	(0.412)	(-0.909)	(0.428)	(2.187)*	(0.008)	(2.501)*
Vocational training	0.10374	-0.09230	-0.04153	0.13768	0.49718	0.55198
	(0.679)	(-0.359)	(-0.426)	(0.686)	(1.536)	(3.466)*
Diploma		-				
Elementary diploma	-	-	-0.05540	-0.20037	-0.46645	0.28583
	-	-	(-0.359)	(-1.187)	(-1.471)	(1.996)*
Second. 1c	-	-	0.04525	0.03194	-	-
	-	-	(0.356)	(0.168)	-	-
Second 2c	0.08609[12]	-0.11323	0.30894	0.33158	0.16628[7]	0.47729
	(0.772)	(-0.430)	(2.372)*	(1.208)	(0.464)	(2.718)*
Higher	-	-	0.48275	-0.04958	0.10522[8]	0.04024
	-	-	(2.744)*	(-0.093)	(0.366)	(0.320)
Apprenticeship	-0.09728[13]	0.11745	-0.14799	-0.33958	0.30963	-0.06649
	(-0.573)	(0.408)	(-0.802)	(-1.661)**	(1.079)	(-0.515)
Age						
Age	-0.14337	0.10656	0.01916	-0.15951	0.07358	0.10005
	(-1.530)	(0.717)	(0.331)	(-1.642)**	(1.023)	(2.187)*
(Age)²/100	0.21499	-0.11003	-0.00890	0.19196	-0.06573	-0.07530
	(1.728)**	(-0.566)	(-0.128)	(1.611)	(0.491)	(-1.227)
Job experience						
Experience	0.01715	0.02690	0.01524	0.12664	-0.15778	0.10970
	(0.717)	(0.583)	(1.675)**	(3.705)*	(-1.588)	(1.659)**
(Experience)²	-0.02682	-0.03656	-0.01217	-0.36617	0.49984	-0.33860
	(-0.329)	(-0.175)	(-1.627)**	(-2.429)*	(1.414)	(-1.100)
Sex[4]	-0.09300	0.13296	0.15282	-0.13146	0.04575	0.25171
	(-0.511)	(0.417)	(1.570)	(-0.764)	(0.242)	(2.140)*
Nationality[9]	-	-	-	-	-0.52974	0.44737
	-	-	-	-	(-2.658)*	(4.736)*
Lambda						
Lambda0	-0.48574	-0.14398	-0.17715	-0.91842	-0.16902	0.19698
	(-1.686)**	(-0.302)	(-0.887)	(-2.699)*	(-0.575)	(1.159)
Lambda1	0.07774	-	-0.02970	-	0.02684	-
	(1.042)	-	(-0.531)	-	(0.280)	-
Lambda2	-	-0.010265	-	0.02654	-	-0.14781
	-	(-0.058)	-	(0.218)	-	(-1.360)
Constant	4.96164	-0.61900	2.39367	6.56546	1.80238	1.74595
	(2.429)**	(-0.176)	(1.777)**	(2.819)*	(1.019)	(-1.720)**
R²	0.359	0.660	0.520	0.583	0.680	0.622
Adjusted R²	0.277	0.568	0.466	0.486	0.578	0.585
F	4.396	7.195	9.603	6.036	6.635	16.699
Sig F	0.000	0.000	0.000	0.000	0.000	0.000

Table J (contd.):   Regression coefficients of the equations of salaries
in the public and private sectors French-speaking Africa[1]

Country/sector	Guinea		Madagascar		Mali		Senegal	
Indep. var.	Public	Private	Public	Private	Public	Private	Public	Private
Education[2]								
Primary	0.51648	-0.25402	-	-	0.10309[11]	-0.05717	0.77697	-0.00817
	(2.633)*	(-1.224)	-	-	(0.703)	(-0.364)	(2.589)*	(-0.041)
Second. 1cg	0.64074	0.17238	-	-	-	-	-	-
	(3.474)*	(0.879)	-	-	-	-	-	-
Second. 2cg	0.71262	0.00214	-0.10038	-0.19815	0.11288	-0.23559	0.71098	0.05575
	(3.428)*	(0.009)	(-0.425)	(-1.113)	(0.524)	(-0.610)	(2.389)*	(0.210)
Second. 1ct	0.75112	0.26877	-	-	-	-	-	-
	(3.344)*	(0.608)	-	-	-	-	-	-
Second. 2ct	0.68358	0.57631	-	-	0.19582	-0.18296	1.34841	0.32143
	(2.866)*	(1.322)	-	-	(0.912)	(-0.490)	(3.886)*	(0.968)
Higher	0.78571	0.43073	0.20188	0.39824	0.20441	-1.44309	0.87002	0.82587
	(2.791)*	(1.132)	(0.761)	(1.633)**	(0.546)	(-1.894)**	(2.267)*	(1.159)
Training[3]								
Apprenticeship	-0.05419	-0.32754	-0.28434	-0.05916	-0.27503	0.11563	-	0.37250
	(-0.376)-	(-1.549)	(-1.507)	(-0.210)	(-1.131)	(0.559)	-	(1.192)
Voc. training	0.14844	-0.16412	-0.17586	0.09838	-0.20616	-0.17416	0.04305	0.14902
	(-1.642)**	(-0.842)	(-0.904)	(0.430)	(-2.410)*	(-0.867)	(0.225)	(0.551)
Diploma								
Elementary	-0.03541	-	0.55778	0.30484	0.04736	-0.46502	0.07119	0.39047
	(-0.103)	-	(1.516)	(1.133)	(0.246)	(-2.307)*	(0.333)	(1.897)**
Second. 1c	-	-	-	-	-	-	0.24497	0.81855
	-	-	-	-	-	-	(1.134)	(2.781)*
Second. 2c	-0.13548[10]	-0.43437[10]	1.02114[7]	0.51975	-0.03271	-0.24953	0.02813	0.64353
	(-1.152)	(-1.531)	(2.557)*	(1.498)	(-0.154)	(-0.759)	(0.154)	(1.423)
Higher	0.02428	-0.23934	0.14596[8]	0.36616	0.43575	1.06364	0.51563	0.83816
	(0.905)	(-0.637)	(0.701)	(1.292)	(1.248)	(1.398)	(1.785)**	(1.174)
Apprenticeship	0.13498	0.59569	0.02366	0.22788	-	-	-	-
	(1.318)	(3.125)*	(0.117)	(0.847)	-	-	-	-
Age								
Age	0.01781	0.00952	-0.01845	0.24846	0.01294	-0.04004	0.11156	0.05220
	(0.316)	(0.130)	(0.787)	(3.516)*	(0.240)	(-0.762)	(1.917)*	(1.794)**
(Age)²/100	0.00064	0.00058	0.03561	-0.27040	-0.01912	0.02878	-0.09766	-0.05426
	(0.009)	(0.006)	(0.454)	(-3.518)*	(-0.360)	(0.529)	(-1.411)	(-1.720)**
Job experience								
Job experience	-0.03641	0.06842	0.05656	0.01327	0.01670	0.07455	-0.00260	-0.01031
	(-2.413)*	(1.808)**	(2.019)**	(0.608)	(1.099)	(3.064)*	(-0.112)	(-0.414)
(Job experience)²	0.11258	-0.28382	-0.13343	-0.01684	-0.01625	-0.23265	-0.00115	0.03667
	(2.197)*	(-1.690)**	(-1.733)**	(-0.279)	(-0.336)	(-2.781)*	(-0.012)	(0.406)
Sex[4]	0.08595	0.05526	0.20547	0.30569	-0.05305	0.48866	0.13794	0.63860
	(0.819)	(0.242)	(1.654)**	(1.945)*	(-0.460)	(2.793)*	(0.856)	(3.585)*
Lambda								
Lambda0	-0.26586	-0.12999	-0.32836	0.31449	-0.53335	-0.71886	0.06906	0.34967
	(-1.579)**	(-0.569)	(-1.736)**	(1.419)	(-3.844)*	(-2.861)*	(0.388)	(1.260)
Lambda1	0.11512	-	0.36214	-	-0.13941	-	0.01452	-
	(0.588)	-	(2.306)*	-	(-0.312)	-	(0.059)	-
Lambda2	-	0.12810	-	0.20371	-	-0.63699	-	-0.00059
	-	(0.604)	-	(0.686)	-	(-1.406)	-	(-0.002)
Constant	1.92334	2.49968	1.70845	-3.28219	2.45392	3.22751	-0.49637	0.18652
	(1.310)	(1.302)	(1.162)	(-1.983)*	(1.533)	(3.313)*	(-0.354)	(0.183)
R²	0.375	0.472	0.494	0.513	0.388	0.428	0.468	0.457
Adjusted R²	0.303	0.276	0.410	0.412	0.341	0.360	0.353	0.377
F	5.168	2.404	5.872	5.072	8.372	6.277	4.079	5.713
Sig F	0.000	0.000	0.000	0.000	0.000	0.000	0.000	0.000

(1) The public sector comprises administrtions and State companies; the private sector makes no distinction between the formal and informal sectors. The dependent variable is the log of the wage; the t test is indicated between parentheses; (2) base = without education; (3) without training = base; (4) 1 = male; (5) base = illiterate/primary; (6) including technical secondary education; (7) diploma ≥ general secondary; (8) diploma ≥ technical secondary; (9) base = national; (10) Secondary diploma of the first and second cycles; (1) Base 1 + 2; (12) several diplomas of any kind; (13) technical diploma of any kind; * = statistically significant to 5 per cent; ** = statistically significant to less than 10 per cent.
Source: Household pilot employment surveys in the capitals of Burkina Faso, 1991; Cameroon, 1990-91; Côte d'Ivoire, 1986-87; Guinea, 1991; Madagascar, 1989; Mali, 1991; Senegal, 1991.

Table K: Regression coefficients of the equations of employees in the para-public and private sectors in Côte d'Ivoire, Abidjan, 1979-1989[1]

Year/sector	1979				1989			
	Para-public		Private		Para-public		Private	
Indépendent var.	ϕ	Sig F	ϕ	Sig F	ϕ	Sig F	ϕ	Sig F
Education[2]								
Primary	0.11980	0.52	0.56633	**0.00**	0.17086	0.23	0.11700	**0.00**
Secondary first cycle	0.38814	**0.00**	0.80653	**0.00**	0.54756	**0.00**	0.40030	**0.00**
Secondary 2nd cycle	0.83918	**0.00**	1.25199	**0.00**	0.84405	**0.00**	0.72638	**0.00**
IUT, BTS	0.77098	**0.00**	1.49578	**0.00**	1.18690	**0.00**	1.12446	**0.00**
Higher, schools of adm.	1.48854	**0.00**	1.83283	**0.00**	1.88011	**0.00**	1.61982	**0.00**
Sector[5]								
Secondary	0.72494	**0.00**	0.36364	**0.00**	-	-	-	-
Tertiary	0.96872	**0.00**	0.40529	**0.00**	-	-	0.17768	**0.00**
Diploma								
General	0.22360	0.15	0.15266	**0.02**	-0.83211	**0.00**	0.37249	**0.00**
Technical	0.58324	**0.00**	0.62766	**0.00**	-0.17736	0.24	0.59713	**0.00**
Vocational training	0.28551	**0.00**	0.42977	**0.00**	-0.46132	0.18	0.53053	**0.00**
Age								
Age	0.04387	**0.05**	0.02513	**0.01**	0.00987	0.16	0.02498	**0.00**
$(Age)^2/100$	-3.93182	**0.09**	-0.26678	0.80	-1.84036	**0.02**	-0.44015	0.49
Nationality[4]	-0.17901	**0.08**	0.01250	0.80	0.18602	**0.00**	-0.14081	**0.00**
Sex[3]	0.15624	0.52	-0.27168	**0.00**	-0.05247	0.73	-0.02241	0.64
Job experience								
Job experience	0.02864	**0.00**	-0.01364	**0.00**	0.03509	**0.00**	0.05758	**0.00**
$(Job experience)^2/100$	-0.04274	**0.00**	0.07223	**0.00**	-0.04518	**0.00**	-0.13602	**0.00**
Lambda1	0.18883	0.73	-	-	-0.76199	**0.01**	-	-
Lambda2	-	-	-0.46043	**0.06**	-	-	0.46440	**0.00**
Constant	1.60904	0.11	2.12695	**0.00**	4.74169	**0.00**	3.071399	**0.00**
R^2	0.680		0.591		0.671		0.521	
Adjusted R^2	0.679		0.590		0.669		0.520	
F	891.999		811.663		447.960		527.794	
Sig F	0.00		0.00		0.00		0.00	
N	7136		9562		3528		7756	

(1) The para-public sector includes State enterprises and enterprises in which the State has a participation – irrespective of the amount of this participation; the private sector includes the formal sector, i.e. establishments which maintain accounts and which have an annual turnover of at least 12 million CFA francs. The dependent variable is the logarithm of the gross monthly wage; (2) Base = without education; (3) 1 = male; (4)1 = Ivorians; (5) Base = primary.

Source: Manpower surveys in the modern sector, 1979 and 1989, ONFP.

3. The labour market in Tunisia: structure, imbalance and adjustment[1]

I. Introduction

The implementation of the economic stabilization and structural adjustment programmes in Tunisia from the mid-1980s have significantly modified the economic transition process and the social dimension of development. The labour market is an essential element in the social effort towards a new structure of social relations.

The initial mixed results – in terms of employment and balance of payments – of the import substitution policies and the promotion of exports which were successively introduced during the period 1960-1980, coupled with new constraints, led the Government to launch an investment programme focused on labour-intensive and export-oriented sectors, without disregarding the more capital-intensive spheres. When this new economic policy ran up against internal and external obstacles, economic growth and employment dropped and the balance of payments deficit and foreign debt increased. The resulting destabilization of the Tunisian economy explains the introduction of a structural adjustment policy in 1986.

According to some analyses, this economic policy has produced some positive results.[2] The country's real output, which had increased at an average annual rate of 6.5 per cent between 1965 and 1980, was only 3.6 per cent a year during the period 1980-1990.[3] As a result of the high rate of population growth,[4] per capita GDP rose by only 0.6 per cent a year, in real

---

[1] This chapter is based on a study already published by the Institute for Labour Studies (Discussion Paper Series No. 35). It summarizes various contributions presented at a meeting of the network of institutes or researchers on the urban labour market in the Maghreb countries, which was organized jointly by the National Institute of Labour and Social Studies (INTES) of Tunisia and the International Institute for Labour Studies (IILS) of the ILO in Tunis on 6-7 December 1990. Use has also been made of papers prepared for the seminar on employment organized by the Development Financing Institute of the Arab Maghreb (IFID), in collaboration with USAID, which was held in Tunis from 13 to 16 June 1990.

[2] Larbi [1990].

[3] World Bank [1992].

[4] Approximately 2.6 per cent per year.

terms, between 1980 and 1988.[5] Despite a revamping of the production apparatus in 1991, the overall unemployment rate is still more than 15 per cent. The pursuit of economic reform, expected to lead to a reorganization of social systems, generated open conflict or hidden pockets of resistance – hardly conducive to a speeding up of the economic transition process. It is within the context of this recent macroeconomic evolution that the functioning of the Tunisian labour market must be examined.

Any analysis of labour market mechanisms is closely linked to conceptual and methodological choices. Tunisia has a wealth of data on its labour market and a study such as this could not be carried out in any other country of the Maghreb. For the last fifteen years, several statistical sources have made it possible to apprehend certain aspects of the urban and rural labour markets: population and housing censi – 1975, 1984; household employment surveys – 1977, 1980, 1983, 1986-87, 1989; various studies of the preceding data or based on specific information.[6]

Despite this wealth of statistical data, any examination of the functioning of the Tunisian labour market faces a number of difficulties. First, the employed active population is not really uniformly defined in the various studies. In particular, the identification of "marginal active persons" and their inclusion or non-inclusion in the employed population increases the uncertainty about the real size of the latter.[7] Second, confusion about what constitutes unemployment raises questions concerning its under-estimation or over-estimation. The definition adopted in 1984 is more restrictive than both the previous one adopted in 1975 and the one used internationally – unemployed persons include only persons aged between 18 and 59, age limits which are not the same as those used for persons with a job. The criterion of availability for work also lacks precision. Finally, the quality of data varies from survey to survey.[8] In these circumstances, the apparent continuity between the various empirical studies probably does not give them the degree of comparability which has often been thought to be the case.[9]

---

[5] The per capita GNP is estimated to have risen by 3.8% during the period 1988-90.

[6] For a detailed analysis of these statistical sources see Kriaa, Bouziz, Trabelsi [1990a].

[7] For example, marginal active persons were included in the 1984 survey but not automatically so in the 1989 survey.

[8] Kriaa, Bouaziz, Trabelsi [1990a].

[9] Under-estimation of female unemployment in 1984 as compared with 1975; under-estimation of marginal active persons in 1989 as compared with 1984.

The heterogeneous nature of theoretical and doctrinal references has itself a profound influence on labour market research. The major aspects of labour market analysis can be grouped around two ideas.[10] First, some studies have concentrated on static imbalances in the labour market, with special reference to the optimal allocation of resources. Secondly, labour market analysis is more often examined from the standpoint of the dynamics of labour supply and demand. These two methodological options lead to a distinction being made between the "problem of employment" and the "problem of unemployment", a distinction which has implications at the economic policy level. The thesis of the dysfunctioning of the labour market results in special attention being given to "labour market policies" which can increase the efficiency of the market. Policies to increase labour demand and reduce labour supply could have less effect on the conditions of under-employed persons than policies designed to improve the efficiency of the labour market.

In Tunisia's case, both methodological options have been used, although implicit preference has been given to the thesis of the inefficiency of the labour market. Thus, on the basis of the previously mentioned statistical sources – the only available data with a real interest at the beginning of the 1990s –, the presentation of labour market studies in this country can be centred successively on the structure, imbalances, dysfunctionings and adjustments of the labour market.

II. The stratification of the labour market

An analysis of the structure of employment and income makes it possible to identify some of the elements inherent in the stratification of the labour market in Tunisia.

1. Employment structure

An analysis by sector of activity shows that the structure of employment prevalent in Tunisia to some extent reflects the process of economic transition. At the end of the 1980s, the "agriculture and fisheries" sector was no longer the main source of employment and accounted for only one quarter

---

[10] Lachaud [1989].

Table 1: Breakdown of production systems and employment in Tunisia, 1984-89

Parameter Sector	1984		1989		Annual growth
	'000s	%	'000s	%	(%)
Non- competitive sector	909.6	52.0	957.8	49.1	1.0
Competitive sector	841.1	48.0	991.8	50.9	3.4
Manufacturing (except chemicals)	370.3	21.2	435.5	22.3	3.3
Construction and publics works	174.3	10.0	172.8	8.9	-0.2
Services (except transport)	296.5	16.9	383.5	19.7	5.3
Overall[1]	1750.7	100.0	1949.6	100.0	2.2
Competitive sector	841.1	48.0	991.8	50.9	3.4
Exports: textiles, tourism	227.4	13.0	264.9	13.6	3.1
Local market	613.7	35.0	726.9	37.3	3.4

(1) Excluding "undeclared" jobs.
Source: Zouari-Bouattour, Zouari [1990].

of jobs,[11] whereas the share of industrial employment was 33.6 per cent. Although the growth of industrial employment is inherent in the development process, it must be stressed that industry is dominated by a few activities which play a key role in terms of jobs. In 1989, textiles absorbed 50 per cent of employment in manufacturing, whereas building and public works accounted for 87.6 per cent of jobs in the non-manufacturing branch. Of the other branches of activity, trade and administration employed 8.5 per cent and 9 per cent respectively of the labour force. Between 1975 and 1989, employment in these two branches practically doubled.

Since 55.5 per cent of active persons in 1984 were employed in urban areas, an analysis of the structure of this employment is not without interest. The urban labour market could be organized around two productive systems which function in different ways.[12] A "protected sector" including the administration and a few monopolistic or public activities – chemicals, mining, oil, electricity, water and transport – and a "competitive sector" of small and medium-sized enterprises, grouping together, in particular, in sectors such as textiles, building materials, mechanical and electrical

---

[11] Agricultural employment is predominant in rural areas, where it encompassed 51 per cent of active persons in 1984.

[12] Zouari-Bouattour, Zouari [1990].

engineering, building, tourism and trade (see Table 1).

The distinctive features of these two productive systems explain the relative importance of their contribution to employment and the existence of specific labour market segments. The protected sector is sluggish, capital-intensive, highly unionized and with high wage rates (in part responsible for the weak growth in employment) and use labour with a level of training allowing workers to acquire specific skills on the job. In these circumstances, the integration of this labour force leads to the establishment of internal markets. In the competitive sector, however, competition has led to a reduction of labour costs and the adoption of management methods which permit some degree of flexibility. Furthermore, industries in this sector have a relatively weak and stable capital/labour ratio, which accounts for their significant contribution to employment in recent years.[13]

This statification overlaps the distinctions between the public/private and formal/informal sectors. According to some analyses,[14] the State share in overall employment in Tunisia (including public service employment) was around 25 per cent in 1989. In fact, at the beginning of the 1990s, the relative share of public employment probably fell, as one of the objectives of the new macro-economic policies was the restructuring of public enterprises through the revision of the legal framework, financial reorganization, the withdrawal of the State from some enterprises in the competitive sector and the reabsorption of surplus staff. An analysis of the employment structure according to modern and informal production systems is more difficult because of the lack of appropriate statistical sources.[15]

These observations are strengthened by an analysis of the active employed population by occupation status showing that the economic transition process in Tunisia has been accompanied by a relative increase in wage employment. During the last fifteen years, salaried employees increased from 58.4 per cent to 65.9 per cent in the employed population, equal to an annual growth of 3.6 per cent. Self-employment has declined in relative terms although there has been a slight increase in absolute figures,

---

[13] Even in export-oriented sectors – textiles, tourism – where productivity gains have been higher than in industries working for the local market – building, metal and electrical industries, agro-food industries, miscellaneous services – employment growth has been substantial.

[14] Bouguerra [1990].

[15] According to an already old study – Charmes [1982] – in the mid-1970s the urban and rural informal market, both localized and non-localized, accounted for 39.3 per cent of total non-agricultural employment.

Table 2: Distribution of the active employed population by status in occupation in Tunisia, 1975-1989

Parameter	1975		1989		Variation annuelle
Status	'000s	%	'000s	%	(%)
Employee	798.0	58.4	1304.0	65.9	3.6
Self-employed/employer[1]	403.4	29.5	463.0	23.4	1.0
Family help	111.0	8.1	175.0	8.8	3.3
Apprentice	33.7	2.5	20.7	1.0	-3.4
Other/not declared	20.5	1.5	16.0	0.8	-1.8
Overall	1366.6	100.0	1978.7	100.0	2.7

(1)The 1989 survey does not distinguish between "employers" and "self-employed persons".
Source: Kriaa, Bouaziz, Trabelsi [1990].

while the relative and absolute share of apprenticeships has also declined (see Table 2).

The structural development of Tunisian production systems explains the current stratification of the labour market, with a relative decline in the agricultural sector, the rapid growth of the textiles industry – which employed 76.5 per cent of women workers in 1989 – and the expansion of building – to the advantage of male wage earners – and services (banking, teaching), which has led to a growth in the number of female employees. Thus, although the proportion of women in the active employed population in Tunisia has stabilized at around 20 per cent since 1975, the relative share of female wage employment rose from 12.8 per cent in 1975 to 17 per cent in 1989. Most of this wage employment is of course located in metropolitan areas a result of urban growth.[16]

The growth in wage employment has been accompanied by a rise in the level of training. Whereas in 1975, primary school was the top education level attained by 83.9 per cent of employed active persons, this figure dropped to 69.4 per cent in 1989. Women have most improved the level of their education and training. In 1989, 56.6 per cent of women had completed at most their primary education, compared with 84.6 per cent in 1975. The respective percentages for male workers are 74.7 per cent and 83.7 per cent. Regarding higher education, differences in training levels by sex are even more marked. However, although the growth in female wage employment

---

[16] Around two thirds of employees work in urban areas.

must be set in the context of the increase in their human capital, two qualifying factors must also be noted. First, there are important training differences by sex between urban and rural areas. Second, given the lesser role played by women in Tunisian society, vocational and technical training is mainly pursued by men.[17] This differentiation in access to employment is quite clear in public financial enterprises, where 84.4 per cent of women workers are office employees, and only 15.6 per cent hold managerial posts.

Meanwhile, the development of wage employment has had two consequences. First, increasing labour market vulnerability can be seen in the emergence or permanence of precarious forms of employment: greater flexibility in the management of labour, the development of internal markets in competitive sectors and the relative importance of the informal sector – more than one third of wage employment – and non-localized activities – more than half of urban informal employment – and the existence of much under-employment.[18] Second, the economic transition has accentuated the differences between labour market integration processes.

In the protected sector, skilled labour is relatively more important than in the competitive sector. For example, in 1984, the former absorbed 77.3 per cent of university graduates and graduates of higher education accounted for 14 per cent of employment – 0.3 per cent to 1.5 per cent according to the branch of activity in the competitive sector in 1984. The structure of employment in the protected sector can be explained by reasons of a technical, economic (capital intensive activity, relatively large size of production units, public nature of enterprises) and political kind, whereas in the competitive sector, the small scale of enterprises, the lower quality production for the local market and the need to reduce labour costs are the main factors leading the minority share of skilled labour. In the context of structural adjustment, this process of differentiated access to employment is of great interest in the identification of the main features of the way in which the labour market functions.

2. Income structure

Despite the fragmentary data available, some observations can be made on the disparity between incomes and on certain factors which determine wages and salaries.

---

[17] Kefi, Zouari-Bouattour, Boyle [1990].

[18] In Tunisia, 26.9 per cent of employed active persons are employed for less than six months a year – 15 per cent of employees.

Figure 1 shows the structure and evolution of various kinds of income by employed person during the period 1971-1988. In 1988, income per employed person was twice as high for self-employment as for wage employment. This difference is mainly due to the relative share of income of self-employed persons. As for wages, earnings per employed person were highest in the administrative sector. In this respect, wages in the non agricultural production sector are comparable to the average wage, whereas agricultural workers are poorly paid. In the rural sector, where the level of skills is low, the wage level is fairly close to the minimum wage (SMAG).[19] The relative growth rates of income of employed persons can be seen in Figure 1. However, some elements suggest that the more rapid growth of non-wage income per employee might also be due in part to the lower relative increase in the level of wages.

Two additional remarks can be made on income levels. First, relatively marked wage differentials exist between the various branches of activity. The public sector – oil, mining, electricity, administration, etc. – pays salaries which are higher than the average wage in the economy as a whole, whereas the reverse is the case in the private sector. Second, a comparison between wages fixed institutionally and wages determined by the market shows that in the period 1971-1989, the former increased more rapidly than the latter (Figure 2). Between 1971 and 1989, the various minimum wage rates increased by around 5.7 times, whereas the average wage increased by 4.6 times. However, as can be seen in Figure 2, the most rapid increase in institutionally fixed wages was from 1980. According to some analyses, this change in the relative cost of labour probably helps explain the slower growth of employment in agriculture and industry.[20]

On the basis of data from a sample of 7,561 employees from the 1980 household survey on employment, some estimations of earnings functions[21] help identify certain aspects of the differences in wages. As regards wage determinants by sex, the human capital model is more applicable to women. In addition, the average wage of women is 12 per cent lower than that of

---

[19] The preceding remarks are in line with previous observations on the structure of employment. In fact the relative growth of non-wage income must be linked to the increase in employees in the employed active population (table 2).

[20] Zouari-Bouattour [1990]; Zouari [1990].

[21] The dependent variable is the logarithm of monthly income; the independent variables are age, square age, the number of years of schooling and the square number of years of schooling. The latter two variables are a proxy for occupational experience. See Zouari-Bouattour, Zouari [1990].

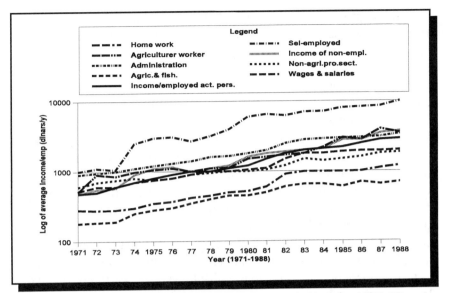

Figure 1: Log of income by employed active persons in Tunisia, 1971-88

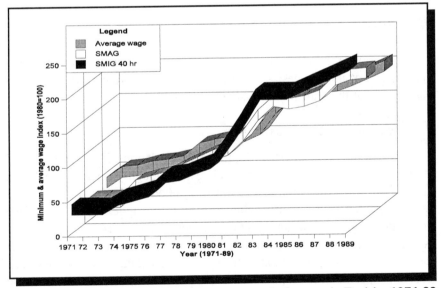

Figure 2: Evolution of minimum and average nominal wages in Tunisia, 1971-89

men, although women have more schooling than men. Furthermore, the marginal yield rates of education and occupational experience are higher for women than for men. Thus contrary to some conclusions which have been drawn, the human capital factors seem to play an important role in the determination of women's earnings, and the age-earnings profiles are not systematically to the detriment of the latter, in particular if they have heavily invested in training. The fact that the average wages of women are lower than those of men could be due to two factors: the precarious nature of some jobs held by women, particularly in textiles, and discrimination by employers. However, this model is too rudimentary to allow any final conclusions to be drawn. When the sample is differentiated according to State officials and employees in enterprises, the average salary in the administrative sector is higher – by 43.5 per cent – that in the production sector.[22] This result must be set alongside the fact that the marginal yield rate of education is twice as high in the administrative sector. In this context, it might be interesting to examine to what extent in recent years the flow of graduates has helped modify these differences in remuneration.

III. Labour market imbalances

In Tunisia the functioning of the labour market seems to reveal two major types of imbalances: a decline in labour absorption[23] and the inadequacy of the educational system.

1. Decline in labour absorption

During the period 1975-1989, the total population of Tunisia increased at an annual rate of 2.5 per cent (Table 3). Although Tunisia's population growth rate was lower than that of most of the other Maghreb countries, it remains nevertheless high. Table 3 seems to suggest that the active population is growing faster than the total population. In fact, however, this is improbable for two main reasons. First, comparability over time of the data on the active population is uncertain. According to some analyses, during the period 1975-89, the total active population increased at an annual

---

[22] However, higher and middle management staff in the production sector have significantly higher salaries.

[23] See Kriaa, Bouaziz, Trabelsi [1990b]; Azabou, Talbi, Skouri [1990]; Zouari-Bouattour, Zouari [1990].

Table 3: Evolution of the total population, active population and participation
rates by urban/rural distribution and sex in Tunisia, 1975-1989

Total/active population (annual growth)	1984/75	1989/84	1989/75
Total population	**2.5**	**2.5**	**2.5**
Total active population[1]	3.1	2	2.7[2]
Male active population	2.7	2.1	2.5
Female active population	4.6	1.6	3.5
Urban active population[3]	**3.9**	**4.7**	**4.2**
Male urban active population	3.7	4.7	4
Female urban active population	4.5	5	4.7
Rural active population[4]	**2.3**	**-1.7**	**0.8**
Male rural active population	1.7	-1.2	0.7
Female rural active population	4.8	-3.9	1.6
Participation rate (percentage)	1975	1984[5]	1989
Overall	**50.2**	**50.5**	**48.1**
Men	81.1	78.6	75.2
Women	18.9	21.8	20.4

(1) Population aged 15 or above estimated at 1,622,000, 2,137,000 and 2,360,000 persons respectively in 1975, 1984
and 1989. For the same years, the male active population was respectively 1,318,000, 1,681,000 and 1,866,000, whereas
the female active population was respectively 304,000, 456,000 and 494,000; (2) 2.6 per cent after correction of the
female active population of 1975 using the 1989 structure; 2.4 per cent after correction of the female active population
of 1975 using the 1984 structure; (3) Population aged 15 or above estimated at 828,900, 1,166,340 and 1,470,131
persons respectively in 1975, 1984 and 1989. For the same years, the male active population was respectively 650,530,
901,700 and 1,132,594, whereas the female active population was respectively 178,370, 264,640 and 337, 537; (4)
Population aged 15 or above estimated at 792,000, 970,240 and 980,461 persons respectively in 1975, 1984 and 1989.
For the same years, the male active population was respectively 667,760, 779,330 and 733,713, whereas the female
active population was respectively 125,140, 190,910 and 156,748; (5) The participation rates for men in urban and
rural areas were 76.1 per cent and 82.7 per cent respectively; the rates for women were 22.8 per cent and 20.7 per
cent respectively.
Source: Kriaa, Bouayiy, Trabelsi [1990b]; Zouari-Bouattour, Zouari [1990].

rate of between 2.4 per cent and 2.6 per cent, whereas the female
population increased at an annual rate of between 1.8 and 2.9 per cent,[24]
with a participation rate in the labour market between 20.7 per cent and 24
per cent. Second, the structural effect of the slight drop in participation rates
has had a negative impact on the evolution of the active population. The fall
in the overall activity rate is probably due to the drop in the activity rates
of young persons (15-29 years) – which itself is mainly the result of the
higher school retention rates at the secondary and higher levels – and to

---

[24] See Kriaa, Bouaziz, Trabelsi [1990a].

Table 4: Employed population by sex and urban/rural distribution in Tunisia, 1975-89

Year Parameter	1975 ('000s)	1984 ('000s)	1989 ('000s)	1984/75 (% p.a.)	1989/84 (% p.a.)	1989/75 (% p.a.)
Total employment	1367	1786	1979	3,0	2,1	2,7
Male	1106	1398	1593	2,6	2,6	2,6
Female	261	388	386	4,5	-0,1	2,8
Urban employment[1]	719	992	1220	3,6	4,2	3,8
Rural employment[1]	648	794	759	2,3	-0,9	1,1

(l)For 1989, the distribution of rural/urban employment has been estimated on the basis of unemployment rates, with account being taken of the non-employed population aged 15-59.
Source: Kriaa, Bouaziz, Trabelsi [1990b]; Zouari-Bouattour, Zouari [1990].

international migration.[25] Labour supply in urban areas has grown rapidly (Table 3). This rural-urban differential in labour supply appears irrespective of sex and can beexplained to a large extent by migration.[26] Migration has also helped accentuate regional differences in the growth of the active population, in particular to the benefit of the east of the country – Tunis and Sfax. The relative progress in male education in rural areas has accelerated this exodus.[27] However, in general, the development process has also accentuated differences in available educational and economic infrastructure and led to an increase in the urban labour supply.

Labour demand in Tunisia must be set within the context of major structural changes: the decline of the share of agriculture in total production, the drop in the share of the active population in agriculture and the growth of the urban population. The share of agriculture in the GDP fell from 22 per cent in 1965 to 16 per cent in 1990, whereas that of industry rose from 24 per cent to 32 per cent during the same period, with services falling slightly from 54 per cent to 52 per cent.[28] In the same way, the share

---

[25] Above all towards Libya at the end of the 1980s. However, special factors may apply according to sex. In the case of men, given the relative increase in the urban active population, the encouragement to take up early retirement helped reduce the participation rate. For women, the drop in real income and structural and social changes may have played an important role.

[26] Although fertility is higher in rural areas.

[27] Women have a lower level of education in rural areas.

[28] World Bank [1992].

òf the active population in agriculture fell from 56.1 per cent in 1960 to 25.8 per cent in 1989, whereas between 1965 and 1989 the percentage of the urban population rose from 40 per cent to 54 per cent. Table 4, which is largely based on the employment series prepared by the Institute of Quantitative Economics, shows that between 1975 and 1979, employment rose at an average annual rate of 2.7 per cent. Differences by sex are slight, with male employment rising by 2.6 per cent a year, while female employment increased by 2.8 per cent a year. Differences in the growth of employment are more marked in time and space, with growth slowing down markedly in the second half of the 1980s, in particular in urban areas. Furthermore, the growth rate of employment depends on both the growth rate of production and labour productivity, with the latter in turn being influenced by technical progress, substitution elasticities, labour intensity and changes in the real cost of labour. Some analyses[29] have tried to take account of these factors and shown that between 1975 and 1989 structural and productivity effects reduced by 50 per cent the impact of production on the level of employment.

The above analysis suggests a tendency towards a reduction in the overall absorption of labour. A labour surplus already existed at the beginning of the period – 15.7 per cent of the active population aged 15 and above, i.e. 13.3 per cent and 18 per cent respectively in urban and rural areas. Although the overall growth rates of the active population and employment appear to be almost identical – around 2.7 per cent per year – during the period 1975-89, two major imbalances occurred. First, female employment grew much less quickly than the female labour supply. Between 1975 and 1989, female employment increased at an annual average rate of 2.8 per cent, whereas the female active population rose by an average of 3.5 per cent per year. Second, a marked gap exists between the growth rates of urban employment and the urban labour supply. In the former, average annual growth was only 3.8 per cent between 1975-89, whereas in the latter case, the increase was 4.2 per cent per year.[30] In rural areas, the imbalance between supply and demand showed a slight tendency towards reabsorption, thanks in part to migration to the cities: the size of the urban active population in 1989 was approximately twice that of the rural active population, whereas in 1975 their distribution was virtually equal. Finally, the fact that after 1984 the number of unsatisfied job applications by women

---

[29] On the basis of work by Banerji and Riedel. See Zouari-Bouattour, Zouari [1990].

[30] The imbalance in urban areas is particularly marked in the case of women.

increased by almost three times is another factor which tended to confirm the relative decline in the absorption of labour.

2. The inadequacy of the educational system

Imbalances in the Tunisian educational system must be examined in the context of demographic changes which have increased dependency ratios and added an increasing proportion of educated persons to the labour market.[31]

The Tunisian educational system is inadequate in two ways. First, a gap exists between the number of new graduates and the rate at which they can be absorbed by the production system. During the period 1975-1984, the average annual growth rates in the number of graduates from secondary or higher educational establishments were 8.1 per cent and 13.5 per cent respectively. Skilled labour was thus an important component of the labour supply in the following years. However, during the period 1984-1989, the employment of graduates from secondary or higher educational establishments rose at an annual rate of only 4.8 per cent and 10 .5 per cent respectively.

Second, an examination of labour absorption by sector indicates that the net demand for skilled labour remained relatively predominant in branches which were not very dynamic, in particular in the protected sector. Between 1975 and 1984, the share of the net labour demand for graduates of secondary and higher education was, respectively, 11 per cent and 44.9 per cent of the additional employment. The tertiary sector absorbed most of the graduates: 80 per cent of higher education graduates and 60 per cent of secondary education graduates. Manufacturing and construction absorbed only 10 per cent and 29 per cent of persons holding, respectively, a university or secondary education diploma. This situation seems to have persisted throughout the second half of the 1980s, despite the unreliability of available data. Structural adjustment programmes, with the deliberate intention of reducing public sector employment, may make such imbalances more marked.

Third, in the mid-1980s, graduates were absorbed into the production system at a low rate. Three and a half years after obtaining their final diploma, only 30.2 per cent of men and 22 per cent of women graduating

---

[31] For example, between 1975 and 1989, the proportion of the active population with at least secondary education doubled – from 14 per cent to 27.9 per cent.

from secondary school had been integrated into the labour market.[32] It is important to examine how this imbalance might be reduced – through rationing the quantity or adjusting of costs – because of its implications in terms of the social returns of education.

The problem of absorption is compounded by graduates' lack of technical skills. While the Tunisian educational system continues to produce graduates in relatively saturated specializations – in particular in the tertiary sector – there appears to be a shortage of the technical skills required by the production process. Thus the manager/worker ratio of the Tunisian economy is relatively low compared with that of comparable economies, and some studies recently carried out in the manufacturing industries – textiles, leather and footwear – have pointed to a marked shortage of technical managers, production technicians and skilled labourers.[33] Data from introductory vocational training indicate that courses which went unfilled in 1989 were mainly in technical sectors, while most of the surplus demand was for courses in the general disciplines.

IV. Labour market dysfunctionings

Some analysts have claimed that the institutional environment is one of the obstacles to the functioning of the labour market in Tunisia.[34]

1. Institutional environment

In Tunisia, the public authorities and the trade unions play a major role in wage-fixing and labour legislation. The current wage policy is based on the collective agreement of 1973, which was signed by the workers' (UGTT) and employers' (UTICA) organizations under the supervision of the State. This agreement marked a turning point in wage policy, which had hitherto been of a regulatory nature in which the structure of wages was closely related to the structure of skills. At the beginning of the 1970s the increase in the real production capacity of the Tunisian economy on the one hand and the growing number of labour disputes on the other led to the introduction of a new wage policy.

---

[32] Ratio between final jobs and the total number of diploma holders of the cohort. See Ben Sedrine [1990].

[33] Baccar [1990].

[34] This argument is developed by: Zouari [1990]; Nabli, Nugent [1989], in the context of the "new institutional economics".

By strengthening the power of the trade unions, the 1973 collective agreement sought to fill the gaps in labour legislation, in particular the social organization and rights of employees in enterprises, the regulation of individual labour relationships and the regulation of general conditions of work. But as this process of homogenization predetermined the general structure of sectoral[35] works agreements, it could prove to be an obstacle to the decentralized organization of labour relations.[36] The 1973 collective agreement regulates employees' career development and remuneration: (i) determination of the status and actual grading of an employee in the enterprise by reference to an occupational classification of work places; (ii) horizontal promotion of employees – from one step to another on the basis of period of service – or vertical promotion in the event of a vacancy or the creation of a post; (iii) remuneration system determined by a wage grid which according to the occupational category, minimum wages and additional components by reference to the guaranteed inter-occupational minimum wage (SMIG), establishes the minimum remuneration of an unskilled labourer. The base wage is the fixed component of the remuneration established by the collective agreement, whereas bonuses – the criteria governing their payment are not always clearly established – and allowances are considered as variable additional elements. Because of its strategic importance, the SMIG is specifically examined by a commission which transmits its proposals to the Government; however, irrespective of the final decision of the public authorities, the raising of the SMIG helps reduce wage differences.

Several aspects of Tunisia's Labour Code play a major role in determining the rules of social relations in enterprises. The most important regulatory provisions give the State a monopoly over the recruitment of employees. As the employer is not required to recruit the person proposed by the placement office, the latter covers only part of the volume of recruitment on the labour market.[37] This situation inevitably leads to arguments in favour of private employment offices. However, two inherent features of collective agreements restrict freedom of recruitment: non-

---

[35] During the period 1974–77, 42 sectoral agreements were signed between trade unions. The negotiation framework was the branch of activity, irrespective of the kind of enterprises concerned.

[36] Thus at the plant level, working conditions may not be less favourable than those established by the framework agreement. Zouari [1990].

[37] 65 per cent in Tunisia. See Zouari [1990]. In sub-Saharan African countries, coverage appears to be even lower. For Mali, see Lachaud [1990a].

discrimination by sex or trade union status; and the priority given to certain categories of persons, in particular permanent, temporary or casual workers.

As regards forms of contracts of employment, contracts of unlimited duration are the general rule, while fixed term contracts may exist only in a written form – unless proof is provided of the non-lasting nature of the work – and if they are for work of a temporary nature. The renewal of a fixed term contract implies its transformation into a contract of unlimited duration. Provisions of the Labour Code regulate the suspension and resiliation of contracts of employment. Under labour legislation, dismissals may be made for either economic reasons or serious misconduct. However, in the first case, dismissals require prior authorization by a supervisory committee and may not be made effective until after a lengthy period of time required for the processing of dossiers and conciliation procedures. Thus the advance notice of dismissal and prior authorization are of a relatively dissuasive character.

Finally, the Labour Code establishes the procedure governing working time in the private sector; the social life of the enterprise is organized by joint advisory committees which must be set up in enterprises with more than 20 employees. These committees have gradually replaced the worker's committees in order to ensure the predominant role of the trade unions in enterprises.

2. Static imbalances on the labour market

The institutional context outlined above has contributed to labour market dysfunctioning. First, differences in protection have been reinforced. In Tunisia, the labour legislation examined above applies theoretically only to persons employed in the non-agricultural production sector and, as such, covers only 37.1 per cent of the members of the active population. Assuming that the wage policy has above all benefited those who earn the SMIG or SMAG, together they accounted for only 16.8 per cent of wage employment in 1988 and 11.1 per cent of total employment. This situation could reduce the performance of the production system in terms of labour productivity, investment efficiency and job creation as well as limit the outlook for generalized application and allow trade unions to consolidate their acquired benefits.[38]

---

[38] Zouari [1990]. This type of argument is linked to the hypothesis than there is no gap between labour law and practice.

Second, the efficiency of labour market mechanisms has been partly wiped out by the disconnecting of market wages and institutional wages.[39] Minimum wages have increased more rapidly than the average market wage (Figure 2) and wage differentials between skill levels have been significantly reduced – from 1 to 5.8 in 1975 and 1 to 4.1 per cent in 1985. This tendency is essentially due to the effect of collective agreements, which have helped standardize the structure of wages and reduce the range of monthly remuneration according to skills. This relative evolution in wages may partly explain the shortage of technical staff noted earlier.

Third, the distortion of factor prices has become more marked. Wage policy established by collective agreements has led to an increase in labour costs, despite differences within the production system. Between 1975 and 1988, per capita labour costs increased by 3.5[40] and in 1985, 71.3 per cent of the wage bill borne by production units was made up of the actual remuneration paid to employees. The increase in the relative cost of labour, coupled with the weakness of interest rates, encouraged the substitution of capital for labour and led to a reduction in the number of new jobs created. In Tunisia, between 1975 and 1988, capital-intensity was multiplied by 1.7. This modification in the allocation of resources helped reduce the level of profits and equity capital of enterprises, with the final result for the latter being an increase in their bank debts. The increase in the relative cost of labour might also lead to an increase in the cost of finished products and a reduction in competitivity on foreign markets.

Notwithstanding labour supply dynamics, preference must be given to economic policies designed to reduce the static imbalances of the labour market, implying a change at the institutional level. On the one hand, the social consensus process must be redefined through a reexamination of the role of the social partners.[41] On the other, the restoration of labour market mechanisms requires greater flexibility in the use of labour and the determination of wages, which will in turn require profound changes in labour legislation.[42]

---

[39] Zouari [1990].

[40] Zouari-Bouattour, Zouari [1990].

[41] According to some analyses, the UGTT helped encourage rigidity on the labour market by sidestepping the essentail objective of collective bargaining. Zouari [1990].

[42] Particularly as regards recruitment and dismissal procedures.

V. Labour market adjustments

Labour market adjustments in Tunisia have mainly affected urban areas and seem to take various forms.

1. Growth of urban unemployment

Over the last decade, one of the most important labour market adjustments in Tunisia has been the growth in the rate of urban unemployment. During the period 1975-89, the overall unemployment rate rose from 12.7 per cent to 15.3 per cent and from 15.7 to 16.2 per cent respectively for persons aged between 18 and 59 and persons aged 15 or above. During the same period, whereas there seemed to be a relative stabilization of unemployment in rural areas, urban unemployment rose by 51.5 per cent for persons aged between 18 and 59: from 10 .3 per cent to 15.6 per cent. In Tunis, 16.7 per cent of the active population was unemployed in 1989, equal to an increase of more than 4 percentage points over 1984. The rise in urban unemployment explains the differentiation in regional unemployment rates: in 1989, 19 per cent of the active population in the west of the country was unemployed, compared with only 14.8 per cent in the east.

In reality, this kind of adjustment incorporates a degree of selectivity. First, the unemployment rate of persons aged between 18 and 24 – 29.8 per cent in 1989 – is twice as high as the national average for persons aged between 18 and 59. Furthermore, of these unemployed, a high percentage of people aged 18 or above are looking for their first job – from 21.6 per cent in 1984 to 42.7 per cent in 1989. Selectivity in terms of unemployment can also be seen according to sex. The unemployment rate for women aged between 18 and 59 rose from 10 .6 per cent in 1975 to 20.9 per cent in 1989, whereas for men in the same age group, the level and growth of unemployment during the same period were relatively lower – 13.4 per cent in 1975 and 13.9 per cent in 1989. The relative importance of unemployment amongst women can be explained by the precarious nature of their jobs and discrimination. Third, adjustment in terms of unemployment has affected an increasing number of graduates. Although relatively low, unemployment amongst graduates of higher education practically doubled between 1984 and 1989.[43] If people with no education

---

[43] In 1984, unemployment amongst university graduates was twice as high amongst women (3.7 per cent) as amongst men (1.8 per cent).

are excluded, unemployment rates increase as the level of education falls, although they tend to increase more rapidly as the level of education rises.

2. Employment stagnation in the modern sector

Several indicators seems to reveal a relative stagnation of employment in the modern sector over the last decade. Despite the recent impetus given to the production system, the deceleration of the growth rate of the Tunisian economy in the 1980s suggests a stabilization of employment growth in the modern sector. In addition, the economic performance of the "non competitive" sector, which is responsible for most of modern employment, was relatively mediocre in the second half of the 1980s. The annual growth rate of value added was only 2 per cent between 1984 and 1989. During the same period, employment rose by only 1 per cent a year (Table 2). Finally, the introduction of the structural adjustment programme brought about an 11.8 per cent reduction in employment in the public production sector between 1985 and 1989. This sector showed both a quantitative – 7.7 per cent of employees – and a qualitative – 5 percent of employees – surplus.[44] Although the qualitative surplus can be reabsorbed by measures from within the enterprise – such as, training, redeployment – employment in the public production sector will probably continue to fall over the coming years.

3. The drop in real wages

Figure 3 shows that real wages have declined considerably since 1983.[45] Between 1983 and 1989, the drop in real wages was 26.7 per cent, 22.5 per cent and 20.8 per cent respectively for the SMIG, SMAG and the average wage. However, during the same period, this was not the case with non-wage income per active person.[46]

Thus, despite a drop in real wages, unemployment increased. In the short term, adjustment policies may lead to temporary unemployment, since the drop in the production of non-tradable goods is faster than the growth in the production of tradeables.

---

[44] Bougerra [1990].

[45] Real wages have been calculated by comparing the appropriate wage index and the cost of living index. The data are taken from: Zouari-Bouattour, Zouari [1990].

[46] It is true that the latter concept is relatively heterogeneous. The average income per active person of non-wage earners encompass the income of the following categories: agricultural workers; self-employed persons and employers; home workers.

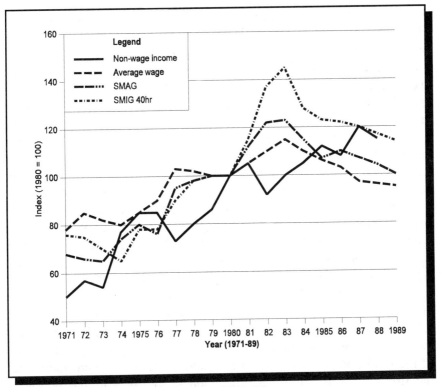

Figure 3: Real wage indices in Tunisia, 1971-89

However, in the long term, real wages may increase, as the surge in growth in the tradeables sector – supposedly more "labour intensive" – increases demand for labour beyond the increase in labour supply resulting from the decline in the production of tradeables.[47] The drop in real wages in Tunisia has probably helped reduce the gap between rural and urban incomes and encouraged recourse to a second job, in particular in urban areas.

4.   Employment and the informal sector

Although the data is incomplete, the informal sector in Tunisia would appear to play an increasing role in employment, income distribution and the balance of the overall social system. The growth of modern employment does not have the capacity to absorb the increase in the active population,

---

[47] See Lal [1984].

especially in expanding urban areas (Table 2). Unemployment, although clearly rising over the last ten years, does not seem to have reached the necessary level to bridge the growing gap between the growth of the active population and the development of employment in the modern sector. It is logical to suppose that the growth of employment in the informal sector – as well as the drop in real wages – is one of the major adjustment processes in the Tunisian labour market, especially in urban areas.

Second, during the 1980s, the sharp growth of the private sector is probably a reflection of the dynamism of the informal sector (table 1). Other analyses have emphasized that enterprises with less than 10 employees, which probably encompass the informal sector, accounted for 95 per cent of all enterprises in 1981, and around 35 per cent of total employment.[48] In addition, the distribution of the active population by status also shows the relative dynamism of the informal sector (table 2). Despite the growth in wage employment, self-employment and family-help work increased significantly in absolute terms between 1975 and 1989.

Finally, the growth of the informal sector has helped absorb some of the surplus graduates. A study of the integration secondary vocational school graduates shows that in the 1980s they tended increasingly to accept the conditions of employment of the informal sector. During the second half of the 1980s, 44 per cent of male graduates entered the labour market for the first time in the informal production sector. In addition, non-wage employment offered vocational school graduates a method of integration – 20 per cent of young men and 36 per cent of young women set themselves up as independent workers. Although employment in the informal sector is often seen as of a temporary nature, replacing unemployment benefits in the case of graduates of secondary education and study grants in the case of graduates of higher education, it is tending to become an increasingly widespread form of labour market adjustment in Tunisia.[49]

5. Migration

Migration is another type of labour market readjustment in Tunisia. Migration takes two forms, external and internal. During the 1980s, natural population growth – 2.4 per cent – was higher than the growth of the population of the country – 2.3 per cent – and migration towards the Gulf

---

[48] In fact 71 per cent of these production units had less than 3 workers, and accounted for 45 per cent of informal employment. Zouari [1990].

[49] Ben Sedrine [1990].

countries was a major form of adjustment in the domestic labour market. This process continued throughout the 1980s, although it slowed down considerably with the evolution of the economic and political situation in the Gulf countries.

Internal migration implies a reallocation of labour which is both intra and inter-governorates, although it is above all the latter which has been studied in detail. The volume of inter-governorate migratory flows – above all from the interior to the coastal areas, especially Tunis – fell slightly in the second half of the 1980s as compared with the period 1975-80. However, during the period 1984-89, approximately 10% of the active population – above all persons aged under 15 and those in the 20-29 age group – moved from one governorate to another.

Conclusion

The present structure of the labour market in Tunisia, although profoundly influenced by the development strategies adopted between 1960-80, must be set within the context of the new economic policies introduced from the mid-1980s which have significantly modified the economic transition process. This study has highlighted several major results of this process.

Despite the conceptual, statistical and methodological unreliability of Tunisian labour market data, analysis does show the dynamism of the private sector, as compared to the protected sector (that is, the administration and public or monopolistic activities) and reveals the marked growth in urban wage employment, particularly amongst women. Furthermore, the protected sector distributes the highest wages and absorbs most of the graduates.

However, the 1980s accentuated two imbalances in the Tunisian labour market: the inability to absorb labour and the inadequacy of the education system – with its surplus of graduates and shortage of technical skills. In the context of the Tunisian economy, an examination of the dynamics of the determinants of labour demand – the lesser dynamism of the production system, structural changes – and labour supply – excessive population growth, progress in education, in particular amongst women, increasing urbanization – sheds much light on the nature of these imbalances. However, some analyses suggest that the main labour market imbalances are mainly due to the evolution of the institutional context. Indeed, State and trade union interference in wage fixing and labour legislation has strengthened differences in protection, helped weaken the efficiency of labour market mechanisms by disconnecting market wages from institutional salaries and encouraged the emergence of distortions in factor prices.

Whether economic or institutional criteria are used to examine the Tunisian labour market, several types of adjustments seem to have become more accentuated during the 1980s: the growth in urban unemployment, the stagnation of employment in the modern sector, the drop in real wages, the expansion of employment in the informal sector and the intensification of migration.

Although our knowledge of the Tunisian labour market is still undoubtedly imperfect, the preceding analysis may lead to a better identification of the premises governing employment policies in this country. Within the framework of the new macro-economic constraints, the introduction – or extension – of policies geared to the labour market could contribute to the development of social progress. The intensification of self-employment, the re-examination of the conditions governing access to education, the re-structuring of the training system and the re-organization of the institutional framework of the labour market are probably the unavoidable objectives to be promoted during the 1990s.

Bibliographical references

Azabou, M., Talbi, B., Skouri, M. 1990. "Projections de la main d'oeuvre et perspectives de l'emploi", in *Institut de financement du développement du Maghreb arabe (IFID) (ed.)*, Politique de l'emploi en Tunisie, Tunis, IFID, proceedings of the seminar organized by the IFID from 13 to 16 June 1990.

Baccar, T. 1990. "Adéquation formation-emploi", in *Institut de financement du développement du Maghreb arabe (ed.)*, Politique de l'emploi en Tunisie, Tunis, IFID, proceedings of the seminar organized by the IFID from 13 to 16 June 1990.

B'chir, A. 1990. *Structure du marché du travail et pauvreté en Tunisie*, Tunis, National Institute of Labour and Social Studies, paper presented to the meeting with a view to the establishment of a network of labour market institutes in the Maghreb, 6 and 7 December 1990.

Ben Sedrine, S. 1990. *Marché du travail et insertion professionnelle en Tunisie*, Tunis, National Institute of Labour and Social Studies, paper presented to the meeting on the establishment of a network of labour market institutes in the Maghreb, 6 and 7 December 1990.

Bougerra, S. 1990. "Problèmes de surplus de main-d'oeuvre dans les entreprises para-étatiques", in *Institut de financement du développement du Maghreb arabe (ed.)*, Politique de l'emploi en Tunisie, Tunis, IFID, proceedings of the seminar organized by the IFID, from 13 to 16 June 1990.

Charmes, J. 1982. *L'évaluation du secteur non structuré: l'exemple de la Tunisie*, Paris, AMIRA.

Chokri, A., Adel, K., Plassard., J.M. 1991. *Le dualisme salarial en Tunisie*, Tunisie, Centre d'études juridiques et économiques de l'emploi (CEJEE), University of Toulouse, mimeo.

El Karm, A. 1990. "La politique monétaire et financière de l'emploi", in *Institut de financement du développement du Maghreb arabe (ed.)*, Politique de l'emploi en Tunisie, Tunis, IFID, proceedings of the seminar organized by the IFID from 13 to 16 June 1990.

Kefi, F., Zouari-Bouattour, S., Boyle, P. (1990): "La femme et l'emploi", in *Institut de financement du développement du Maghreb arabe (ed.)*, Politique de l'emploi en Tunisie, Tunis, IFID, proceedings of the seminar organized by the IFID from 13 to 16 June 1990.

Kouin, R. 1990. *L'intégration régionale des marchés du travail en Tunisie*, Tunis, National Institute of Labour and Social Studies, paper presented to the meeting on the establishment of a network of labour market institutes in the Maghreb, 6 and 7 December 1990.

Kriaa, F., Bouaziz, R., Trabelsi, H. 1990a. "La population active: source et qualité des données", in *Institut de financement du développement du Maghreb arabe (ed.)*, Politique de l'emploi en Tunisie, Tunis, IFID, proceedings of the seminar organized by the IFID from 13 to 16 June 1990.

Kriaa, F., Bouaziz, R., Trabelsi, H. 1990b. "Tendances historiques", in *Institut de financement du développement du Maghreb arabe (ed.)*, Politique de l'emploi en Tunisie, Tunis, IFID, proceedings of the seminar organized by the IFID from 13 to 16 June 1990.

Lachaud, J.P. 1989. "Urban labour market analysis in Africa", *Labour and Society*, Vol. 14, No. 4, October.

Lachaud, J.P. 1990a. *Le marché du travail au Mali*, Washington, International management & development group, mimeo.

Lachaud, J.P. 1990b. "Fonctionnement des marchés du travail en Tunisie: aspects économiques et institutionnels. Quelques commentaries", in *Institut de financement du développement du Maghreb arabe (ed.)*, Politique de l'emploi en Tunisie, Tunis, proceedings of the seminar organized by the IFID from 13 to 16 June 1990.

Lachaud, J.P. 1991. *Le marché du travail en Tunisie: structure, déséquilibres et ajustements*, Geneva, International Institute for Labour Studies, Discussion papers No. 35.

Lal, D. 1984. *Real effects of stabilization and structural adjustment policies: an extension of the Australian adjustment model*, Washington, World Bank, Staff working paper No. 636.

Larbi, E. 1990. "La politique nationale et son environnement", in *Institut de financement du développement du Maghreb arabe (ed.)*, Politique de l'emploi en Tunisie, Tunis, IFID, proceedings of the seminar organized by the IFID from 13 to 16 June 1990.

Mazumdar, D. 1981. *The urban labour market and income distribution: a study of Malaysia*, Washington, World Bank.

Mehran, F. 1990. "La population active: source et qualité des données. Commentaires", in *Institut de financement du développement du Maghreb arabe (ed.)*, Politique de l'emploi en Tunisie, Tunis, IFID, proceedings of the seminar organized by the IFID from 13 to 16 June 1990.

Nabli, M.K., Nugent, J.F. (eds.) 1989. *The new institutional economics and development: theory and applications to Tunisia*, Amsterdam, North-Holland.

Sid-Ahmed, A. (1991): "Emploi et croissance au Maghreb", *Revue Tiers-Monde*, No. 125, January-March.

Squire, L. 1981. *Employment policy in developing countries: a survey of issues and evidence*, Washington, World Bank

Terrell, K., Svejnar, J. 1989. *The industrial labor market & economic performance in Senegal*, London, Westview Press.

World Bank. 1991. *World Development Report 1990*, Washington.

Zouari-Bouattour, S., Zouari, A. 1990. "Aspects économiques du fontionnement des marchés du travail", in *Institut de financement du développement du Maghreb arabe (ed.)*, Politique de l'emploi en Tunisie, Tunis, IFID, proceedings of the seminar organized by the IFID from 13 to 16 June 1990.

Zouari, A. 1990. "Aspects institutionnels du fonctionnement des marchés du travail", in *Institut de financement du développement du Maghreb arabe (ed.)*, Politique de l'emploi en Tunisie, Tunis, IFID, proceedings of the seminar organized by the IFID from 13 to 16 June 1990.